The Pleasures of Book Collecting

DISCARDED BY
WILLARD LIBRARY

090

The Pleasures
of
Book Collecting

SALVATORE J. IACONE

DISCARDED BY
WILLARD LIBRARY

WILLARD LIBRARY
Battle Creek, Michigan

HARPER & ROW, PUBLISHERS

NEW YORK, HAGERSTOWN,

SAN FRANCISCO,

LONDON

090
Iac
c. 1

On pages 183 to 246 are excerpts from *The Delightful Diversion: The Whys and Wherefores of Book Collecting*, by Reginald Arthur Brewer, published by The Macmillan Company; *Fishers of Books* by Barton Wood Currie; *Penny Wise and Book Foolish* by Vincent Starrett; and *A Book Hunter's Holiday: Adventures with Books and Manuscripts*, by Abraham Simon Wolf Rosenbach.

The photographs on pages 16, 26, 35, 37, 39, 41, 48, 59, 60, 62, 66, 69, 76, 79, 81, 82, 93, and 132 are reproduced courtesy of Sotheby Parke Bernet; those on pages 20, 27, 30, 44, 119, and 137 are reproduced courtesy of Swann Galleries; and those on pages 6, 18, 86, 89, 90, 95, 96, 98, 99, 108, 110, and 152 courtesy of Daniel Langdon.

THE PLEASURES OF BOOK COLLECTING. Copyright © 1976 by Salvatore J. Iacone. All rights reserved. Printed in the United States of America. No part of this book may be used or reproduced in any manner whatsoever without written permission except in the case of brief quotations embodied in critical articles and reviews: For information address Harper & Row, Publishers, Inc., 10 East 53rd Street, New York, N.Y. 10022. Published simultaneously in Canada by Fitzhenry & Whiteside Limited, Toronto.

FIRST EDITION

Designed by Sidney Feinberg

Library of Congress Cataloging in Publication Data

Iacone, Salvatore J
   The pleasures of book collecting.
   Bibliography: p.
   Includes index.
   1. Book collecting. I. Title.
Z987.I15   1976   020'.75   76–9194
ISBN 0–06–012141–6

---

76 77 78 79 80 10 9 8 7 6 5 4 3 2 1

*To my wife, Renée
and daughter, Alexis*

Contents

III
SAGE ADVICE AND TIMELESS ANECDOTES

Illustrations

Preface

Long before I even dreamed of collecting books, dozens of volumes concerning the nature of book collecting had been published. To be sure, the works of A. Edward Newton, A. S. W. Rosenbach, John T. Winterich, and John Carter continue to offer a great deal of enjoyment and information. Yet quite a number of changes have occurred since the classic accounts of book collecting first appeared. Many of the titles frequently referred to are either out of favor with collectors or almost impossible to collect nowadays, prices are outdated, and individuals mentioned as outstanding collectors or dealers are long dead.

It is for this reason that I have compiled a guidebook to book collecting in the 1970s, and I trust for the years ahead. I sincerely hope that this volume will not only enlighten aspiring collectors concerning the language and techniques of book collecting, but encourage and inspire them as well, since I believe that the collecting of books is one of life's most enjoyable pursuits.

SALVATORE J. IACONE

Acknowledgments

During the course of writing this book, quite a number of people offered invaluable assistance and suggestions, to whom I want to extend my sincere appreciation.

To Anthony S. Mercatante, an inimitable author in his own right in the field of mythology and folklore, for first suggesting that I submit my initial notes and ideas to his editor at Harper & Row, Harold E. Grove. To Hal Grove, for his wholehearted support and encouragement, and indispensable advice, I shall be always grateful. To Phillip Sperling, for sharing with me his vast knowledge of books. To the great Grolier Club for the warmth extended to me, and the opportunity to use their superb library for my research. To Robert Barry and the Antiquarian Booksellers' Association of America, for permission to reprint their membership list.

To the various rare-book dealers whose knowledge and expertise proved indispensable, with special thanks to John Fleming; Mrs. Marguerite Cohn of the House of Books, Ltd.; John S. Van Kohn, and the staff of Seven Gables Bookshop.

To Herbert Cahoon of the Morgan Library, Dr. James L.

Clifford, and Mrs. Mary Hyde for their warm encouragement. To the great collector Raymond E. Hartz, and his wife, Elizabeth, for offering me the opportunity to see one of the finest private book collections in the world, my warmest appreciation. To Daniel Langdon, for his marvelous photographs. To Mrs. Christina Stile, for her assistance with the manuscript.

And last, but most deeply, to my wife Renée, for her devotion, love, and patience, which sustained my efforts throughout the writing of this book, my love and gratitude.

S.J.I.

May 27, 1976

I

THE NATURE
OF
BOOK COLLECTING

1

The Pleasures of Book Collecting

"... there is nothing that begins so easily and
takes us so far as the collecting of books."

A. EDWARD NEWTON
The Amenities of Book-Collecting

More than forty years ago, the late Dr. A. S. W. Rosenbach,
perhaps the most renowned rare-book dealer of his day, concluded that "after love . . . book-collecting is the most exhilarating sport of all."* While every collector of books may not share
Dr. Rosenbach's intense enthusiasm, none would deny that book
collecting is surely one of the most pleasurable of pastimes. To
be sure, book collecting as a hobby is a lifetime endeavor. Few
ever outgrow it, since its possibilities are infinite, and more
often than not, the enjoyment derived from collecting books
increases rather than diminishes with the passing of time. In
fact, there are some who attribute the unusual longevity of
many collectors to their stubborn determination to acquire a
particular volume that they have been seeking for years.

One reason for the persistence of interest in book collecting
over the years is its appeal to a wide diversity of tastes. George
Washington, Cardinal Richelieu, Queen Isabella of Spain,
Madame de Pompadour, and J. P. Morgan represent collectors
whose interests were as various as their personalities and ca-

---

* *A Book Hunter's Holiday*, page 106.

reers. Whatever one's interest in life may be, that interest can be paralleled in book collecting.

There is hardly a subject around which a collection cannot be built. For instance, there are collectors of the first editions or earliest printings of various works of literature, history, science, philosophy, of bibles, children's books, travel books, almanacs, and on and on.* Many individuals gather fine bindings that represent the most beautiful and skillful examples of the binder's art. Since many of the finest bound books were executed for the various monarchs and members of the aristocracies of Europe over the centuries, they are often prized for their historical associations.

Still other collectors gather books produced by private presses, which are valued for their unique style, their craftsmanship and typographical beauty, or the earliest printed books of the fifteenth century, known as incunabula. Furthermore, there are collectors of manuscripts and illustrated books. It is not difficult to see that the possibilities are virtually endless.

Most appealing of all, one can pursue the pleasures of book collecting without having to spend great sums of money. While there are, to be sure, books that can and do cost many thousands of dollars, a great many desirable items are available for relatively modest prices compared with the huge financial outlay that is often required of collectors of paintings and sculpture. Even the most prominent works of literature—with exceptions, of course—are not always expensive to collect. More than by any other factors, book collecting is affected by the law of supply and demand, and by fashion. What else can explain the fact that while first editions of the works of, say, Charles Dickens can be purchased for a modest sum, the first books of modern

---

* A list of subjects, though by no means complete, is provided at the end of this chapter.

writers such as William Faulkner or Gertrude Stein prove surprisingly expensive. Although the various factors that determine the value of a book will be discussed at length in later chapters, the aspiring collector must be aware that one can collect books costing less than a dollar or more than half a million.

At the same time, and perhaps more importantly, the beginning collector must be conscious of a fact that has somewhat diminished the pleasure of collecting books: namely, that many of the titles that were available in the past are not so readily obtainable today.

This is so because over the years many of the most desirable titles held in esteem by collectors have been absorbed into public institutions, such as the New York Public Library, the Pierpont Morgan Library, also in New York, the Henry E. Huntington Library in California, the Henry Clay Folger Shakespeare Library in Washington, D.C.—which, incidentally, houses the largest collection of Shakespeare's works in the world—and various university libraries, to such an extent that many of the volumes that were available in the past are at best extremely difficult to obtain today, as well as expensive, or at worst assuredly impossible. Thus, we often hear of the wealthiest of collectors changing their pattern of collecting.

Lest the novice become discouraged, I do not mean to suggest that every volume that a collector may desire is either unobtainable or unaffordable. I only want to caution the reader against believing that the books he or she may wish to have are easily obtainable at all times. Certainly, most of the volumes will be available and perhaps affordable, but this will not always be the case.

As one seasoned prominent collector, Raymond E. Hartz, suggested to me, the collector must seek the titles that are to be had in his or her time. In Mr. Hartz's most active period of

A first edition of the King James Bible (1611), believed to be the king's own copy

collecting, which was the 1930s and 1940s, it was still possible to collect the works of William Caxton, the first English printer, or the novels of Jane Austen in their original bindings, or an original etching executed by Thackeray for *Vanity Fair.* These items are rarities today.

At the same time, strangely and happily enough, the improbable sometimes becomes possible. For instance, most of the rare-book dealers and auctioneers I interviewed in the course of writing this book agreed that a copy of a first edition of Henry James's work that also bore his signature was quite uncommon. Yet just recently, after accepting the sad fact that I might perhaps never hope to obtain such a prize, I was offered a copy of the first edition of *The Better Sort,* published in London in 1903, which contains James's classic story "The Beast in the Jungle." The remarkable aspect of this copy, since it is not an uncommon title in the James canon, is that it was inscribed to George Meredith, another important novelist of the nineteenth century, in James's hand. The inscription reads: "George Meredith, his faithful old friend, Henry James." You can well imagine my delight in acquiring this extremely interesting volume after almost giving up all hope.

In addition to the improbable at times turning into the possible, the list of collectible authors and subjects grows yearly due to new collectors and new interests. It is not difficult to see that book collecting still offers the delight and pleasure and personal satisfaction that has been experienced by collectors over the centuries.

As to what constitutes the nature of the collector himself or herself, quite a number of opinions have been expressed, as they have regarding what motivates him or her to pursue such a hobby. Collectors themselves have been most articulate about this issue. In *The Collector's Book of Books,* Eric Quayle defined the collector of books as "a bibliophile; an otherwise rational member of the community consumed by the love of books" (page 8). Other commentators, however, while acknowledging the book collector to be certainly a lover of books, have observed that the pleasure in collecting favorite works of literature, or any other field of interest, had a somewhat selfish basis. John T. Winterich emphatically stated that the joys derived from book collecting lie in "the gratification of possession and the satisfaction of exhibition."* Similarly, Reginald Brewer contended in *The Delightful Diversion* that collectors "may prate all they like about the esthetic and cultural influences of collecting, but underneath all these is the sheer satisfaction of possession" (page 12).

Perhaps as complete and sensible an estimate of the nature of the book collector was offered by Herman W. Liebert in the June 1973 *Gazette* of the famed Grolier Club:

> What is the nature of this drive to collect books and manuscripts? One school of psychiatrists tells us that the collecting instinct is anal-erotic, reflecting the infant's attempt to satisfy his ego by withholding the contents of his bowels when the parent is urging him to excrete them. . . . these psychiatrists and I seem to have met infants that exhibit behavior of very different kinds. . . . As a matter of fact, I think that there are some easily identifiable elements in the collecting mania. One is the satisfaction of starting, and, against all odds, of completing a pattern; all the first editions of a certain author, or all the significant books on a certain subject. Book-collecting has this in common with crossword or jigsaw puzzles, stamp or coin collecting, needle-point. But with this difference, that one can read the books he collects. . . . There is, further, uniquely in book-collecting, the identification with authors, the growing knowledge of

---

* *A Primer of Book Collecting*, pages 179–80.

them and their works, and the creative experience that produced their works. . . . There is, finally, that sense of touch with the past, the vicarious participation in the main stream of man's cultural development, which is especially satisfying in a time like our own, when the fragmented present and the inscrutable future offer little feeling of orientation or identity. [Pages 15–16]

The collector, then, represents a kind of private preserve for the manuscripts and printed landmarks of Western man. What might have been the fate of the Gutenberg Bibles or the folios of Shakespeare, or the now classic poetry and fiction of the eighteenth and nineteenth centuries, had the instinct to collect and preserve them not prompted collectors to gather them up before they disappeared from sight? As Winterich stated succinctly: "If printing is the art preservative of all arts, then book-collecting is the preservative of that preservative."* Thus, the importance of the collector to Western cultural history is undeniable.

At the same time, however, that collectors seek to gather printed works and manuscripts for their intrinsic cultural value, they cannot fail to regard the potential market value that is inevitably a direct by-product of collecting anything worthwhile and desirable to others. A number of years ago, Barton Currie pointed out in *Fishers of Books* that while the "supposed worth of a collection in dollars and cents matters little as against the personal satisfaction" one obtains from collecting books, "it would be ridiculous to say that only a slim minority of book-collectors are influenced in their collecting by the thought of shrewd investment" (pages 150, 187).

The viewing of book collecting as a source of financial investment has always been an extremely controversial issue among collectors. To be sure, most of them believe that one should

---

* *The Grolier Club: 1884–1967* (New York: The Grolier Club, 1967), p. 49.

collect books primarily for pleasure, and that the market value of a particular item is merely incidental to its intrinsic value. It stands to reason that the works of Caxton, the plays of Shakespeare, the poetry of Keats and Browning, and the novels of Dickens and Jane Austen should have substantial market value due to their merit as outstanding milestones in literature. The fact that many books in demand by collectors bring handsome profits upon resale, they believe, should not influence the collector in his or her choice of which author, title, or subject matter to collect, or lead them into thinking that book collecting is comparable to the stock market. The wise collector buys only those volumes he or she deems valuable and of interest, since despite the fact that one can profit financially by pursuing book collecting as a form of speculative endeavor, it is equally true that a great many of the volumes that are bought for substantial amounts of money one day can prove not as valuable the next day, week, month, or year. Book collecting, perhaps more than any other pastime, is extremely vulnerable to fashion, and the beginning collector would do well to bear this fact in mind.

Nevertheless, the sanest attitude toward the financial aspect of book collecting may be the realization that there is really nothing morally wrong with viewing one's collection in terms of market value. After all, stamp or coin collectors, painting connoisseurs, and even electric train hobbyists rejoice over the growth in value of their collections over the years. So why shouldn't the collector of books rejoice? It would not be surprising to learn that many a collector has slept soundly safe in the thought that should it prove necessary, his or her book collection could stave off bankruptcy. There is little harm in knowing that a book purchased today may just be worth twice as much one day as in the future, or feeling a sense of satisfaction that one's judgment was truly sound or that one's tastes were of the highest order. Only the wealthiest of people can collect books with no regard to their market value.

What then, one might ask, truly constitutes the book collector? Is he or she anyone who owns a library, whether it consists of ten or ten thousand books? Does the sizable number of paperbacks stored away in a closet, on a bookshelf, or in the trunk of an automobile form a collection? Quite simply, the book collector can be defined as anyone who truly enjoys retaining those printed works that enriched his mind and provided him with immense enjoyment. Yet among serious book collectors method must accompany purpose. It is for this reason that collectors tend to concentrate upon following some sort of pattern, or method, or guideline. Accordingly, as has been noted, some collect only the first editions of their favorite titles or authors, while others concentrate upon incunabula, private press books, illustrated works, or finely bound volumes.

Yet to do so one must become a kind of detective who constantly searches through rare-book dealers' catalogues and bookshelves, auctioneers' advertisements, secondhand bookshops, library sales, flea markets, antique shops, and an occasional aunt's basement or attic for desired titles. Book collecting can be compared to the great chase undertaken by the huntsman or the detective, in which it is difficult to rest until your game or culprit or volume is caught.

If pursued methodically though casually, book collecting will prove to be an exhilarating enterprise. Yet sometimes, as in any other hobby or interest, one gets virtually carried away to such an extent that the concerns of the everyday world seem trifling. Witness the classic instance of the wealthy collector who bought an entire house and its contents some years ago in Brighton, England, in order to acquire a twelfth-century book of hours that the former owner would not separate for purchase from the other contents of the house. Not all collectors need be as diligently devoted to the game as was this man.

In the preceding pages, I have attempted to provide the aspiring collector with an overview of book collecting and the nature of the collector. The following chapters will treat the various aspects of book collecting in as detailed a manner as possible. The information provided is intended not only to instruct the novice collector, but to serve as a source of entertainment. While it is useful to be acquainted with the various technical terms and tools of the trade, so to speak, I do not want the reader to lose sight of the fact that book collecting is primarily a pleasurable pursuit and that one should derive a great deal of joy and satisfaction from it.

In the hope of providing the beginning collector with some direction, I have compiled a list of subjects on which collections can be focused. The list is hardly complete, since the possibilities of collecting books far exceed the limits of these pages.

Subjects

Literature	Military	Food
History	Mathematics	Cooking
Americana	Fashions	Gardening
Medicine	Psychology	Botany
Finance	Printing	Exploration
Sports	Etiquette	Sea travel
Motion pictures	Interior decoration	Dancing
Travel	Politics	Entomology
Philosophy	Television	Sculpture
Science	Music	Art
Physics	Police	Ships
Magic	Crime	Theology
Occult	Architecture	Old glass
Astrology	Sociology	Pewter
Aviation	Archaeology	China

Subjects (cont'd)

Furniture	Chivalry	Money
Antiques	Armor	Tobacco
Pottery	Automobiles	Real estate
Children	Religion	Science fiction
Fairy tales	Astronomy	

2

The History of Book Collecting

The earliest books collected were perhaps the papyri of Egypt and the ancient scrolls of Greece and Rome. These were gathered into libraries at Alexandria, Constantinople, and Rome, as well as in numerous other locations.

In the Middle Ages, the manuscripts copied by monks in monasteries were collected chiefly by people of wealth and rulers of church and state.* Thus it was that book collecting in the modern sense did not begin until after the invention of the printing press in the mid fifteenth century. For most collectors of the fifteenth and sixteenth centuries, the purpose of acquiring books was to compile a working library that would serve as a source of reference for scholars and humanists. One famous collection, the Bridgewater Library, begun by Sir Thomas Egerton in 1600, was one of the most extensive of its kind. It was purchased intact by Henry E. Huntington of California in 1917, and formed a considerable part of Huntington's world-famous library. Other renowned libraries were formed by Jean Grolier (1479–1565), Jacques Auguste de Thou (1553–1617), and Sir Thomas Bod-

---

* The first book about book collecting was written by Richard de Bury in 1345, and titled the *Philobiblon*. It was not printed until 1473 in Cologne, and in London until 1598–99.

ley, who established the public library named for him in 1598 at Oxford University, the Bodleian.

In the eighteenth century, a group of wealthy men in England began seriously and systematically to collect early printed books of the fifteenth and sixteenth centuries. Among these collectors were such notables as the first and second Earls of Oxford, the first Duke of Roxburghe, the eighth Earl of Pembroke, and the second Duke of Devonshire.

At the same time, an active interest in sixteenth- and seventeenth-century literature took hold, with special emphasis on the printing and literature of the Elizabethan and Jacobean periods. On the continent, a similar pattern occurred, in which collectors transferred their interest from incunabula to later works.

The early part of the nineteenth century witnessed a resurgence of interest in early printed works. Among the more formidable collectors were the second Earl of Spencer, who collected fifty-six Caxtons and first editions of all the classics of Greece and Rome; Richard Heber, who gathered one of the greatest libraries of early English poetry and drama, and Continental literature and history; and Sir Thomas Phillipps, who compiled the most impressive collections of manuscripts ever owned privately.

At this same time, James Lenox of New York acquired the first Gutenberg Bible in the Americas, and his books ultimately represented part of the collection of the New York Public Library. John Carter Brown collected Americana, George Brinley the books of Colonial America, and Robert Hoe English literature. Later though no less formidable American collectors include Henry Clay Folger, Henry E. Huntington, and the illustrious financier J. P. Morgan.

As for the various trends that have developed over the years, it was not until the last quarter of the nineteenth century that

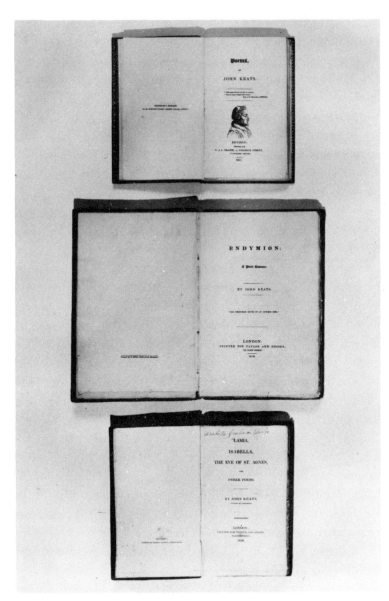

First editions by John Keats

collectors began seeking out contemporary or near-contemporary authors' works. For instance, in England the writings of the Romantic poets Wordsworth, Coleridge, Byron, Shelley, and Keats were first collected. Similarly, the works of Dickens and Thackeray—though at first purchased for their brilliant illustrations rather than their literary merit—were beginning to attract the interest of collectors, as were books by Tennyson, Browning, Ruskin, Swinburne, and George Eliot.

While collectors of literature tended to focus primarily upon poetry, and interest in early printed books and manuscripts still prevailed, the serious collectors of the day began to regard contemporary authors in a more favorable light than did their predecessors.

By the mid 1920s, largely as a result of the sale of the Stephen H. Wakeman estate in 1924, American authors such as Poe, Hawthorne, and Emerson were being sought for their first editions, and after the John Quinn sale in 1923 collectors began to pay attention to the writings of Henry James, Walter Pater, Sir Arthur Conan Doyle, and William Butler Yeats.

Furthermore, prose works slowly began gaining an advantage over poetry, and books by such contemporary authors as Joseph Conrad, George Bernard Shaw, James Barrie, and John Galsworthy were highly sought.

An extremely significant development of the twenties was the vigorous interest many collectors began to express in the works of writers of the eighteenth century. First editions of Samuel Johnson, Daniel Defoe, Henry Fielding, Samuel Richardson, Tobias Smollett, and Laurence Sterne were now sought as eagerly as had been the works of Caxton, Chaucer, Shakespeare, and Boccaccio.

Also, and perhaps just as importantly, collectors began to concentrate upon acquiring works of philosophical, scientific,

Eliza Meynell.

THE

MYSTERIES OF UDOLPHO,

A

ROMANCE;

INTERSPERSED WITH SOME PIECES OF POETRY.

BY

ANN RADCLIFFE,

AUTHOR OF THE ROMANCE OF THE FOREST, ETC.

IN FOUR VOLUMES.

Fate fits on these dark battlements, and frowns,
And, as the portals open to receive me,
Her voice, in sullen echoes through the courts,
Tells of a nameless deed.

VOL. I.

LONDON:
PRINTED FOR G. G. AND J. ROBINSON,
PATERNOSTER-ROW.
1794.

First edition of a classic eighteenth-century Gothic novel

political, and economic importance as fervently as previous collectors had sought the masterpieces of literature.

As for collecting interests today, they have been somewhat limited by the fact that many items available in the past are no longer to be found so readily, such as Chaucer, Shakespeare, and Boccaccio. Still, collectors attempt to acquire these items if and when they appear for sale at auction or in a dealer's catalogue. At the same time, there has been and continues to be interest in the notable works of the seventeenth, eighteenth, and nineteenth centuries, as well as the works of such twentieth-century notables as James Joyce, Ernest Hemingway, F. Scott Fitzgerald, Ezra Pound, T. S. Eliot, Robert Frost, Gertrude Stein, William Faulkner, D. H. Lawrence, W. H. Auden, Joseph Conrad, and Nathanael West.

To be sure, interest persists among collectors for first and rare editions of scientific, philosophical, economic, historical, political, and detective works, as well as those pertaining to natural history, Americana, and sea travel. Science fiction is steadily gaining devotees each year, and as new authors enter the spotlight, and new works aspire to classic status, they attract more collectors. One of the most attractive aspects of book collecting is its capacity to appeal to diversified tastes and interests, thus augmenting the infinite pleasure enjoyed by successive generations of collectors.

A collection of some modern first editions popular with collectors

3

What Makes a Book Worth Collecting?

The initial question usually raised by the aspiring book collector concerns the nature or kinds of books worth collecting. How do I know which books are worthwhile and which ones to ignore? the novice will often ask. Are all books valuable, or should the title of a given work warrant priority over age alone? Should I concentrate on collecting only cloth or hardbound books, or are paperbacks just as desirable? Should the reputation of the author or the work be given the highest consideration, or should one judge a book desirable on the basis of its fine binding? Can newly published books be of interest as readily as old ones? What is the basis or justification for preferring to collect one first edition over another?

The only sensible answer to these questions is that a book's collectibility first and foremost rests solely with each individual's desires, interests, and tastes. What one man regards as a treasure, another may deem suitable for the trash can. Therefore, the first rule of collecting books is to collect only what you like. As Barton Curric said many years ago: "the great mistake in collecting—assuming that you collect for yourself, for a personal library that is to house intimate companions—is to buy what you could not, under any circumstances, bring yourself to read."* Thus, in terms of personal value accorded any book, the decision is entirely dependent upon your individual preferences. Why should it be otherwise?

Once decided upon the kinds of books you desire to collect, you must approach the rare-book dealer or other specialist in your field of interest, or at times the various auction rooms, in order to obtain them. In the dollars-and-cents world of anti-quarian booksellers and auctioneers, the collector soon learns that the market value of a book is hardly determined by personal whim and preference. Therefore, over the years dealers and col-lectors alike, in an effort to establish objective criteria to refer to whenever they attempt to determine a given title's collectible value, tend to honor various factors other than personal prefer-ence, such as the general importance of the given title in relation to comparable works in its field or on its subject, the degree to which that work is in demand by collectors, whether the known existing copies are rare or relatively common, and perhaps most importantly, its physical condition.

Regarding the first of these factors, importance, it stands to reason that collectors over the years have chosen to concentrate on acquiring the outstanding works of their particular field of interest, be it literature, science, history, etc., since the very stat-ure of those works endows them with a great deal of intrinsic interest. In literature, for example, such works as Shakespeare's plays, John Donne's *Poems* (1633), Henry Fielding's *Tom Jones* (1749), Jane Austen's *Pride and Prejudice* (1813), Charles Dickens's *Pickwick Papers* (1836–37), Charlotte Brontë's *Jane Eyre* (1847), and William Thackeray's *Vanity Fair* (1848) stand as undeniable milestone works of unending joy, interest, and value.

---

* *Fishers of Books*, page 113.

At the same time that collectors seek the universally acknowledged landmarks of man's progress in literature, science, exploration, or travel, a number of relatively minor works may also be in demand due to their intrinsic interest to individual collectors.

Therefore, assuming that a title is acknowledged to be one of importance, and of interest to and in demand by collectors, two other factors must also be taken into account in order to assess the value of a book: namely, rarity and condition.

RARITY

Certainly one of the most crucial factors to consider when attempting to judge the value of a book is its rarity. Yet how does one define "rarity"? Is an old book rare merely by virtue of its age? Is a book that is out of print and seemingly unavailable in bookshops automatically to be regarded as a rarity? Or is a book rare when quite a few individuals want to acquire it, but very few are able to locate it? For the majority of collectors and dealers, this last definition most nearly approximates the meaning of rarity, since there is no point in deeming a book "rare" and hence valuable if no one wants it. As in any other field, the law of supply and demand provides the basis of value.

Yet the term "rare" is quite general, and for practical purposes has been refined to various gradations. John Carter points out those distinctions in *Taste and Technique in Book Collecting* (page 134). A book is "rare" that proves difficult to find in the country where it is sought. "Very rare" applies to books that are difficult to find in any country. "Extremely rare" refers to books of which only fifty or sixty copies are known to exist, while "excessive rarity" occurs when the number of copies does not exceed ten. A book that was printed in a very small number is known to be "absolutely rare." Alfred Lord Tennyson's *The Lover's Tale* (1833) and Algernon Charles Swinburne's *Siena* (1868) qualify as being "absolutely rare" since only six copies of each were printed, while Elizabeth Barrett Browning's first book, *The Battle of Marathon* (1828), is "excessively rare" since of the fifty copies originally printed, only nine have been discovered. Similarly, only one copy of the first edition of Shakespeare's *Venus and Adonis* (1593) survives, and that in the Bodleian Library at Oxford University.

Any number of circumstances contribute to a book's rarity. Many times it is printed privately by the author either because he or she is unable to find a publisher, as was the case of Edgar Allan Poe with his first book, *Tamerlane and Other Poems* (1827), or because the author has a specific purpose in mind, as did Robert Frost when he published only two copies of his first book of poems, *Twilight,* in Lawrence, Massachusetts, in 1894, one of which was intended for his fiancée, Elinor, and one copy for himself.

With Poe's first book, the situation is especially interesting. The number of copies which were printed remains uncertain, as well as the reason for which *Tamerlane* never obtained the circulation that Poe may have intended. The only reference that Poe made to the publication of this work appeared in the Advertisement to the second edition of the poem in *Al Aaraff, Tamerlane, and Minor Poems* (1829), which stated that "This poem was printed for publication in Boston, in the year 1827, but suppressed through circumstances of a private nature." Just what those "circumstances" were has never been fully explained. One might guess that perhaps Poe could not pay the printer, and hence the copies were never distributed commercially. More likely, perhaps, as Thomas Ollive Mabbott suggested, " 'suppres-

sion' was a euphemism for 'had no real circulation,' "* and
when Poe realized that copies were neither selling nor gaining
critical favor, he "suppressed" the book, yet only after a number
of copies were either sold or given away.

Or perhaps the printer sold what copies he could after Poe
joined the army, some time before the book was ready for publication, and either destroyed the remaining copies or sold them to
a bookseller, or left them in a box in his shop. No one knows for
certain what happened.

What is certain, however, is that either out of temperament or
by accident, Poe created a rarity that today would bring a small
fortune to anyone who discovers a copy.† At this writing, only
eleven copies have been discovered. Of course, Poe never realized that his actions would have such repercussions long after he
lived, or that the detection of the whereabouts of copies of his
first book would prove perhaps as mystifying and exciting as the
detective stories he created.

Quite often, the publisher of a first book, owing to the author's relative obscurity and the perennially high costs of printing, decides to publish the volume in a low number of copies. As
time passes, and the stature of the author grows, the publisher
will often print successively more copies of each new title. Consequently, anyone seeking to collect the works of a particular
author in first edition form will, more often than not, have less
difficulty in obtaining the later titles than the earlier ones. Such
is the situation with Robert Browning, whose earliest book,
Pauline (1833), is virtually impossible to find, but whose later

---

* *Tamerlane and Other Poems* (New York: The Facsimile Text Society,
Columbia University Press, 1941), page xxxi.

† In 1974, a copy of *Tamerlane* brought $123,000 at a Sotheby Parke Bernet
auction in New York.

The very rare first book by William Faulkner

A nineteenth-century rarity by Stephen Crane; his first book (1893)

volumes, for the most part, are relatively accessible and inexpensive.

In general, then, first and early books of authors in demand by collectors are often more desirable and valuable than later ones. In the case of the poet Edwin Arlington Robinson, who was neither as popular nor as prolific as Browning or Tennyson, only his first book, *The Torrent and the Night Before,* privately printed in Maine in 1896, and his second, *The Children of the Night* (1897), are really held in esteem by collectors. Both are difficult titles to obtain.

Sometimes rarities are created as a result of disasters or accidents. Fires, floods, or wholesale destruction of an author's work will create a market for a book in which the demand far exceeds the supply. Frank Norris's *Yvernelle* (1892) achieved rare status as the result of a warehouse fire that destroyed most of the copies of the first edition. While Norris's most important title, both critically and in terms of book collecting, is *McTeague* (1899), *Yvernelle* exceeds it in value merely by virtue of its accidental rarity.

Another situation in which a rarity is created occurs when publishers print extremely small numbers of a title merely for purposes of securing a copyright. A perfect example of this is Joseph Conrad's *Some Reminiscences,* which was published in New York in 1908 by its English publisher in order that the American copyright be secured. Only six copies were printed. The book did not appear in its regular trade edition until 1912. Hence the fact that extreme value was placed upon those earlier six copies by collectors, not only because they preceded the first trade edition by quite a number of years, but also since so few were printed.

It sometimes occurs, even in times supposedly as advanced as ours, that a book is repressed or censored on either political or moral grounds, and subsequently unavailable to the public. When this occurs, rarities are often the result. Six weeks after D. H. Lawrence's *The Rainbow* (1915) was published, a court order demanded that it be taken off the market on moral grounds. Very few copies had been sold, the result being that today *The Rainbow* is not only a rather difficult book to locate for collectors of Lawrence's works, but expensive as well.

Similarly, James Joyce's *Ulysses* (1922), owing to the presence of language and scenes that were regarded as morally objectionable in its day, was more or less untouchable by the more established publishers in London and New York who feared possible lawsuits for publishing "obscenity." It was published in Paris by Sylvia Beach, a local bookseller who was a friend of Joyce's, in a first edition of one thousand copies, of which the first hundred were signed by Joyce and printed on Dutch handmade paper. A first edition of *Ulysses*, now regarded as perhaps the most important novel of the twentieth century, will cost a collector quite a few thousand dollars as a result of its rarity and critical importance.

Another instance in which a book acquires rare status occurs when the publisher has been in business for a short time and his reputation is not fully established. The first edition of the Brontë sisters' *Poems* (1846) achieved its rare status among collectors because the publisher, Aylott and Jones, a relatively obscure firm, decided to sell the remaining copies of the slow-moving book to the established firm of Smith, Elder, and Company. Upon acquiring the unsold copies, Smith, Elder removed the previous publisher's title page and inserted one that bore its name. The book was then placed upon the market again. Today the true first edition in the collectors' estimation is the volume with the Aylott and Jones title page, which, as it happens, is extremely rare to come by.

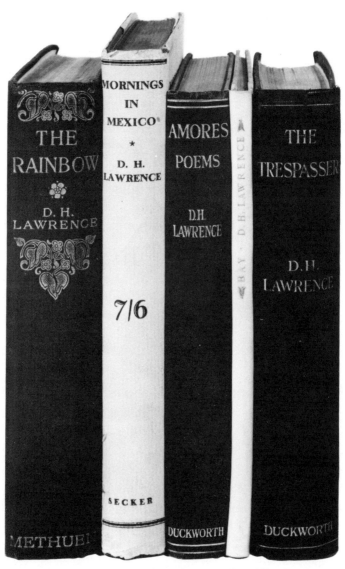

First editions by D. H. Lawrence, including *The Rainbow*,
an extremely rare title

On occasion, a last-minute change in the date of publication produces a rarity. As a result of the postponement of the publication of Lewis Carroll's *Alice's Adventures in Wonderland* from 1865 to 1866, a seemingly inconsequential decision at the time, one of the most renowned rarities of literature was created. Carroll's dissatisfaction with the quality of the printing caused the publisher to suppress the edition originally issued in July 1865, of which only a few copies had been given away by the author.

And so it happened that some copies of the first edition of *Alice*, yet only a very few, escaped the fate of the other copies, and bore the date 1865 on their title page. Had a great number of copies been so published, the atypically title-paged volumes would merely have been preferred by collectors, and perhaps not so feverishly sought. As it stands, however, many a collector dreams of the day when he may encounter the 1865 *Alice*, since if and when he does, he will be in possession of a truly rare and desirable book.

Thus, age alone is never the sole requisite for rarity. What the collector must bear in mind is that while thousands of books may qualify as "rarities" as a result of one or more of the factors mentioned above, only a slim percentage are in demand. For every acknowledged rarity that might prove expensive, there are countless others that can be purchased for a modest sum. In the end, the collector must decide which "rare" books are truly worth collecting.

CONDITION

The physical condition of any book in demand by collectors is always of prime consideration. Even the rarest of titles are compared in terms of their condition, despite the fact that those who want them would perhaps accept them in almost any condition rather than not at all. Of such importance is the condition of a work to collectors that dealers and auctioneers invariably are compelled to describe as accurately as possible the various defects, if any, of the volumes they are presenting for sale or auction in their catalogues.

While each dealer and auctioneer will differ with respect to the detail he will offer regarding the condition of a book, all will at least cite if a book is in "poor," "worn," "fair," "good," "fine," or "mint" condition. Further, they will note if the pages or illustration plates are "foxed"—that is, brown-spotted as a result of age; if the interior covers are cracked; if the dust wrapper is present and whether it is torn or mended with tape; if the color of the binding has faded or darkened, and other indications of physical wear, such as if the corners of the binding are "bumped," or bent; if the text, or body, of the book has become loosened from the binding; if any parts of the spine or covers are "rubbed," or scuffed; and if there are torn or missing pages.

Naturally, first editions and other collectibles should always be secured in the finest condition available. At the same time, the collector must realize that not every desirable title can be obtained in near-perfect condition. In fact, more often than not, collectors are faced with either acquiring a particular title that they have long been seeking, due to its rarity, despite its worn or even poor condition; or passing it by and risking not seeing that item again for some time.

Whenever he is faced with this dilemma, the collector should pay high regard to the degree of frequency with which the particular title is offered by dealers and auctioneers, as well as the possible demand by other collectors. If the book is not that uncommon, or is available to collectors at least once or twice a year and not particularly in demand by other collectors, it would be foolish not to wait until a copy in fine condition turns up.

On the contrary, if a title is so rare as to be hardly ever offered on the market, and the collector's desire to acquire the volume is intense to the point of obsession (which often occurs), the most sensible action to take is to buy the book, provided the price is commensurate with its condition,* in the hope that in the months or years ahead it will be replaced someday by a more perfect copy if and when one appears on the market. Again, this course should be pursued only in instances of extreme rarity.

For the most part, however, the collector would do well to follow the sound guidelines suggested by John T. Winterich in his admirable *A Primer of Book Collecting.* Seasoned as well as beginner collectors can benefit from his advice.

What is good secondhand condition? Something, obviously, short of perfection. A book in good secondhand condition may show signs of having been read, but it should not show signs of having been maltreated. The binding, which makes the book rather farther than clothes make the man, should not be rubbed, scratched, stained, faded, bent or dog-eared. . . . The body of the book should fit snugly into the binding. Misuse tends to loosen the body from the outer garment, and such a condition is difficult to repair. Repairs of any kind, furthermore, do not enhance the value of a rare book, and are resorted to only as a preservative.

The inside of the volume should be clean and whole. A book is not in good secondhand condition if the pages are badly smudged, or worse yet, made hideous by marginal notes.* Tobacco ashes—especially ashes hot enough to scorch the paper

---

* Just as collectors tend to differ, however slightly, in their requirements and definitions of "acceptable condition," so too do dealers sometimes differ in determining a price based upon the condition of a book.

or even burn holes through it—and gingerbread crumbs that leave an unmistakable trail of grease do not enhance the value of a rare book.

The endpapers—the blank leaves at the beginning and end of a book—should not bear writing,* and writing on the title page is, of course, a supreme offense, unless the inscription carries some association interest. [Pages 99–100]

Winterich goes on to define the perfection that occurs "when a book is uncut and unopened" (page 111). "Uncut" refers to any book whose sheets have not been trimmed for binding, while "unopened" applies to volumes whose sheets or leaves have not been separated, an indication that the book in all probability has never been read. The irony of a book being of greater value if its pages have never been separated for reading has long been noted by collectors as bordering on the absurd. Nevertheless, their awareness has never diminished the value of unopened books.

The golden rule of book collecting, therefore, is to buy, whenever possible, only those volumes that are in the best of condition. The collector will never regret acquiring books in fine condition, and should the occasion arise when these books are sold, either because the collector has lost interest in them, has found duplicates, or is in dire need of money, the chances for loss, with respect to original purchase price, are indeed minimal —provided, of course, that the books are in demand at the moment—while the chances for some profit are probable.

In order for a book to be truly desirable, in terms of condition, it should possess the binding in which it was first issued. Sometimes, of course, the original binding is in such a state of disrepair that the only alternative is to have the book rebound,

---

* Unless, of course, in either the author's or other celebrated hand.

First editions by Thomas Hardy in especially fine condition

usually in fine leather. What must be taken into consideration by the collector is whether the book was rebound at a date close to its publication, or at such time as to be regarded as being contemporary with its issue, or many years after its initial appearance—say, one hundred or so—or just recently. The value of a book is determined, by and large, by a combination of its rarity, its condition, and the state of its binding—whether original or rebound, and if rebound, when. While recently bound copies of a work can prove valuable and expensive as a result of the artistry and skill evidenced in the production of its binding, and will enhance any bookshelf, most collectors tend to prefer a book in its original binding—unless they happen to be collectors of fine bindings. A copy of an 1813 *Pride and Prejudice* or an 1847 *Jane Eyre* in its original binding, then, is of infinitely greater value and desirability than a similar copy in a relatively contemporary binding—which, in its turn, is of far greater interest than a copy bound at a much later date.

Let the collector visit any rare-book dealer's shop or witness an auction in which there appear two copies of the same book in different bindings, and he or she will see, as I have recently seen, the astounding difference in value reflected in the prices of a copy in its original binding format and one in either a later or a present-day binding. To the uninitiated, the shock will indeed be great.

As a result of the differing methods and practices by which books have been printed, bound, and distributed for sale since the earliest days of printing, a problem arises regarding what exactly constitutes "original" condition. The collector must be familiar with the various binding procedures that have flourished from time to time in order to be able to truly ascertain the value of the books he or she wishes to acquire. It is indeed imperative for the aspiring collector to know that in books printed from the

A collection of first editions by Jane Austen in original boards with paper labels

fifteenth century to perhaps the middle to late eighteenth century, the bindings tend to vary considerably since it was not the practice of printers to issue their productions ready-bound.

Printing and binding grew as two distinct crafts from the earliest days, and remained so until the eighteenth century, when books were issued bound in paper-covered boards. Before that time, and even somewhat afterward, books were issued in bundles of sheets, sometimes loosely sewn together, but not bound between covers, since it was customary for the purchaser to bring the sheets to his favorite bookseller or binder, and commission him to bind the sheets in whatever binding the buyer found pleasing.

The earliest book buyers were usually persons of considerable wealth, who had their books bound in the best of leather crafted in the hands of a notable craftsman of the day, and often gilded, decorated with silver, or bedecked with jewels. Since the purchaser of a given work could choose to have it bound from a variety of leather bindings, including quarter calf, sprinkled calf, diced calf, mottled calf, tree calf, and marbled calf, with any combination of colors, many first editions or early copies of works produced during those times will appear for sale in different bindings. Thus, in this instance, "original" more or less becomes translated as "contemporary."

From the mid-eighteenth century, books began to be issued with greater frequency between paper-covered boards, their pages uncut primarily as a service rendered by the bookseller to ensure protection of the sheets. Paper or leather labels were usually glued to the spine, bearing the title, and optionally the name of the author. These covers were never expected to last permanently. Hence their rather fragile nature, and their value today since so few survived in acceptable condition. Sir Walter Scott's *Waverley* (1814), John Keats's *Endymion* (1820), and any number of titles by Wordsworth, Coleridge, Byron, and Shelley, to name but a few, are relatively expensive to acquire, though not nearly so costly as when they are offered in their original boards.

First editions of Henry Fielding's *Joseph Andrews* (1742) and *Tom Jones* (1749) in contemporary bindings

Cloth-covered board bindings began to appear on school textbooks around the middle of the eighteenth century. Yet it was not until the early 1820s that the first books published in cloth came into relatively frequent use, and not until the 1830s that cloth-covered bindings became an established publishing practice. In time, titles and authors' names were lettered in gilt on the spine and covers, and various pictorial embellishments were added, along with ornamentation of design. Thus, the collector will find various titles of the period by Charles Dickens, the Brontë sisters, Anthony Trollope, William Thackeray, and a host of others listed as being available in "original cloth," which is, needless to say, the preferred condition.

In the Victorian era, many novels were initially published monthly in parts, and by and large the parts are preferred by collectors, since the first book editions technically do not represent the novels' first appearance in print. Not all the authors of that period utilized this format, but the more popular writers, notably Dickens and Thackeray, invariably published their latest productions in monthly installments. In the nineteenth century, books were still a rather expensive luxury for the majority of the population, and as more and more people learned to read, the demand for reading material increased, while the means to acquire books did not. Consequently, the monthly-part format served as a cheap means of delighting in the stories of popular writers.

To the collector today, monthly parts are not inexpensive. Certainly the most coveted item in the Dickens canon is the complete collection of the monthly installments of *The Posthumous Papers of the Pickwick Club,* which ran from April 1836 to November 1837. So numerous are the various points* that occur in the rare first issue that fourteen pages of bibliographical description were devoted to it by John Eckel when he compiled his classic bibliography of Dickens's works. While the collector will find it rather inexpensive to acquire this novel in its

---

* Eccentricities of type, design, content, or other characteristics which do not appear in all the copies of the first edition of an author's work. See Chapter 14.

Two novels by Charles Dickens in original monthly parts

first-edition book form, which appeared in 1837, he or she will have to search quite some time for the first-issue monthly parts. Once they are found, the collector should be prepared to part with a small fortune if the parts are to grace his library shelves. Thus, in an effort to establish some order of priority with respect to novels that first appeared in monthly-installment form, we might suggest that parts issued earlier than the first book edition are preferable to it (though there are exceptions, as in the cases of George Eliot and Henry James), but that the first book edition in its original cloth may be preferable to an edition bound from the monthly parts, and in a contemporary binding, since according to John Carter,* it was customary for the complete volume in publisher's cloth to be issued immediately prior to the publication of the last part.

Thus it is that the first book edition, although one step removed from the original manner of issuance—that is, in weekly or monthly parts—can often represent the first complete published form of a work. Still, there are collectors who prefer a bound copy containing the monthly parts. It is their prerogative, and they cannot be criticized for their preference.

With respect to modern first editions, to collectors they are hardly ever acceptable in anything but the very finest condition. Of paramount importance also is the presence of the dust wrapper or jacket, if the volume was originally issued with one.

Although dust wrappers date back to the nineteenth century, they were not as commonly provided then as they are today. Many collectors value dust jackets not only for their beauty or ingenuity of design, but because they are an integral part of the book, and are adamant that any title so issued should not be acquired in an incomplete state. In fact, unless a modern first

---

* *ABC for Book-Collectors*, page 113.

edition that does not include its dust jacket is distinguished for the presence of either the author's signature, an important inscription, or an associative feature, most collectors will decline to buy it.

In addition to dust wrappers' being regarded as an essential aspect of a book, they are often used to identify the earliest issues of a first edition that cannot otherwise be distinguished from later ones. For instance, while the first printing of Ernest Hemingway's *For Whom the Bell Tolls* (1940) is distinguished from later printings by the presence of an "A" on the copyright page, the first-stage dust jacket, which encased the earliest copies of the first printing, does not mention the photographer's name, Arnold, beneath Hemingway's photo. For extremely discriminating collectors, no other copy will suffice than the one with the first-state dust wrapper. Similarly, collectors of the works of Thomas Wolfe prefer the edition of *Look Homeward, Angel* (1929) that bears a photograph of Wolfe on the back of the dust wrapper, even though the price may be two hundred dollars more than for a copy of the first edition in a later wrapper.

The difference in value and subsequent cost to the collector between first editions of the same title with and without the dust jacket is astounding. First editions of Hemingway, Fitzgerald, Faulkner, D. H. Lawrence, Gertrude Stein, T. S. Eliot, James Joyce, and Ezra Pound with their dust jackets will often cost anywhere from twice to ten times the price of the same titles without the wrappers.* One bookseller recently told me that most of the libraries he sells modern first editions to won't accept any modern title without its jacket.

One last point concerning dust jackets: they should not be torn and stained, as often occurs since their function initially is

---

* Dust jackets for Fitzgerald's books are notoriously rare.

First editions with dust jackets

protective rather than decorative, nor should they be pasted together with glue or tape, despite the fact that sometimes repair is the only means of preventing the wrapper from disintegrating entirely. If one is going to play the book collecting game, one must abide by its rules, one of the strangest and most unreasonable perhaps being the preference for dust jackets.

To conclude, condition is everything. Buy only those books that are available in the finest condition. To do otherwise is to buy books that cannot be said to be in "collector's condition," and consequently, of collector's value.

4

First Editions

Anyone who owns books, whether they be stored on a bookshelf in a library or living room, in a box in an attic or basement, or in the trunk of an automobile, stands a fairly good chance of being in possession of a first edition. By definition, a first edition is one of any number of copies initially printed upon the publication of a book or pamphlet. That is to say, the first edition of a work is comprised of the copies first printed by the publisher for sale to the public. A first edition of a particular work can consist of any number of copies. If a book is privately printed, the number of copies produced can range from one to one hundred —or even one thousand, although this does not usually occur. Works published by the major firms basically number anywhere from two thousand to twenty thousand, dependent upon public demand for a certain topic, or an author's popularity. Ironically enough, in the view of collectors, though certainly not in that of an author or publisher, the smaller the number of copies printed for the first edition, the better, since rarity serves as the basis for desiring a particular volume—provided, of course, that the author is in current demand with collectors.

Since first editions are held in such high esteem, the majority of collectors will concentrate on them in searching out their favorite authors' works or volumes in their field of interest. Unless some unusual point is attached to them, collectors will not be even slightly interested in later editions. The value of the first edition rests, in their view and rightly so, with the fact that it represents the original or initial manner of appearance in printed form of an author's creative efforts. In Reginald Brewer's opinion, the interest in first editions has its basis in the fact that a "first edition enjoys certain distinctions that can never attach to later printings. . . . First, it was the original form in which contemporary readers were permitted to examine the author's work. . . . Secondly, it was the edition in which his own creative efforts crystallized."*

As to which first editions should be collected and which discarded, that only the individual can determine. In time, every collector learns which titles and authors relative to his or her field are worth acquiring and which are not. Since every published work initially appears in first edition form, some degree of discretion must be applied, else there would be no point to collecting books; the basis for collecting anything is selectivity. As with rarity, the law of supply must be accompanied by the law of demand in order for a first edition to be of any value to the collector. The ironic aspect of any kind of collecting is that despite the infinite possibilities available as a result of discrepancies in their standards of taste, all too often collectors seem to vie for the same titles or authors relevant to their special interest. Collectors of literature seem to seek the first editions, year in and year out, of Milton, Fielding, Johnson, Dickens, Thackeray, the Brontës, Hemingway, Joyce, James, and Eliot, to name but a very few, while collectors of science books often dream of acquiring something by Galileo or Sir Isaac Newton.

---

* *The Delightful Diversion,* pages 24–25.

First edition of Ernest Hemingway's second book

More often than not, the later editions of an author's works can be purchased for one or two dollars while the first edition may be valued at a price that exceeds these figures by five, fifty, five hundred, or five thousand times. An excellent example lies in the incident that occurred quite some years ago when the owner of a New York secondhand bookshop returned from lunch and looked over a number of books that his assistant had bought for ninety cents, noticing among them a first edition of Edgar Allan Poe's *Murders in the Rue Morgue* (1843). He immediately telephoned a noted rare-book dealer, and sold the book for twenty-five thousand dollars.

Lest I mislead the reader, there are a number of ways in which a later edition of a given work can prove of interest and value to collectors. On occasion, an author will issue a revised edition of a previously published work, in which appear added or formerly deleted chapters, noteworthy textual changes, or other substantial alterations in either content or format. One such instance concerns a relatively modern title, *Exile's Return*, Malcolm Cowley's classic account of American expatriate writers who lived abroad in the 1920s. It was first published in 1934; in 1951, Cowley saw fit to revise the format and text of the book, and a revised edition was issued.

Since the changes he effected were of such a decidedly noteworthy nature, the revised format has been regarded ever since as the book in its final and thus truest form. Later printings of this popular work, either in hardbound or paperbound copies, are printed from the 1951 plates. As a result, both the 1934 and the 1951 editions, though issued almost twenty years apart, are considered as the first edition. In instances where authors are infamous for issuing revised editions of their works, as George Moore, author of *Esther Waters* (1894), was, collectors must decide for themselves the course that both their patience and their pocketbooks will permit them sensibly to pursue.

A second instance in which a later edition proves in demand by collectors occurs when and if a book appears in a first "illustrated" edition, with drawings or sketches executed by an artist of widely acknowledged renown, such as George Cruikshank in the nineteenth century, or Rockwell Kent in our own. Both the Cruikshank editions of the works of Fielding and Goldsmith, which represent but a few of his productions, and the Kent editions of Melville's *Moby-Dick* (1930), to name but one example of this fine artist's efforts, are prized by collectors for the beauty and skill of their illustrations.

At other times, the inclusion of a preface or an afterword by someone held in esteem by collectors—that is, either another author or a noted expert on a particular subject—in a work that person did not write often endows it with collectible interest. For instance, in a collection of short stories by Guy de Maupassant, *The Old Number: Thirteen Tales,* issued by Harper's in 1889, Henry James provided an introduction. This volume is of special interest for James collectors since it includes a critical essay which they may value not only for its intrinsic literary merit, but also because it appeared in no other previous publication.

It sometimes happens that an author will autograph a later edition of a work for an admirer or as a gift expressing the author's affection or esteem. While a great deal more will be said about this in a later chapter, it suffices at this point to know that any book containing writing in the hand of an author who is in demand by collectors will be of intense interest to anyone who collects books.

Lastly, later editions of a writer's works in their first "collected edition" form are frequently of interest to collectors. It often happens that a publisher will issue a complete edition of an author's novels, poems, plays, essays, or critical writings. Sometimes the collected edition is issued during the writer's lifetime, in which case extensive revision may distinguish the individual works from the manner in which they originally appeared. Thus, the collected edition becomes of interest since it represents final versions of the author's writings.

When Scribner's published the New York Edition of Henry James's novels and tales in 1907–9, James made quite a number of changes in such novels as *The American* and *The Portrait of a Lady*. Similarly in demand are the first collected editions of the writings of Charles Dickens, William Wordsworth, Percy Shelley, and Jane Austen, to name but a few.

Notable poets and writers of short stories will often have either a first "collected edition" or a first "selected edition." Generally speaking, unless the poems or stories were selected by the author himself, the first collected edition is preferable. The first collected editions of T. S. Eliot, W. B. Yeats, Marianne Moore, and E. E. Cummings, to note a few modern poets, are of decided interest to some collectors, though hardly, of course, as valued as the first editions of these writers.

5

Impression, Issue, and State

In collecting first editions, three important factors must be taken
into consideration before a book can truly be determined a first
edition: impression, issue, and state.

Technically speaking, a first edition is composed of any number of copies printed at the earliest date from one setting-up of
type plates. If the type is removed, and changes possibly made in
the text or format of the book, subsequent copies printed represent the second or later editions.

A problem arises for the collector, however, when the type
plates are left "standing" after the initial number of copies have
been printed, in order that various numbers of copies can be
printed at various times thereafter. The total number of copies
printed each time afterward comprise later "impressions." Thus
it is that a book may represent a second impression of the first
edition since theoretically it was printed from the same plates as
the first impression of the first edition, though at a later date.
Yet, for a book to be truly desirable to collectors, it should
represent one of the copies that comprise the first impression or
printing of a first edition. Collectors will usually accept no other.
The collector should always pay close attention to the verso—or
back—of the title page to see if there is any indication that the

volume represents the "second impression" or "third impression," which would usually be printed beneath the copyright date. Rarely there will be some notation of the impression on the face of the title page. One problem that arises when attempting to distinguish the first impression from later ones is due to the fact that some publishers either neglect to note the varying impressions, or do so in such a manner as to baffle the most adroit and experienced of collectors. For this reason, the collector should refer to Henry S. Boutell's excellent *First Editions and How to Tell Them** for a complete list of devices used by publishers to differentiate first from later editions and first from later impressions. Most library reference rooms contain a copy of this most useful guide for collectors. If it should prove difficult to consult this work, the obvious recourse is to consult your local rare-book dealer for advice.

Another extremely important factor to consider concerns the "issue" of a first edition. Just as there are varying impressions of a first edition, there are at times available different issues. Issues are created as a result of alterations made during the printing of the first edition, by the author's changes in textual content or format; by the correction of errors in printing which appear in some copies and not in others; by the inclusion or deletion of illustrations; or by other variations between copies that have already been sent from the publisher to distributors or booksellers, and those printed afterward. In any case, for a book to be regarded as having appeared in two or more issues, there must be present some variation of either text or format among the copies that constitute the first edition.

There are many classic examples of books that have appeared in various issues of first edition form. Since there are too many

---

* See also Jack Tannen, *How to Identify and Collect American First Editions: A Guidebook* (New York: Arco, 1976).

to mention here, I have devoted all of Chapter 14 to discussing the various characteristics or points that distinguish one issue of a title from another. For the sake of example, however, some items should be noted. The first issue of the first edition of Sinclair Lewis's *Elmer Gantry* (1927) is detected by looking to see if on the back of the spine, near the top of the binding, a "C" appears for "G" in the spelling of "Gantry." This error was the result of a discrepancy that occurred during the initial printing of the book and was not noticed until several hundred copies had been printed, bound, and distributed for sale. Later issues of the first edition read correctly and hence are not as highly regarded by collectors as the first issue. Another instance in which an error in spelling distinguishes the first from later issues of a first edition concerns John Dos Passos's *Three Soldiers* (1921), in which the word "signing" appears for "singing" on page 213.

Of course, errors do not always occur in the first issue. Sometimes they appear later, as in Stephen Crane's *The Red Badge of Courage* (1895), in which the last line of type on page 225 is printed perfectly in the first issue, but damaged in the second. It occasionally happens that errors or omissions in type or spelling are discovered after the book has been printed, but before it has been bound. In such cases, the usual practice of publishers is to print a separate small slip of paper bearing the correction and insert it in the book when it is bound. This paper is known as an errata slip, from the Latin word meaning "erred, strayed." Thus, collectors will often be informed by dealers and auctioneers if a particular volume contains the errata slip that may be called for when attempting to determine the priority of various issues of a first edition.

On other occasions, priority of issue is determined by the inclusion or exclusion of content. The second issue of Bret

Harte's *The Luck of Roaring Camp* (1870), for example, contained the short story "Brown of Caleveras," which was not included in the first issue.

Sometimes the presence or absence of an illustration serves to determine priority of issue. In Thackeray's *Vanity Fair* (1848), the first issue has a woodcut illustration on page 336 of Lord Steyne, a distasteful character in the story. A member of the aristocracy protested at the time of publication that the sketch bore too great a resemblance to himself, and the illustration was suppressed from later printings.

Advertisements also serve to distinguish priority of issue, as in Nathaniel Hawthorne's *The Scarlet Letter* (1850), which must include four pages of advertisements at the front of the book. Also of significance can be differing types of paper upon which the text is printed, as in Edna St. Vincent Millay's first book, *Renascence and Other Poems* (1917), which initially was printed on paper watermarked "Glaslan," while the watermark of a later issue was "Ingre d'Arches."

Among the factors that can separate one issue of a first edition from another is the color or design of the binding cloth, as in the case of D. H. Lawrence's *The Prussian Officer* (1914), the first issue of which appeared bound in dark blue cloth stamped in gold decoration, while later issues were bound in lighter blue cloth stamped in dark blue. There is also the size of the book: James Branch Cabell's *Jurgen* (1919) measured exactly one and seven-eighths inches from cover to cover in the first issue. The second issue was one-quarter inch thicker.

The "state" of a book is another important consideration. States result from textual corrections, additions, and excisions, as well as changes in design or format, instituted during the manufacturing of the book. The difference between issues and states lies in the fact that books appearing in two or more states are usually distributed simultaneously, while issues often come from the publisher at separate times. A classic example concerns the first American edition of Mark Twain's *The Adventures of Huckleberry Finn* (1885), which is known to exist in two states, one in blue cloth, intended for sale by subscription, and the other in green cloth, designated as the first trade edition for the public. Both copies can be said to represent the first edition, since they were issued simultaneously for sale, even though they represent two distinct states. Whenever precedence is discovered concerning a book's state, then of course preference is given to whichever copy represents the first state. The importance of a book's issue and state should never be disregarded by the collector, however ridiculous adherence to this practice may seem, since sometimes there is no other way in which one copy of a first edition can be given priority over another.

No discussion of first editions can be considered adequate without some mention of books that achieve their first publication in magazine or newspaper serial form. Titles as various as Charles Dickens's *David Copperfield* (which appeared in book form in 1850 after issue in monthly parts from May 1849 to November 1850), Sir Arthur Conan Doyle's *The Adventures of Sherlock Holmes* (which ran from July 1891 to June 1892 in *The Strand Magazine*, not appearing in book form until October 1892), and Ernest Hemingway's *A Farewell to Arms* (published by Scribner's in 1929, after initially appearing in six numbers of *Scribner's Magazine* from May to October of 1929) represent this practice. Many other titles, such as Charlotte Brontë's *Jane Eyre* (1847) and Somerset Maugham's *Of Human Bondage* (1915), never were serialized. The problem that arises out of this practice of publishing works in serialized parts first is whether the book form that follows can truly represent the first edition. In his essay "Serial Fiction" in John Carter's *New Paths in Book-Collecting*, Graham Pollard attempts to come to terms with this dilemma. With respect to priority, he writes: "There can be no doubt that, if first appearance is in itself a virtue, it belongs almost exclusively to the serial issue" (pages 249–50). He further notes that a great deal of importance rests with the serial issue since "its illustrations and its differences from the final text may sometimes throw a vivid light on the original form from which the story developed" (page 252). He then poses the inevitable question of why serial issues are "so rarely noted in the bibliographies, and hardly ever found on the collector's shelves" (page 252). The answer, Pollard feels, lies in a variety of reasons.

In the first place a serial is not advertised in any permanent form, as a new volume is in *The English Catalogue*, and consequently it is difficult to trace its whereabouts without access to the author's private accounts or some other external clue. When it has been traced in the files of a newspaper in some public library, the most difficult part is still to come: old newspapers and magazines do not come on to the book market, they go to the pulping mill or the fried-fish shop. Even when the desired periodical is at last found, it is not without its embarrassments to the fastidious or the hidebound collector. No newspaper file fits tidily into the bookcase; and when a place has been found for it, still further doubts arise. Only a small portion is the work of the favoured author, and shelf-room has to be wasted on a mass of irrelevant matter. On the other hand, even if all the numbers containing the desired serial are present, what is it but an imperfect file of a periodical; and imperfections of any kind are repulsive to a thorough collector. [Pages 252–53]

Despite these shortcomings, Pollard still believes that the fact cannot be denied that serial issues often represent the first or original manner of publication for books, short stories, and poems, and that closer attention should be paid them by the collector. Only the individual can decide on a personal format for collecting a first edition, and though he or she may be theoretically wrong to prefer the book form to the serial issue, the right to decide for oneself provides the basis for the freedom that is at the heart of the pleasures derived from collecting books.

FOLLOW THE FLAG

Among collectors of nineteenth- and twentieth-century American and English authors, the phrase "follow the flag" can be of utmost importance. This term applies to collecting and regarding as first editions only works published in an author's native country. With a great many writers who had all their works published first either in England or in America, such as Willa Cather or Charles Dickens, the first edition is truly the one appropriate to their place of birth. But in the case of expatriate writers, such as Henry James and T. S. Eliot, or writers whose works were sometimes first published in England, and at other times in America, as were the writings of Joseph Conrad and Somerset Maugham, the collector must decide whether to accept the first published edition of their work as the true first, which indeed it is, or the first edition published in their native land.

Should the collector of John Galsworthy, for example, accept as the first edition of *The Forsyte Saga* (1922) the English edition or the American, which preceded the English edition by two months? The most American of writers, Mark Twain, first published the *Adventures of Huckleberry Finn* in London in December of 1884, only three days before the first American edition. Similarly, the first two books of poems by Robert Frost, *A Boy's Will* (1913) and *North of Boston* (1914), were initially published in London. Further examples include Joseph Conrad's

First editions by Joseph Conrad, slightly rubbed at tops of spine

Binding variants of the first edition of Robert Frost's second book

Victory (1915), first published in America, Somerset Maugham's *Of Human Bondage* (1915), which had its American publication prior to its London printing, and Robert Louis Stevenson's *Dr. Jekyll and Mr. Hyde* (1886), which, when published in New York, preceded the London edition by only a few days.

The works of expatriates present their collectors with particularly frustrating situations. Henry James, though born and educated in America, decided that his native country offered little to stimulate him either culturally or aesthetically, and he settled in England while still a young man. His writings, though, were often published simultaneously in England and America. Where one edition clearly predates the other, there is no problem in deciding the precedence. But what of his later works, such as *The Better Sort* (1903) or *A Small Boy and Others* (1913), which were published at the same time in both America and England? Also, despite the fact that James acknowledged his preference for European values and culture, the greater portion of his work illustrates either admiration for Americans and their values, or at least an obsessive fascination with the American girl, who almost always achieves greater nobility than her European counterpart. James, it seems, remained an American at heart despite his own open preferences for European ways. Therefore, should anyone collecting the works of Henry James favor the editions published not only in his place of birth but so often about its people, or the English editions? To complicate matters further, James became a British subject shortly before his death in 1916.

T. S. Eliot, like James, became a British subject, but much earlier in life. Strangely enough, while the bulk of his writing was published first in England, his most famous pieces, *The Waste Land* (1922) and *Four Quartets* (1943), had prior pub-

The very rare first edition of Melville's *Moby Dick*, (1851) published in London before the American edition

lication in America. With the exception of these two works, Eliot's first editions are for the most part preferred in the English first-edition format.

Perhaps the answer to the "follow the flag" dilemma is for the collector to acquire both first editions. The only problem with this policy is that in the case of extremely prolific writers, such as Conrad, James, and Eliot, it could take years to gather a complete collection of their works, not considering the cost.

More sensibly, the collector might decide to regard the first edition of an author's work as being just that, the first, despite place of publication, and to hell with following the flag!

6

Early Printed Books and Printers

The book as a work of art has long been of interest to collectors. Many specialize in acquiring the earliest printed books, or incunabula, of the fifteenth and sixteenth centuries, while others seek works bearing the imprint of famous printers or publishing houses, private-press productions, or books with fine bindings.

In order for the reader to gain an overview of the earliest printed books and their printers, as well as acquaintance with some of the most desirable titles (though, of course, many are either unavailable today or astronomically priced), here is a rather brief history of the printed book.

The invention of movable type signifies the beginning of printing as we know it today. Although such a method of printing was in use in the Orient from the eleventh century, the earliest printing from movable type in Western Europe was practiced in Mainz, Germany.

The first printed material intended for public circulation appears to be a form of indulgence from Nicholas V to anyone who would aid the King of Cyprus against the Turks (the sheet is dated August 15, 1454). The first book commonly believed to have been printed from movable type is the famed Gutenberg Bible, printed by Johannes Gutenberg in Germany in 1455.

This book is the most highly prized of volumes throughout the world not only for its historical significance, but also because it represents one of the most superb examples of the printer's art. It is the dream of all dealers, auctioneers, and collectors to someday happen upon another copy of this Bible. Very recently, in an old church attic in a small town in Germany, the forty-seventh copy was discovered. Needless to say, at today's prices, a newly discovered Gutenberg can bring possibly millions of dollars to its discoverer. It remains the most expensive of rare books to acquire, as well as one of the most difficult to find.

From Mainz the art of printing spread to Italy, and by 1469 Venice was established as the center of printing in Italy. In 1470, printing reached the shores of France. It expanded from Paris, where a press was begun at the Sorbonne, to Lyon and then to Toulouse in 1476. From France, printing spread to Switzerland, notably to Basel and Geneva, and from there to Valencia, Spain, in 1474, to Denmark in 1482, Portugal in 1489, and Sweden in 1495.

The history of early printed books in England is essentially the history of William Caxton, generally regarded as the first English printer. Having been engaged in commerce for the greater part of his life, Caxton gave up his business pursuits in about 1470 and entered the service of Margaret, Duchess of Burgundy, the sister of Edward IV. Supposedly Caxton was introduced to the art of printing in 1471, while on a visit to Cologne. From there he traveled to Bruges, where he worked until 1477 with the press established by Colard Mansion.

It was at Bruges in 1474 that Caxton printed what is regarded as the first book in English, a translation of *The Recueil des Histoires de Troye*. When his patron, Margaret, retired into private life in 1476, Caxton left Bruges for England, where in 1477 he printed *Dictes and Sayings of the Philosophers* at Westminster, the first dated book printed in England.

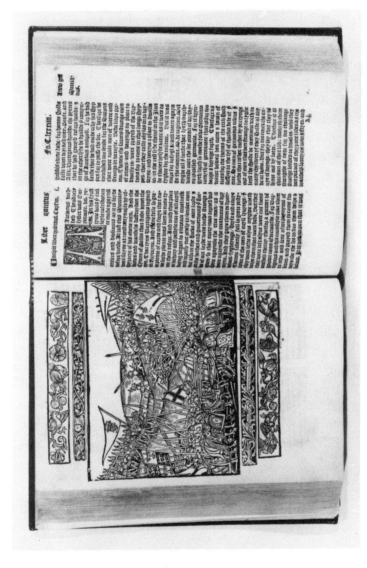

Polychronichon produced by Wynkyn de Worde, William Caxton's successor, 1495

Perhaps the most important of Caxton's printings, in a literary sense at least, was Chaucer's *The Canterbury Tales* in 1478. Caxton also printed Thomas Malory's classic account of King Arthur and the Knights of the Round Table, *Le Morte d'Arthur*, in 1485. When Caxton died in 1491, his distinguished press passed into the able hands of his former assistant, Wynkyn de Worde, whose various works, printed until his death in 1535, are also eagerly sought today.

It must be remembered by the aspiring collector of early printed books, or incunabula, as they are often referred to (from the Latin for "swaddling clothes"—hence, beginnings), that virtually hundreds of items were produced in the fifteenth and sixteenth centuries. Though only a relatively small proportion of those works are of interest and value to the most serious collector, this does not mean that the majority of early printed books are of little or no value. Many of the early printed books are available and affordable to the collector of average means. One does not have to spend tens of thousands of dollars in order to collect incunabula. It is this possibility that underscores the premise that book collecting need not be limited to individuals of limitless financial resources.

To return to some of the highlights of early printing, the *Opus grammatices*, printed by Pynson in 1494, contains numbered pages for the first time: "Pagina prima," "pagini ii," etc.; and a *Bull of Pope Pius II*, Mainz, 1463, and the *Sermo ad Populum*, Cologne, 1470, are the earliest examples of works that contain a printed title page. The earliest book in English bearing a printed title page is the *Treatise of the Pestilence*, which appeared before 1490.

Additionally, the *Mainz Psalter*, printed by Johann Fust and Peter Schoeffer in 1457, is regarded as the first European book to bear a colophon, noting the printer and date, while Caxton's *The Myrrour of the World* (1481) is the first English illustrated book.

Perhaps one of the most desirable items among collectors is the first sporting book, *The Book of Hawking, Hunting, and Heraldry* published in 1486 by an unknown printer. In addition to its historical precedence over all other sporting books, this volume is important for being one of the first to contain English poetry.

The Aldine Press was founded in Venice in 1494 by Aldus Manutius, whose goal was to publish not only beautiful but textually accurate editions of the Greek and Roman classics. His first production was an edition of Lascaris's *Greek Grammar* in 1496. At his death in 1515, the press was carried on until Aldus's son Paolo took control in 1533, supervising the various productions until his death in 1574, at which time he was succeeded by his son, Aldus.

As with all rare books, some of the numerous works of the Aldine Press are more in demand by collectors, and consequently more expensive to acquire. Yet for the most part, while the *Nine Plays by Aristophanes* may not prove an inexpensive title to acquire, many other Aldine books can be obtained at a relatively modest cost.

Of the great printing families of the sixteenth century, none is more illustrious than the Estiennes of France. In 1500, Henri Estienne founded his press at Paris. Although he produced many admirable works, the fame of the house rests upon the endeavors of Robert Estienne, who printed editions of the Bible in Latin, Hebrew, Greek, and French, as well as several editions of Latin grammars for use in schools.

In Holland in the sixteenth century, the outstanding printing house was that of Christopher Plantin, established at Antwerp in

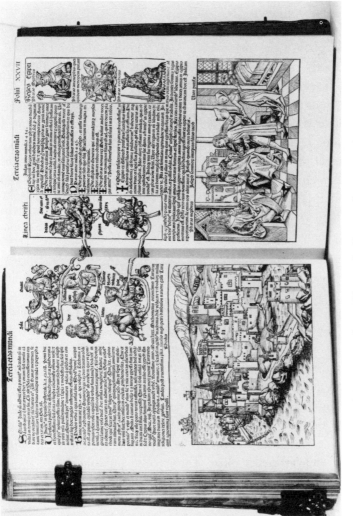

The Nuremberg Chronicle, Latin edition, 1493

1563. A Bible produced in 1572 remains the touchstone of his art.

In England, John Day was responsible for many admirable productions between 1546 and 1584, among them William Cunningham's *Cosmographical Glass* (1559), Sleiden's *Chronicle* (1560), Foxe's *Acts and Monuments* (1563), and the first English translation of *Euclid* (1570).

As time passed, printing became more and more a commercial endeavor, but though the days of the scholar-printer seemed over, one family in Holland, the Elzevirs, continued to produce a number of excellent works. While their focus was upon Latin and French classics, one of the most notable productions of the Elzevir Press is *Le Patissier Francois* (1665), among the earliest of cookbooks.

Strangely enough, while the seventeenth century is highly distinguished in literary terms by the names of Milton, Donne, and Dryden, few advances were made in the art of printing. With the exception of the Oxford University Press, no one press produced enough examples of the printer's art to be singled out for distinction. Yet toward the end of the seventeenth century, in 1677, Jacob Tonson opened a bookseller's shop in London and began purchasing the copyrights of the works of the more notable authors of the day, one of whom was John Dryden.

In those days, the bookseller was often the nearest approximation to the publisher, and in 1684 Tonson issued an edition of Dryden's *Miscellany Poems,* which proved a great success for author and bookseller alike. Tonson also published editions of Alexander Pope's earlier work in 1709, and in 1725 he published Pope's famous edition of Shakespeare.

In addition to Tonson, another bookseller-publisher of note was Bernard Lintot, who published not only Pope, but Gay and Steele as well. And were it not for Robert Dodsley, Samuel

Johnson's *The Vanity of Human Wishes* (1749) and *Rasselas, Prince of Abissinnia* (1759) may have never seen the light of day.

As the nineteenth century dawned, the scholar-printer and the bookseller-publisher slowly gave way to the large publishing firms. From that time to the present day, printing moved further away from an experimental and unique art to become an increasingly big business. As more and more people learned to read, the business of printing books coincided with the growth of the middle classes, who would prove to be the backbone of the reading public in the nineteenth and twentieth centuries.

7

Private Press Books

Will Ransom, in *Private Presses and Their Books*, defines the private press as being "the typographic expression of a personal ideal, conceived in freedom and maintained in independence" (page 22). To be sure, private presses often utilize their freedom from the limitations of the commercial publishing world to create works that are representative of the book as an art form—that is, truly outstanding examples of typography and book design. More often than not, private press productions are further enhanced by the use of the highest quality of paper.

There are various reasons, other than the desire to create typographical works of art, for establishing a private press. Some individuals enjoy working with paper, ink, and type to such an extent that for them the operation of a private press serves as a hobby and means of entertainment. In such instances, the private press is the source of pleasure rather than profit.

Many an author might never have seen his work in print were it not for a private press. On occasion a writer cannot find a suitable publisher for his or her material due to the controversial nature of its contents, and its liability to censorship. Other authors, obscure and as yet unpublished, are unable to interest a major, or even a minor, established publisher in printing their works. A great many writers who later became highly renowned, such as Edwin Arlington Robinson and T. S. Eliot, had their first works published by a private press.

Of course, a writer does not always have to be obscure or previously unpublished in order to seek the services of a private printer. Virginia Woolf published many of her novels and essays through the Hogarth Press, founded in England by her husband, Leonard, and herself. Sometimes established authors have their work published privately with the intention of giving copies only to members of their family, close friends, or business acquaintances. Tennyson and T. S. Eliot, to name but two, utilized private presses for just those reasons after their reputations had been established.

Lastly, colleges and universities often establish presses in order to publish scholarly material under their own auspices. This material may appeal to only a select number of individuals; hence the more commercial firms must often reject such works since their production would prove unprofitable.

Collectors have their own preferences in private presses. In many cases, the printer and his press have achieved universally acknowledged respect over the years. In other instances, both printer and press may be obscure. For beginning collectors who feel that they would prefer to collect private press books, a brief and by no means complete history of private presses and their printers follows. Only the more illustrious names are mentioned, those whose productions have proved to be favorites of collectors over the years.

For further reference, various titles pertaining to private presses have been included in the bibliography at the end of the book.

The first privately printed book in English may well have been William Caxton's *Recuyell of the Historyes of Troye*, published in Bruges in 1474. The book was ordered by his patroness, Margaret, Duchess of Burgundy, and was not intended for commercial purposes. Hence its designation as a privately printed book.

The sixteenth and seventeenth centuries witnessed little advance in the use of private presses. The eighteenth century, however, provides what may be one of the most famous examples of a private press: Sir Horace Walpole's Strawberry Hill Press. Founded at Twickenham, England, in 1757, this celebrated press published the writings not only of Sir Horace, but of a number of other authors, including Thomas Gray.

A gentleman turned master craftsman, Walpole obtained a great deal of personal satisfaction from his efforts, as well as widespread respect from his contemporaries. While Strawberry Hill Press productions can prove costly to the collector, there are some items available at a modest cost.

In the same year, 1757, another famous press was founded, this time by John Baskerville at Birmingham, England. The most desirable production from this press, in the view of many collectors, is the Baskerville Bible of 1763; most of the other productions can be obtained for a reasonable price.

Across the English Channel at this time, Benjamin Franklin, no stranger to the printing press, was producing a variety of items from a small press at his home in Passy, while serving as ambassador to France. These productions can prove quite expensive, and are generally not easy to come by.

The earliest private presses of the nineteenth century were the Hafod Press, founded in 1803, and the Press at Frogmore Lodge, 1809. Also, quite a number of publications issued from the Private Press of Lee Priory from 1813 onward. Other presses of note include the Middle Hill Press (1819); the Great Totham Press (1831–49); the Beldornie Press, founded in 1840 by Edward Vernon Utterson of the Isle of Wight; and the renowned Daniel Press (1845–1903), which enjoyed perhaps the greatest longevity of all private presses.

The most outstanding private press of the late nineteenth century was William Morris's Kelmscott Press, founded at Hammersmith, England, in 1891. Kelmscott items tend to be rather expensive, the *Works of Chaucer* being among the most highly prized.

Another important late-nineteenth-century press was the Ashendene Press of C. H. St. John Hornby, which began printing in 1894 at Ashendene, England. All publications were printed on handmade paper. Most esteemed of all its productions are Dante's *Divine Comedy* and Spenser's *The Faerie Queene*.

Another press of note was the Merrymount Press, which began printing skillful examples of typographical art in 1893.

In America at this time, the earliest private presses of renown are the Fair Hill Press (1867) and the Appledore (1879–95), as well as the Kingate Press, which was maintained at Canton, Pennsylvania, from 1901 to 1905, and the Village Press, which originated in Park Ridge, Illinois, in 1903.

The turn of the century in England witnessed the founding of the famed Doves Press by T. J. Cobden-Sanderson in 1900. Although this press closed its doors as relatively recently as 1917, its publications, for the most part, are on the expensive side today, the most desirable item perhaps being the Doves Bible.

The Cuala Press, founded in Ireland and supervised by Elizabeth Yeats, first published the works of her brother, William Butler Yeats. Who knows what the possibilities might have been for the great Irish poet to attain early publication had it not been for this small press?

The Golden Cockerel Press, founded by Harold M. Taylor in

And loveth him, the which that right for love
Upon a cros, our soules for to beye,
First starf, and roos, and sit in hevene above;
For he nil falsen no wight, dar I seye,
That wol his herte al hoolly on him leye.
And sin he best to love is, and most meke,
What nedeth feyned loves for to seke?

Lo here, of Payens corsed olde rytes,
Lo here, what alle hir goddes may availle;
Lo here, these wrecched worldes appetytes;
Lo here, the fyn and guerdon for travaille
Of Jove, Appollo, of Mars of swich rascaille!
Lo here, the forme of olde clerkes speche
In poetrye, if ye hir bokes seche.

O moral Gower, this book I directe

To thee, and to the philosophical Strode,
To vouchen sauf, ther nede is, to corecte,
Of your benignitees and zeles gode.
And to that sothfast Crist, that starf on
rode,
With al myn herte of mercy ever I preye;
And to the Lord right thus I speke and seye:

Thou oon, and two, and three, eterne on lyve,
That regnest ay in three and two and oon,
Uncircumscript, and al mayst circumscryve,
Us from visible and invisible foon
Defende; and to thy mercy, everichoon,
So make us, Jesus, for thy grace digne,
For love of mayde and moder thyn benigne!
Amen.
Explicit Liber Troili et Criseydis.

Kelmscott

The Kelmscott *Chaucer* (1896), from the press of William Morris

1921, and the Nonesuch Press, which began publication in 1923, produced works by classical and contemporary authors in a most skillful manner. Many of the items produced by these two presses are continually sought after by collectors, as are, though not as greatly now as in past years, the works of the Mosher Press of Thomas B. Mosher, who introduced many English writers of the late nineteenth and early twentieth centuries to Americans from 1891 to 1923. Among the authors published under the auspices of the Mosher Press were Swinburne, Rossetti, and Housman.

Each year, numerous private presses produce items that may prove of interest to collectors. The modern book enthusiast need not feel limited by the preferences of past collectors, but free to chart his or her own course toward collecting private press books.

8

Fine Bindings

Although books have been known to have been bound in one form or another from the earliest times, and beautifully jeweled and embroidered bindings were designed for use on church altars, the art of binding books in decorated leather seems to have been first practiced in the monasteries of Egypt in the eighth century.

In Europe, the earliest known decorated leather binding is that of the Stonyhurst Gospels from the tomb of St. Cuthbert, perhaps the work of a late seventh-century craftsman. Between the twelfth and fifteenth centuries, bindings were often embellished with highly imaginative designs which were stamped or impressed into the leather covers, and during the fifteenth century the art of gold-tooling, as perfected by Moorish craftsmen in Spain, was introduced to Venetian craftsmen, and soon afterward spread to France and England.

Strangely enough, the various styles of bindings obtained their names from the wealthy individuals who purchased them, rather than from the craftsmen who skillfully produced them. The most famous of bindings, and perhaps one of the most expensive, is the "Grolier" binding, which was executed for Jean Grolier, who served as Treasurer of France in the sixteenth century. The

Exquisitely decorated fine binding

famous Grolier Club in New York is named for this illustrious gatherer of fine books.

Other famous bindings are the "Maioli," the "Canevari," and the "Wotton." In England in the eighteenth century, renowned bindings came from the hands of three master craftsmen: Roger Payne of Windsor, Edwards of Halifax, and John Whitaker. The collector should remember that examples of these fine bindings can often be very expensive to acquire, if they are available at all. Yet there are innumerable examples of finely bound books that require little more than the collector's interest in acquiring them and a modest sum of money.

Many rich buyers throughout the eighteenth and early nineteenth centuries were reluctant to place on their shelves books bound in paper boards, as was the standard practice of publishers. They insisted that their books be finely bound in any variety of exquisite leather grains, and as a result, untold numbers of finely bound books are available to the modern collector.

In fact, even after the 1830s, when cloth bindings became popular among publishers and readers alike, many who could afford it still preferred to have their books rebound in leathers of the highest quality. This preference has persisted to this day, and the lover of fine bindings will soon discover that many another collector shares his ardent interest and passion for finely bound books.

A binding by De Creuzevault (1930)

A binding by Edwards of Halifax

9

Signed, Inscribed, and Presentation Copies

SIGNED COPIES*

At a recent New York auction, a copy of the first edition of Joseph Conrad's *Lord Jim* (1900), certainly one of his most celebrated works, brought fifty dollars, while a more obscure title of his, *Notes on My Books* (1921), fetched $120. Wouldn't the more famous title be in greater demand, one might ask, and subsequently sell for the greater amount of money? Generally speaking, the answer would be a resounding Yes! provided, of course, that both works are in similar physical condition and that neither outweighs the other in terms of rarity. But in this instance, the lesser known title contained Conrad's signature, while the more famous one did not.

At the same auction, a first edition of a book that merely included an introduction by Oscar Wilde, yet was signed and dated in his hand, brought an astounding four hundred dollars. More astonishing, a rare-book dealer who only a short time ago offered a copy of the first edition of F. Scott Fitzgerald's *Tender Is the Night* for sixty-five dollars, lists a signed copy of the same

---

* Copies of books autographed by their authors need not be first editions to be of interest to collectors.

title in his latest catalogue for $850. Obviously there's a lesson
here, one might surmise: namely, that copies of first editions
signed by their authors are of much greater value than unsigned
copies. In general this is true, and the aspiring book collector
would be correct in assuming that his or her collection should
preferably contain signed copies of an author's works.

Yet just as not every first edition is worth collecting, so not
every signed one is valuable. There would be little point to collecting books if this were otherwise, since the very act of collecting in itself, be it of coins, bottles, or stamps, implies selectivity
and discretion. What, then, the puzzled novice might ask, determines the value of a signed copy of an author's work? The
answer, to be sure, is not a simple one since quite a few factors
must be taken into account before one signed copy can be
judged collectible, another worthless.

A safe rule that can be applied whenever attempting to judge
the value of a signed work is to consider the degree to which first
editions of the author in question are sought and esteemed by
other collectors. The most reliable sources of reference for this
question are the antiquarian or rare-book sellers' catalogues,
both past and present, and the records of the more widely known
auctioneers, which are for the most part available in *American
Book Prices Current.** The persistent presence of an author's
name and works in either the dealers' catalogues or auctioneers'
ledgers over the years is one indication of a writer's durability in
terms of market value.

Another factor to be considered is the reputation and historical worth of an author and his works. Writers of such universally
acknowledged classic stature as Fielding, Wordsworth, Byron,
Coleridge, Shelley, Keats, Dickens, Thackeray, Hardy, George

---

* Volumes are issued annually and are available in the reference rooms of
most libraries.

Eliot, and the Brownings will perhaps always be interesting and desirable to collectors. Yet the signed copies of their works are not cheaply obtained, if available at all nowadays, and the collector of somewhat modest means might decide it is more practical to concentrate upon acquiring the signed works of the virtually hundreds of other worthwhile authors.

Autographed first editions by authors whose work holds interest for the individual collector, and perhaps an enduring literary quality as well, need not be expensive. Of course, with any author, there is always the possibility that one or two titles, signed or not, might prove exceptionally expensive, yet signed copies of works by say, Conrad Aiken, James Branch Cabell, Archibald MacLeish, John Masefield, Katherine Anne Porter, and Ogden Nash can usually be acquired for a modest cost. Signed first editions by some of the more major writers of the twentieth century, such as Theodore Dreiser, Joseph Conrad, Edna St. Vincent Millay, John Dos Passos, and Thornton Wilder, often cost somewhat more, with signed titles by Hemingway, Fitzgerald, Joyce, Gertrude Stein, Ezra Pound, T. S. Eliot, and D. H. Lawrence growing more expensive each year.

With respect to contemporary authors, such as Saul Bellow, Norman Mailer, Gore Vidal, Joyce Carol Oates, Anthony Burgess, Bernard Malamud, Philip Roth, and Truman Capote, the collector can often obtain signed copies of their works relatively inexpensively. This is not to imply that their work does not have an enduring quality, or that all contemporary authors' signed works can be cheaply obtained. What is suggested, however, is that the very fact that a contemporary author's work cannot be time-proven, in terms of literary endurance and collector's interest, in most instances accounts for its relatively low cost to the collector.

At the same time, should the beginning collector feel any

THE DRY SALVAGES

by

T. S. ELIOT

T. S. Eliot

FABER AND FABER
24 Russell Square
London

First edition signed on the title page

degree of skepticism toward investing money in the signed works of authors whose reputations have not been securely established, he or she would do well to think back upon those wise collectors who acquired the signed first editions of Hemingway, Pound, Joyce, and Fitzgerald when they were merely contemporary authors of the day. Such collectors can now congratulate themselves for their shrewd foresight in acquiring books that today cost many times what they paid for them then.

One last note. Sometimes signed editions are extremely valuable to collectors if an author has been known to autograph his or her books rarely, or if very few signed copies have been discovered over the years. While every writer at one time or another affixes his signature to one or more of his books, some tend to sign more books than others. Either Henry James, Stephen Crane, Edith Wharton, William Makepeace Thackeray, George Meredith, Frank Norris, and Virginia Woolf were not particularly inclined toward signing many copies of their works, or so few have survived or have been located that autographed copies of their first or even later editions often prove quite valuable. At a recent auction in New York, a rather worn yet signed copy of the first edition of *The Pit* (1903), usually one of Frank Norris's least expensive titles, brought $175.

Other authors whose signatures prove rare and extremely expensive include Alexander Pope, Oliver Goldsmith, Jonathan Swift, Matthew Arnold, John Keats, and especially Jane Austen. Even works by Alfred Tennyson, Charles Dickens, James Boswell, Horace Walpole, and Sir Walter Scott, whose signatures are deemed rare, though by no means as rare as the above-mentioned ones, as will often cost the collector a rather large sum of money, if they can be located at all in a dealer's shop or at auction. Thus, it should never be forgotten by the aspiring collector that the cornerstone for collecting signed as well as unsigned first editions is the law of supply and demand.

SIGNED LIMITED EDITIONS

Whenever issued simultaneously with the first trade edition,* the "signed limited number" first edition of an author's work generally is of greater interest to collectors and dealers alike. Very often, the first printing of an author's work numbers into the thousands, while the signed edition may consist of five to five hundred copies. Consequently, since rarity is to a large degree the raison d'être of any collector's library, there is far greater advantage to possessing a copy of a first edition that is not only signed by its author, but limited in number as well. Hence the preference among many collectors for the signed limited first edition of an author's book.

In addition, the signed limited number first edition often differs physically from the first trade edition in that the paper upon which the text is printed may be of larger size and heavier weight, the covers may be specially hand-crafted or decorated, and the book itself issued in a cloth or cardboard slipcase to protect it from wear or soilage.

Strangely enough, the issuance of signed limited number first editions has generated quite some controversy among collectors as to which first edition, the signed limited or the trade, should be given precedence. In some instances the issue can be decided very easily by securing information from the publisher concerning the actual date of publication of both editions. As sometimes happens, the trade edition is published a few days or even a few weeks before the signed limited edition. In this case, the decision

---

* The ordinary or regular first edition intended for general public sale.

STREET HAUNTING

BY VIRGINIA WOOLF

THE WESTGATE PRESS
SAN FRANCISCO ~ 1930

Title page of limited first edition

THIS EDITION, limited to five hundred copies, has been printed by The Grabhorn Press of San Francisco in May, 1930. The type used is Weiss Antiqua, hand-set. Each copy is signed by the author,

Virginia Woolf

Copy No. 93

Signed limited edition page (much magnified) of Virginia Woolf's *Street Haunting* (1930)

regarding the value to be accorded each edition is simply left to the individual collector. Yet dealers' catalogues and auctioneers' records attest that collectors prefer signed limited editions, though they will make every effort to secure a copy of the first trade edition as well.

The discrepancy in price between signed limited and trade first editions is often rather huge. For example, one rare-book dealer's latest catalogue lists a copy of the signed limited first edition (256 copies) of Aldous Huxley's *Point Counter Point* (1928) for $160. Directly beneath this item is listed a copy of the first trade edition of the same title; the price is twenty-five dollars, which is approximately one-sixth the cost of the signed limited copy. Similarly, a signed limited edition copy of Theodore Dreiser's classic *An American Tragedy* (795 copies) brought fifty dollars at auction, while one of the fifteen thousand first trade editions would hardly fetch twenty dollars.

By the same token, an author's work that is first issued in an extremely limited signed edition format is well worth its weight in gold, provided, of course, that there are interested collectors. For instance, Hart Crane's now classic poem *The Bridge* was first printed in Paris in 1930 and issued in a signed limited edition of only fifty copies. Only a short time ago, a well-known and highly respected New York bookseller who specializes in modern first editions offered a copy for $1,500. While this price may seem a staggering amount of money to pay for a signed modern first edition, it should be remembered that the author's reputation is well established, and that Crane not only ranks very highly in the hierarchy of modern poets in terms of intrinsic literary value, but is popular with collectors as well, and this particular volume represents his greatest poetic achievement. Of greater interest to collectors is the fact that this issue of the first edition of *The Bridge* was printed in a relatively small number of copies, and that the author's signature accompanies the volume.

Thus, the preference among collectors appears very strong indeed for signed limited number first editions, despite the controversy that has perennially surrounded them—provided that such copies either precede or be issued simultaneously with the first trade edition.

Whenever faced with deciding which first edition of a contemporary writer's latest work should be bought, assuming that the collector is interested in that author's works in general and that the latest volume is issued in both a signed limited number and an ordinary trade edition format, one would do well to remember that though the former may be more expensive to acquire, it may also prove a far wiser investment in terms of personal value in the long run.

INSCRIBED COPIES

An inscribed copy is one that its author has autographed for a particular recipient—a close friend or associate, a member of the family, or even a complete stranger. Very often, authors will not only sign their names, but will add a few lines of praise, gratitude, or cordiality. Since inscriptions tend to be more personal in tone than mere autographs, they are held in higher esteem by collectors. In fact, the value of an inscribed copy is usually determined by the intensity or depth of the author's message.

The value of an inscribed copy rests on three factors: the reputation of the author, the degree of rarity and desirability, and the relationship of recipient to author. This last factor is of extreme importance. For instance, there are presently listed in a dealer's catalogue two copies of T. S. Eliot's poem *Marina*, pub-

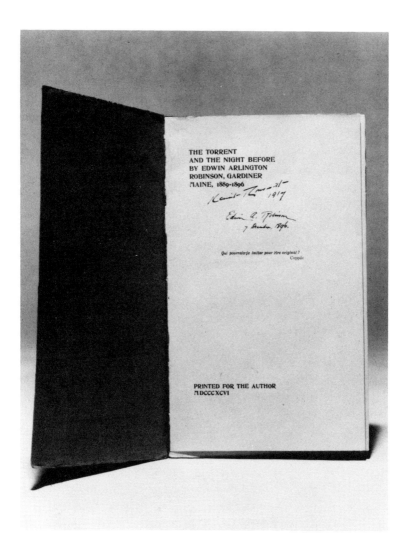

THE TORRENT
AND THE NIGHT BEFORE
BY EDWIN ARLINGTON
ROBINSON, GARDINER
MAINE, 1889-1896

Qui pourrais-je imiter pour être original?
Coppée

PRINTED FOR THE AUTHOR
MDCCCXCVI

An inscribed copy of the very rare first book by Edwin Arlington
Robinson

lished in London in 1930. The signed copy of a limited edition of four hundred is priced at ninety-five dollars, while the first trade edition is offered at fifteen dollars. In London, however, at Sotheby's auction of May 22, 1973, a copy of the first trade edition inscribed by Eliot to Edith Sitwell sold for £140 (approximately $350)! Had Dame Edith not been one of the notable literary figures of the first half of the twentieth century, the copy most probably would have been sold for less.

Of course, not every inscribed copy need be dedicated to a celebrated figure or to a close acquaintance of the author to be of interest to collectors. More often than not, the recipients will be obscure individuals. Yet this fact will not diminish the value of an inscribed copy provided the author's signature is in demand among collectors. Witness the April 1973 auction at Swann Galleries in New York, where a first edition of Eliot's most famous play, *Murder in the Cathedral* (London, 1935), though inscribed to no one of particular importance either to Eliot or to posterity, brought $110. Strangely enough, this figure is exactly double the amount asked by a noted dealer in his present catalogue for a copy of the same title that bears only Eliot's signature.

First-edition copies of E. M. Forster's *A Passage to India* (London, 1924) were sold at auction by Sotheby Parke Bernet in New York for eighty dollars on February 20, 1973, and by Christie and Sotheby's of London on April 4, 1973, and July 16, 1973, for thirty pounds (approximately seventy-five dollars) and thirty-eight pounds (one hundred dollars) respectively. All these copies were in good condition, though unsigned. Only the power and fascination connected with an inscribed copy can account for the fifty-five pounds (one hundred fifty dollars) paid at Sotheby's on July 17, 1973, for a worn yet inscribed copy of the same title. Even more surprising, a copy of the first edition of

MATISSE PICASSO
AND GERTRUDE STEIN

WITH

TWO SHORTER STORIES

BY

GERTRUDE STEIN

First edition of Gertrude Stein's *Matisse, Picasso and Gertrude Stein*
(1932)

Inscribed presentation end paper; the inscription reads "A cook does not mean that there is cooking"

Ernest Hemingway's *Green Hills of Africa* (New York, 1935), inscribed by the author to an admirer, brought $225 at the June 5, 1975, auction at Swann Galleries. Not only is this one of Hemingway's least successful titles, in critical terms, but the physical condition was less than satisfactory. The backstrip was dulled and faded, and the dust jacket torn in several places. Yet this book fetched forty-five dollars above its quoted bid price of $180 merely by virtue of Hemingway's inscription on the inner end paper.

PRESENTATION COPIES

A presentation copy is one that is not only inscribed but given by the author as a gift to the recipient. As with inscribed copies, the relationship between author and recipient is of prime consideration. A first edition of Robert Frost's *A Boy's Will* (London, 1913) that read on the endleaf: "Leonora Dougan from Robert Frost," was offered in a catalogue of some years ago for $1,150. Leonora Dougan began teaching at the New Hampshire State Normal School in 1911, as did Frost. He remained only a year (she stayed for eleven), and the following year, his first book of poems was published in England. The value of this presentation copy rests with the inference that can be drawn from his remembrance of Miss Dougan.

At times, presentation copies are of interest to collectors not only for their uniqueness or rarity, but also for the insights they can provide into literary history. At a recent display at the New York Public Library of first editions, letters, and other memorabilia relating to both the Brownings, there were copies of the first editions of Edgar Allan Poe's *The Raven* and Alfred Tennyson's *Maud*. Both volumes were presentation copies inscribed to Elizabeth Barrett Browning, and they serve to add to our knowl-

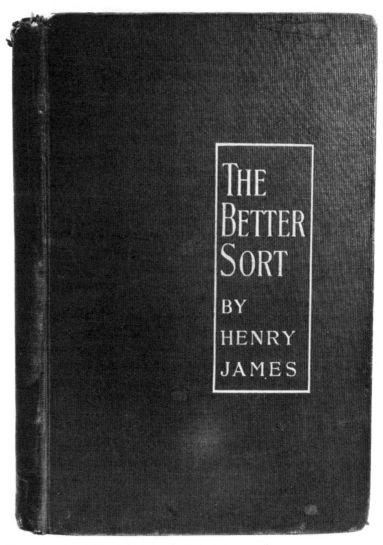

First edition of *The Better Sort* (1903) bearing inscribed end paper

A most interesting inscription on the front end paper of
The Better Sort

edge of Poe and Tennyson. We learn that Poe must have thought highly of the English poet to send her a copy of his most famous poem inscribed "with respect," despite the fact that they had never met. And Tennyson's warm feeling toward Mrs. Browning after his reading of *Maud* at the Brownings' home on the evening of September 27, 1855, is evidenced by his gift.

John Carter, in his *ABC for Book-Collectors* (pp. 155–56), noted the collector's order of preference with respect to presentation copies:

1 With a signed presentation inscription in the author's hand to a named recipient; dated before, on, or near publication.

2 Ditto, but dated considerably later than publication or undated.

3 With the recipient's name, but having *from the author* or *with the author's compliments* instead of signature.

4 Without autograph inscription, but showing evidence of having been sent by the author or on his instruction by the publisher.

5 With a note in the hand of the recipient stating that the book was a gift of the author.

6 With a later note making a similar statement at secondhand, from family tradition or the like.

Needless to say, not all presentation copies need be as valuable in personal association as the Frost copy, or as interesting and informative in a historical sense as the Poe and Tennyson volumes. Quite often the collector can obtain a presentation copy of a work by a favorite author for a modest sum. At all times, however, one should pay high regard to the importance of the author, either to oneself or in collecting circles, and the relationship of the recipient to the author, before writing a check for copies of first or later editions that are inscribed presentation copies.

Signed, inscribed, or presentation copies of first or later editions of works by the following authors are particularly worthwhile to collect:*

Henry Adams
George Ade
James Agee
Conrad Aiken
Richard Aldington
Nelson Algren
Hervey Allen
Sherwood Anderson
Maxwell Anderson
Guillaume Apollinaire
Michael Arlen
Matthew Arnold
W. H. Auden
Jane Austen

James Baldwin
Djuna Barnes
Sir James Barrie
John Barth
Donald Barthelme
Samuel Beckett
Sylvia Beach
Max Beerbohm
Hilaire Belloc
Marie Belloc-Lowndes
Saul Bellow
Stephen Vincent Benét

Arnold Bennett
John Berryman
John Betjeman
William Blake
Heinrich Böll
James Boswell
Elizabeth Bowen
Kay Boyle
Bertolt Brecht
Rupert Brooke
Van Wyck Brooks
Anne Brontë
Charlotte Brontë
Emily Brontë
Elizabeth Barrett Browning
Robert Browning
William Cullen Bryant
Bulwer-Lytton
Anthony Burgess
Edgar Rice Burroughs
William Burroughs
Samuel Butler
George Gordon, Lord Byron

James Branch Cabell
George W. Cable
Erskine Caldwell

---

* This list is intended to serve merely as a guide, and in no way attempts to include every author whose signature bears importance.

Albert Camus
Truman Capote
Thomas Carlyle
Lewis Carroll
Joyce Cary
Willa Cather
Raymond Chandler
Anton Chekhov
G. K. Chesterton
Kate Chopin
Agatha Christie
Sir Winston Churchill
Humphrey Cobb
Irvin S. Cobb
Jean Cocteau
Samuel Taylor Coleridge
Colette
Wilkie Collins
Ivy Compton-Burnett
Cyril Connolly
Joseph Conrad
James Fenimore Cooper
A. E. Coppard
Gregory Corso
Noël Coward
Malcolm Cowley
James Gould Cozzens
Hart Crane
Stephen Crane
Aleister Crowley
Robert Creeley
E. E. Cummings

Charles Darwin
Daniel Defoe
Walter de la Mare
Thomas De Quincey

August Derluth
Charles Dickens
James Dickey
J. P. Donleavy
Hilda Doolittle (H.D.)
John Dos Passos
Norman Douglas
Sir Arthur Conan Doyle
Theodore Dreiser
Lord Dunsany
Lawrence Durrell

Ralph Ellison
George Eliot
T. S. Eliot
Ralph Waldo Emerson
John Erskine

James T. Farrell
William Faulkner
Edna Ferber
Eugene Field
Rachel Field
Henry Fielding
Ronald Firbank
F. Scott Fitzgerald
Janet Flanner
Ian Fleming
Paul Leicester Ford
Ford Madox Ford
E. M. Forster
Anatole France
Harold Frederic
Sigmund Freud
Robert Frost
Christopher Fry

John Galsworthy
Federico García Lorca
Erle Stanley Gardner
Hamlin Garland
Mrs. Gaskell
Jean Genêt
André Gide
Allen Ginsberg
George Gissing
Ellen Glasgow
Oliver Goldsmith
Robert Graves
Kate Greenaway
Graham Greene
Lady Gregory
Zane Grey

Dashiell Hammett
Thomas Hardy
Frank Harris
Joel Chandler Harris
Bret Harte
L. P. Hartley
Nathaniel Hawthorne
Lafcadio Hearn
Ben Hecht
Joseph Heller
Lillian Hellman
Ernest Hemingway
O. Henry
Joseph Hergesheimer
Hermann Hesse
Maurice Hewlett
Oliver Wendell Holmes
James Hilton
Gerard Manley Hopkins
A. E. Housman

Laurence Housman
William Dean Howells
W. H. Hudson
Langston Hughes
James Huneker
Fannie Hurst
Aldous Huxley
J. K. Huysmans

Henrik Ibsen
William Inge
Eugene Ionesco
Washington Irving
Christopher Isherwood

Shirley Jackson
Henry James
William James
Randall Jarrell
Robinson Jeffers
Sarah Orne Jewett
Samuel Johnson
James Jones
James Joyce

Franz Kafka
John Keats
Jack Kerouac
Rudyard Kipling

Charles Lamb
Ring Lardner
D. H. Lawrence
T. E. Lawrence
Richard Le Gallienne
Doris Lessing

Sinclair Lewis
Wyndham Lewis
Vachel Lindsay
Jack London
Henry Wadsworth Longfellow
Anita Loos
Amy Lowell
James Russell Lowell
Robert Lowell

Compton Mackenzie
Archibald MacLeish
Norman Mailer
Bernard Malamud
André Malraux
Thomas Mann
Katherine Mansfield
J. P. Marquand
John Masefield
Edgar Lee Masters
W. Somerset Maugham
Mary McCarthy
Carson McCullers
William McFee
Herman Melville
H. L. Mencken
George Meredith
Alice Meynell
John Stuart Mill
Edna St. Vincent Millay
Arthur Miller
Henry Miller
A. A. Milne
Margaret Mitchell
George Moore
Marianne Moore
Alberto Moravia

Christopher Morley
Iris Murdoch

Vladimir Nabokov
Ogden Nash
Anaïs Nin
Frank Norris

Joyce Carol Oates
Sean O'Casey
Flannery O'Connor
Eugene O'Neill
George Orwell
John Osborne
Wilfred Owen

Dorothy Parker
Boris Pasternak
Kenneth Patchen
Harold Pinter
Luigi Pirandello
Sylvia Plath
Edgar Allan Poe
Katherine Anne Porter
Ezra Pound
T. F. Powys
J. B. Priestley
Marcel Proust
Thomas Pynchon

John Crowe Ransom
Dorothy Richardson
Samuel Richardson
Conrad Richter
James Whitcomb Riley

Edward Arlington Robinson
Philip Roth

Antoine Saint-Exupéry
J. D. Salinger
Carl Sandburg
George Santayana
William Saroyan
Jean-Paul Sartre
Siegfried Sassoon
Dorothy Sayers
Delmore Schwartz
Karl Shapiro
George Bernard Shaw
Percy Shelley
William Gilmore Simms
Neil Simon
Upton Sinclair
Edith Sitwell
Osbert Sitwell
Sacheverell Sitwell
Tobias Smollett
C. P. Snow
Stephen Spender
Gertrude Stein
John Steinbeck
James Stephens
Wallace Stevens
Robert Louis Stevenson
David Storey
Harriet Beecher Stowe
Lytton Strachey
William Styron
Jonathan Swift
Algernon Charles Swinburne
Arthur Symons
John Millington Synge

Booth Tarkington
Allen Tate
Sara Teasdale
Alfred, Lord Tennyson
William Makepeace Thackeray
Dylan Thomas
Henry David Thoreau
James Thurber
Alice B. Toklas
Lee Tolstoy
Mark Twain

Louis Untermeyer
John Updike

Paul Valéry
Gore Vidal

John Wain
Robert Penn Warren
Evelyn Waugh
H. G. Wells
Eudora Welty
Glenway Wescott
Nathanael West
Rebecca West
Edith Wharton
Walt Whitman
Kate Douglas Wiggin
Richard Wilbur
Oscar Wilde
Thornton Wilder
Tennessee Williams
William Carlos Williams
Edmund Wilson
Owen Wister

P. G. Wodehouse   Elinor Wylie
Thomas Wolfe
Leonard Woolf   W. B. Yeats
Virginia Woolf
William Wordsworth   Emile Zola
Richard Wright   Louis Zukofsky

10

Association Copies

Very recently, a neighbor of mine, Robert H. Smyth, remarked to me that he had heard I was writing a book about book collecting, and thought I might be interested in seeing some books that were once owned by his great-grandfather, who happened to be no less illustrious a figure than Nathaniel Hawthorne. He added that while the books were not written by Hawthorne, they still represented interesting curiosities. When I asked him how he had come to acquire these books, he answered that they were Christmas gifts from his father, whose mother had been the daughter of Julian Hawthorne, Nathaniel's son.

Unable to restrain my curiosity, I asked if I could see the books as soon as possible. He was kind enough to bring the books to me. As it turned out, both books were early-nineteenth-century works of Americana, the most interesting being *Inchiquin, The Jesuit's Letters* (1810), which bore Hawthorne's signature and the date 1829 on the title page, as well as a note written in Hawthorne's hand, signed, and dated, which acknowledged that the book was a gift to him from one Richard Manning. The other volume was *Memoir of the Life and Writings of Rev. Jonathan Mayhew, D.D.* (1838), in which Hawthorne's signature appeared on the front inner cover.

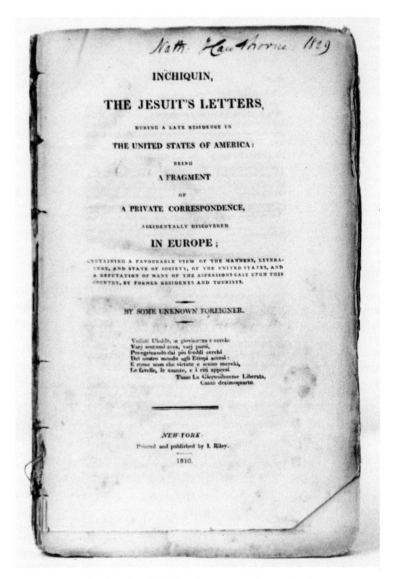

Nath. Hawthorne 1829

INCHIQUIN,

THE JESUIT'S LETTERS,

DURING A LATE RESIDENCE IN

THE UNITED STATES OF AMERICA:

BEING

A FRAGMENT

OF

A PRIVATE CORRESPONDENCE,

ACCIDENTALLY DISCOVERED

IN EUROPE;

CONTAINING A FAVOURABLE VIEW OF THE MANNERS, LITERA-
TURE, AND STATE OF SOCIETY, OF THE UNITED STATES, AND
A REFUTATION OF MANY OF THE ASPERSIONS CAST UPON THIS
COUNTRY, BY FORMER RESIDENTS AND TOURISTS.

BY SOME UNKNOWN FOREIGNER.

Veduti Ubaldo, in giovinezza e cerchi
Varj costumi aver, varj paesi,
Peregrinando dai piu freddi cerchi
Del nostro mondo agli Etiopi accesi:
E come uom che virtute e senno merchi,
Le favelle, le usanze, e i riti appresi.
       Tasso La Gierusalemme Liberata,
         Canto decimoquarto.

NEW-YORK:

Printed and published by I. Riley.

1810.

Fine Nathaniel Hawthorne association book

In terms of intrinsic value, these two works would probably be of most interest to collectors of Americana; but as association books, each title was more than desirable to collectors of Hawthorne's works, of American literature, or of literature in general. This is so since the books were once owned by a famous literary figure, and bore his signature as proof of ownership. Furthermore, to the scholar the books might possibly not only shed light on Hawthorne's reading interests but also suggest possible influences upon his own works of fiction.

Association books do not have to be first editions to be of interest to collectors. Often books from an author's childhood, such as school textbooks or copybooks, Bibles, or even such things as birth or marriage certificates, postcards, or Christmas cards can be of value because of association. Also, association books need not have been owned by persons of literary importance only, but by anyone who either distinguished himself in one way or another, or was related in some way to the author, or was a close friend or associate of the famous individual.

Sometimes association books are later editions of noted works, which were once owned by famous individuals—again not necessarily written by them—or inscribed by them to either another noted person or someone closely related or associated to them.

In any case, proof of ownership must somehow be indicated, whether by the owner's signature or autograph, a presentation inscription, a bookplate, a letter inserted stating ownership of the book, or any other mark of possession or association.

Association copies sometimes emerge from private libraries, having belonged to either the noted individual, or a member of his or her family, or a close acquaintance. For instance, a few months ago a noted rare-book dealer offered a copy of the first edition of Ezra Pound's *'Noh' or Accomplishment* (1916),

CURIOSITIES

OF

LITERATURE.

CONSISTING OF

ANECDOTES, CHARACTERS, SKETCHES,

AND

OBSERVATIONS,

LITERARY, CRITICAL, AND HISTORICAL.

Jane Austen

An extremely desirable association copy

which had been owned by the poet's father, Homer, and bore his signature. The interest in this associative copy rests with the family relationship. A collector could feel much sentimental interest in owning a book that clearly associates a poet with his father.

Many times a presentation copy of a work can doubly serve as an association copy when the book is inscribed either to another famous person or to one closely related to the author. Examples of this would be F. Scott Fitzgerald's presentation copy of *The Great Gatsby* (1925) to T. S. Eliot, or Eugene O'Neill's copy of C. E. Montague's *A Writer's Notes on His Trade* (1930), presented to his wife Carlotta.

As in the case of presentation copies, the value of association copies rests upon the degree of importance of the individuals involved—in the view of the rest of the world and especially collectors—the contents or nature of the works themselves, and the manner in which ownership or association is expressed.

For this reason, association copies vary in price and value. The beginning collector, to be sure, must determine carefully the extent to which his or her pocketbook will allow for the acquisition of association books.

II

THE MECHANICS
OF
BOOK COLLECTING

11

A Plan for Collecting

The seasoned book collector, upon being asked for advice by the novice as to the manner in which book collecting should ideally and practically be pursued, will on most occasions suggest that the beginner develop some kind of plan, and not collect at random.

The basis for this insistence on order may well rest with the experienced collector's realization that one must either limit one's scope or sphere of interest, or else go mad or bankrupt. After all, no one can collect everything of interest, importance, and value (though some have tried), since to do so would necessitate living at least two lifetimes. Despite this improbability, as well as the sound advice of more experienced collectors, most beginners will undoubtedly embark upon a course of acquisition in which everything and anything will be collected. This is only natural, since in the early stages of the book collecting fever, the most unlikely titles will be gathered up in the hope that they are surely worth having.

A great many years ago, Barton Currie concluded in *Fishers of Books* that there were essentially three stages of book collecting that every collector inevitably passed through.

The first stage was "assimilation." As mentioned previously, this is the least desirable phase of bibliomania, since the collector is usually not very discriminating. At its best, the collector with, let us say, an interest in literature might collect a first edition or two of Charles Dickens, one of Thackeray, three of Henry James, one of James Joyce, two of Hemingway, five of T. S. Eliot, and one of Gertrude Stein. What is wrong, it might now be asked, with collecting the first editions of these highly regarded authors? There is nothing at all wrong with collecting their works, but what usually occurs in the course of assimilating any number of books into one's collection is that for every Dickens or James item, there will most likely be thirty unexciting titles which may later prove to be of little interest to the collector. While it is every collector's prerogative to collect whatever he or she chooses, we might ponder how many more Dickens or Joyce items might have been acquired with the money spent on those thirty or so other titles.

It is perhaps in recognition of this that even the hardiest of assimilators enters the second stage of book collecting: "discrimination." To begin with, the discriminating collector has a decided advantage over the assimilator in that he knows what he wants, and is subsequently somewhat less (though not always) at the mercy of his impulses. The discriminator acquires a method for collecting, that of selectivity, which not only brings a great deal of satisfaction, but also assures greater success in acquiring the books he wants simply by virtue of the fact that he knows what he wants. While it is often by chance that the assimilator stumbles upon a title he wants to include in his collection, the discriminator achieves his goal primarily through diligent procedure. Of course, even with the careful methodology of the discriminator, luck and the probable availability of a given title play a large role. Many a collector who has set out to acquire works by Shakespeare or early publications by Caxton has had to forgo his plans simply as a result of the improbability of acquiring a Shakespeare quarto or folio, or a volume printed by Caxton.

The third stage of collecting involves the skillful "integration" of various titles concerning diverse fields of interest that somehow have something in common with one another. For instance, the collector of books about the sea and possibly whale-hunting may have the opportunity of acquiring a first edition of Herman Melville's *Moby-Dick* to integrate with his collection.

Similarly, the collector of the historical novels of Sir Walter Scott or James Fenimore Cooper will want to integrate them with books that pertain to the specific period in history in which a particular novel's plot occurs. Or the collector of sporting books might want to consolidate his stock with works by Ernest Hemingway, which often have sports such as hunting, fishing, and bullfighting as their background. Thus, the ability to integrate the items in one's collection approximates an art, and is an admirable achievement for any collector.

Insofar as specific plans for collecting are concerned, there are several that the collector may utilize. Perhaps the easiest plan focuses on the collecting of the works of a single author or one specific title. Single-author collections, in particular, are not only pleasurable to amass, but can often prove valuable as well.

With the exception of Shakespeare, whose works in first edition form either are impossible to locate or, if discovered, will cost a fortune, many authors are not expensive to collect in entirety. Perhaps it would be more accurate to say that almost every author in demand by collectors has one or two titles that are difficult to acquire, and consequently costly.

For instance, at the moment most of the first editions of D. H. Lawrence can be purchased for relatively small sums, but when one attempts to obtain a copy of the Florence edition of *Lady*

Chatterley's Lover (1928), or *The White Peacock* (1911), or *Sons and Lovers* (1913), the price will be rather higher than the other first editions.

Similarly, the first editions of even so illustrious a writer as Charles Dickens are within reach of many collectors of modest means, but when one attempts to acquire Dickens's novels in their originally issued monthly-part form, the prices can reach astronomical heights. And so, while the single-author plan often proves satisfying, the collector should be aware that gaps may be difficult to close as a result of either the excessive rarity or the high cost of one or more volumes.

The single-title plan offers just as great variety as the single-author plan, while allowing the collector to maintain a limited scope. In choosing a title, the possibilities are of course infinite. Some people collect foreign-language editions of the Bible from the fifteenth century onward. Others concentrate upon classic titles in literature, such as Cervantes's *Don Quixote*, Dante's *The Divine Comedy*, Henry Fielding's *Tom Jones*, Jane Austen's *Pride and Prejudice*, Emily Brontë's *Wuthering Heights*, Charles Dickens's *Great Expectations*.

Still another approach to collecting is the "high-spot" plan of the outstanding works of literature, science, natural history, or whatever field of interest appeals to the collector. One might love detective fiction and seek out works by such masters of the genre as Sir Arthur Conan Doyle, Agatha Christie, and Dashiell Hammett.

Someone interested in twentieth-century literature might want to acquire first editions of the finest expressions of the art of Theodore Dreiser, James Joyce, Ezra Pound, Ernest Hemingway, F. Scott Fitzgerald, William Faulkner, D. H. Lawrence, T. S. Eliot, and Gertrude Stein. With each author, the collector is entirely free to select whatever title he feels may represent that

Important first editions by Gertrude Stein

writer's outstanding achievement. With each field of interest, the collector is also free to choose the titles believed to highlight that subject. The selection of a plan, as well as the procedure for pursuing it, rests entirely with the taste and judgment of the collector. Ideally, each individual eschews the time-worn patterns of past collectors and charts a plan that is both original and unique.

Yet since many beginning collectors seek some sort of guidance, I have prepared and in some cases reprinted lists of titles in various genres sought by collectors over the years, or at present. It must be understood that some of the items listed are extremely difficult to obtain—in some cases impossible—or very expensive. Also, these lists are not intended to serve as a shoppers' guide to book collecting, but are presented to point out to the beginner past collectors' focuses of interest. Needless to say, the lists are by no means authoritative. Each collector must determine his or her own pattern of collecting in an effort to achieve the greatest amount of private pleasure.

Twentieth-Century American Literature

Sister Carrie (Dreiser), 1900
The Wonderful Wizard of Oz (Baum), 1900
The Octopus (Norris), 1901
The Wings of the Dove (James), 1902
The Call of the Wild (London), 1903
The Ambassadors (James), 1903
Rebecca of Sunnybrook Farm (Wiggin), 1903
The Sea-Wolf (London), 1904
The Golden Bowl (James), 1904
The House of Mirth (Wharton), 1905
The Jungle (Sinclair), 1906
The Four Million (O. Henry), 1906
Poems (W. C. Williams), 1909

Three Lives (Stein), 1909
Personae (Pound), 1909
Jennie Gerhardt (Dreiser), 1911
Ethan Frome (Wharton), 1911
A Boy's Will (Frost), 1913
North of Boston (Frost), 1914
Spoon River Anthology (Masters), 1915
Mountain Interval (Frost), 1916
The Man Against the Sky (Robinson), 1916
Chicago Poems (Sandburg), 1916
Men, Women and Ghosts (Amy Lowell), 1916
Renascence and Other Poems (Millay), 1917
Prufrock and Other Observations (Eliot), 1917
Cornhuskers (Sandburg), 1918
The Magnificent Ambersons (Tarkington), 1918
My Ántonia (Cather), 1918
Winesburg, Ohio (Anderson), 1919
Poems (Eliot), 1920
Main Street (Lewis), 1920
Smoke and Steel (Sandburg), 1920
The Age of Innocence (Wharton), 1920
The Emperor Jones (O'Neill), 1920
This Side of Paradise (Fitzgerald), 1920
A Few Figs from Thistles (Millay), 1920
Three Soldiers (Dos Passos), 1921
The Waste Land (Eliot), 1922
Babbitt (Lewis), 1922
The Enormous Room (E. E. Cummings), 1922
Harmonium (Wallace Stevens), 1923
in our time (Hemingway), 1924
An American Tragedy (Dreiser), 1925
Arrowsmith (Lewis), 1925
The Great Gatsby (Fitzgerald), 1925
Roan Stallion (Jeffers), 1925
Gentlemen Prefer Blondes (Loos), 1925
Cantos (Pound), 1925
The Sun Also Rises (Hemingway), 1926

Soldier's Pay (Faulkner), 1926
The Bridge of San Luis Rey (Wilder), 1927
Men Without Women (Hemingway), 1927
Strange Interlude (O'Neill), 1928
John Brown's Body (S. V. Benét), 1928
A Farewell to Arms (Hemingway), 1929
Look Homeward, Angel (Wolfe), 1929
The Sound and the Fury (Faulkner), 1929
Dodsworth (Lewis), 1929
Ash Wednesday (Eliot), 1930
The Bridge (Crane), 1930
As I Lay Dying (Faulkner), 1930
Flowering Judas (Porter), 1930
Mourning Becomes Electra (O'Neill), 1931
The Good Earth (Buck), 1931
Sanctuary (Faulkner), 1931
Tobacco Road (Caldwell), 1932
Young Lonigan (Farrell), 1932
Light in August (Faulkner), 1932
Mutiny on the Bounty (Hall and Nordhoff), 1932
1919 (Dos Passos), 1932
The Autobiography of Alice B. Toklas (Stein), 1933
Winner Take Nothing (Hemingway), 1933
Anthony Adverse (Allen), 1933
The Daring Young Man on the Flying Trapeze (Saroyan), 1934
Tender Is the Night (Fitzgerald), 1934
The Children's Hour (Hellman), 1934
The Petrified Forest (Sherwood), 1934
The Young Manhood of Studs Lonigan (Farrell), 1934
Tropic of Cancer (Miller), 1934
Life with Father (Day), 1935
Tortilla Flat (Steinbeck), 1935
Absalom, Absalom! (Faulkner), 1936
Gone with the Wind (Mitchell), 1936
Of Mice and Men (Steinbeck), 1937
To Have and Have Not (Hemingway), 1937
Our Town (Wilder), 1938

The Grapes of Wrath (Steinbeck), 1939
The Day of the Locust (West), 1939
Native Son (Wright), 1940
The Heart Is a Lonely Hunter (McCullers), 1940
You Can't Go Home Again (Wolfe), 1940
For Whom the Bell Tolls (Hemingway), 1940
Watch on the Rhine (Hellman), 1941
The Last Tycoon (Fitzgerald), 1941
Go Down, Moses (Faulkner), 1942
The Skin of Our Teeth (Wilder), 1942
Four Quartets (Eliot), 1943
The Glass Menagerie (Williams), 1945
Wars I Have Seen (Stein), 1945
A Streetcar Named Desire (Williams), 1947
The Naked and the Dead (Mailer), 1948
Other Voices, Other Rooms (Capote), 1948
The Age of Anxiety (Auden), 1948
The Young Lions (Shaw), 1949
Death of a Salesman (Miller), 1949
The Man with the Golden Arm (Algren), 1949
The Cocktail Party (Eliot), 1950
The Caine Mutiny (Wouk), 1951
From Here to Eternity (Jones), 1951
The Catcher in the Rye (Salinger), 1951
The Old Man and the Sea (Hemingway), 1952
Invisible Man (Ellison), 1952
The Adventures of Augie March (Bellow), 1953
Cat on a Hot Tin Roof (Williams), 1955
A Good Man Is Hard to Find (O'Connor), 1955
Howl (Ginsberg), 1956
A Long Day's Journey into Night (O'Neill), 1956
A Death in the Family (Agee), 1957
The Wapshot Chronicle (Cheever), 1957
On the Road (Kerouac), 1957
The Assistant (Malamud), 1957
Poems (Wilbur), 1957
Goodbye, Columbus (Roth), 1959

Naked Lunch (Burroughs), 1959
Rabbit, Run (Updike), 1960
The Sot-Weed Factor (Barth), 1960
The Colossus (Plath), 1960, 1962
Nobody Knows My Name (Baldwin), 1961
Catch-22 (Heller), 1961
One Flew Over the Cuckoo's Nest (Kesey), 1962
Who's Afraid of Virginia Woolf? (Albee), 1962
Ship of Fools (Porter), 1962
V (Pynchon), 1963
Herzog (Bellow), 1964
A Moveable Feast (Hemingway), 1964
Julian (Vidal), 1964
In Cold Blood (Capote), 1966
The Painted Bird (Kozinski), 1966
The Confessions of Nat Turner (Styron), 1967
Couples (Updike), 1968
Lost in the Funhouse (Barth), 1968
Portnoy's Complaint (Roth), 1969
Slaughterhouse-Five (Vonnegut), 1969
Bech (Updike), 1970

Twentieth-Century British Literature

Lord Jim (Conrad), 1900
The Shadowy Waters (Yeats), 1900
Erewhon Revisited (Butler), 1901
Kim (Kipling), 1901
Poems of the Past and Present (Hardy), 1901
Youth and Two Other Stories (Conrad), 1902
The Hound of the Baskervilles (Doyle), 1902
The Way of All Flesh (Butler), 1903
Typhoon and Other Stories (Conrad), 1903
Romance (Conrad and Hueffer), 1903
The Private Papers of Henry Ryecroft (Gissing), 1903
Ballads (Masefield), 1903
Nostromo (Conrad), 1904

Green Mansions (Hudson), 1904
The Dynasts (Part I) (Hardy), 1904
The Return of Sherlock Holmes (Doyle), 1905
Where Angels Fear to Tread (Forster), 1905
Will Warburton (Gissing), 1905
The Scarlet Pimpernel (Orczy), 1905
The Man of Property (Galsworthy), 1906
The Dynasts (Part II) (Hardy), 1906
Poems, 1899–1905 (Yeats), 1906
The Secret Agent (Conrad), 1907
The Longest Journey (Forster), 1907
Chamber Music (Joyce), 1907
Major Barbara (Shaw), 1907
The Playboy of the Western World (Synge), 1907
The Old Wives' Tale (Bennett), 1908
A Room with a View (Forster), 1908
The Dynasts (Part III) (Hardy), 1908
Last Poems (Meredith), 1909
Tono-Bungay (Wells), 1909
Howard's End (Forster), 1910
The History of Mr. Polly (Wells), 1910
The Green Helmet and Other Poems (Yeats), 1910
Under Western Eyes (Conrad), 1911
The White Peacock (Lawrence), 1911
The Crock of Gold (Stephens), 1912
Sons and Lovers (Lawrence), 1913
Love Poems and Others (Lawrence), 1913
Chance (Conrad), 1914
Dubliners (Joyce), 1914
The Prussian Officer and Other Stories (Lawrence), 1914
The Widowing of Mrs. Holroyd (Lawrence), 1914
The Thirty-Nine Steps (Buchan), 1915
Victory (Conrad), 1915
The Rainbow (Lawrence), 1915
The Good Soldier (Ford), 1915
Of Human Bondage (Maugham), 1915
The Voyage Out (Woolf), 1915

Images (1910–1915) (Aldington), 1915
The Mother and Other Poems (E. Sitwell), 1915
1914 and Other Poems (Brooke), 1915
A Portrait of the Artist as a Young Man (Joyce), U.S., 1916
Amores (Lawrence), 1916
The Shadow Line (Conrad), 1917
South Wind (Douglas), 1917
His Last Bow (Doyle), 1917
The Wild Swans at Coole (Yeats), 1917
The Old Huntsman and Other Poems (Sassoon), 1917
Poems (Hopkins), 1918
Exiles (Joyce), 1918
Seven Men (Beerbohm), 1919
The Moon and Sixpence (Maugham), 1919
Night and Day (Woolf), 1919
The Arrow of Gold (Conrad), 1919
The Rescue (Conrad), 1920
Women in Love (Lawrence), private printing, N.Y., 1920
Bliss and Other Stories (Mansfield), 1920
Crome Yellow (Huxley), 1921
The Forsythe Saga (Galsworthy), 1922
Ulysses (Joyce), Paris, 1922
Jacob's Room (Woolf), 1922
The Garden Party and Other Stories (Mansfield), 1922
Late Lyrics and Earlier (Hardy), 1922
Last Poems (Housman), 1922
The Rover (Conrad), 1923
Antic Hay (Huxley), 1923
Whose Body? (Sayers), 1923
Kangaroo (Lawrence), 1923
Some Do Not (Ford), 1924
A Passage to India (Forster), 1924
No More Parades (Ford), 1925
Suspense (Conrad), 1925
The Painted Veil (Maugham), 1925
Mrs. Dalloway (Woolf), 1925
A Man Could Stand Up (Ford), 1926

Seven Pillars of Wisdom (T. E. Lawrence), limited edition, 1926
To the Lighthouse (Woolf), 1927
Pomes Penyeach (Joyce), Paris, 1927
October Blast (Yeats), 1927
The Last Post (Ford), U.S., 1928
Point Counter Point (Huxley), 1928
Lady Chatterley's Lover (Lawrence), Florence, 1928
Anna Livia Plurabelle (Joyce), U.S., 1928
Poems (Auden), 1928
The Tower (Yeats), 1928
Pansies (Lawrence), 1929
The Virgin and the Gypsy (Lawrence), 1930
The Edwardians (Sackville-West), 1930
Vile Bodies (Waugh), 1930
The Waves (Woolf), 1931
Brave New World (Huxley), 1932
Lost Horizon (Hilton), 1933
Goodbye, Mr. Chips (Hilton), 1934
A Handful of Dust (Waugh), 1934
18 Poems (Thomas), 1934
The Hobbit (Tolkien), 1937
The Years (Woolf), 1937
Mister Johnson (Cary), 1939
After Many a Summer Dies the Swan (Huxley), 1939
Finnegans Wake (Joyce), 1939
The Power and the Glory (Greene), 1940
Portrait of the Artist as a Young Dog (Thomas), 1940
Between the Acts (Woolf), 1941
The Horse's Mouth (Cary), 1944
The Razor's Edge (Maugham), 1944
Animal Farm (Orwell), 1945
Brideshead Revisited (Waugh), 1945
The Heart of the Matter (Greene), 1948
The Loved One (Waugh), 1948
The Heat of the Day (Bowen), 1949
Nineteen Eighty-Four (Orwell), 1949
The Grass Is Singing (Lessing), 1950

Lucky Jim (Amis), 1954
Lord of the Flies (Golding), 1954
Look Back in Anger (Osborne), 1956
The Alexandria Quartet (Durrell): *Justine,* 1957; *Balthazar,* 1958;
    Mountolive, 1958; *Clea,* 1960
The Birthday Party (Pinter), 1958
This Sporting Life (Storey), 1960
A Clockwork Orange (Burgess), 1962
The Unicorn (Murdoch), 1963
The Homecoming (Pinter), 1965
Rosencrantz and Guildenstern Are Dead (Stoppard), 1967

One Hundred Books Famous in English Literature*

The Canterbury Tales (Chaucer), 1478
Confessio Amantis (Gower), 1483
Le Morte d'Arthur (Malory), 1485
The Booke of the Common Praier, 1549
The Vision of Piers Plowman (Langland), 1550
A Myrrour for Magistrates (Baldwin, Sackville, et al.), 1563
Songes and Sonettes (Howard), 1567
The Tragidie of Ferrex and Porrex (Norton and Sackville), 1570 (?)
Chronicles of England, Scotlande, and Irelande (Holinshed), 1577
Euphues (Lyly), 1581
The Countesse of Pembroke's Arcadia (Sidney), 1590
The Faerie Queene (Spenser), 1590
Essaies (Bacon), 1598
*The Principal Navigations, Voiages, Traffiques, and Discoueries of
    the English Nation* (Hakluyt), 1598
The Whole Works of Homer (Chapman), 1609 (?)
The Holy Bible, 1611
The Workes (Jonson), 1616
The Anatomy of Melancholy (Burton), 1621
Comedies, Histories and Tragedies (Shakespeare), 1623
The Tragedy of the Dutchesse of Malfy (Webster), 1623

---

* Selected by the Grolier Club of New York, 1902.

A New Way to Pay Old Debts (Massinger), 1633
The Broken Heart (Ford), 1633
The Famous Tragedy of the Rich Jew of Malta (Marlowe), 1633
The Temple (Herbert), 1633
Poems (Donne), 1633
Religio Medici (Browne), 1642
The Workes (Waller), 1645
Comedies and Tragedies (Beaumont and Fletcher), 1647
Hesperides (Herrick), 1648
The Rule and Exercises of Holy Living (Taylor), 1650
The Compleat Angler (Walton), 1653
Hudibras (Butler), 1663
Paradise Lost (Milton), 1667
The Pilgrim's Progress (Bunyan), 1678
Absalom and Achitophel (Dryden), 1681
An Essay Concerning Human Understanding (Locke), 1690
The Way of the World (Congreve), 1700
The History of the Rebellion and Civil Wars in England (Clarandon), 1702
The Tatler, 1710
The Spectator, 1711
The Life and Strange Surprizing Adventures of Robinson Crusoe (Defoe), 1719
Travels into Several Remote Nations of the World (Swift), 1726
An Essay on Man (Pope), 1733
The Analogy of Religion (Butler), 1736
Reliques of Ancient English Poetry (Percy), 1765
Odes (Collins), 1747
Clarissa (Richardson), 1748
The History of Tom Jones (Fielding), 1749
An Elegy Wrote in a Country Church Yard (Gray), 1751
A Dictionary of the English Language (Johnson), 1755
Poor Richard Improved (Franklin), 1758
Commentaries on the Laws of England (Blackstone), 1765
The Vicar of Wakefield (Goldsmith), 1766
A Sentimental Journey Through France and Italy (Sterne), 1768
The Federalist, 1788

The Expedition of Humphry Clinker (Smollett), 1771
An Inquiry into the Nature and Causes of the Wealth of Nations (Smith), 1776
The History of the Decline and Fall of the Roman Empire (Gibbon), 1776
The School for Scandal (Sheridan), Dublin, 1780
The Task (Cowper), 1785
Poems (Burns), 1786
The Natural History and Antiquities of Selborne (White), 1789
Reflections on the Revolution in France (Burke), 1790
Rights of Man (Paine), 1791
The Life of Samuel Johnson, LL.D. (Boswell), 1791
Lyrical Ballads (Wordsworth and Coleridge), 1798
A History of New York . . . by Diedrich Knickerbocker (Irving), 1809
Childe Harold's Pilgrimage (Byron), 1812
Pride and Prejudice (Austen), 1813
Christabel, Kubla Khan, A Vision: The Pains of Sleep (Coleridge), 1816
Ivanhoe (Scott), 1820
Lamia, Isabella, The Eve of St. Agnes, and Other Poems (Keats), 1820
Adonais (Shelley), 1821
Elia (Lamb), 1823
Memoirs (Pepys), 1825
The Last of the Mohicans (Cooper), 1826
Pericles and Aspasia (Landor), 1836
The Posthumous Papers of the Pickwick Club (Dickens), 1837
Sartor Resartus (Carlyle), 1834
Nature (Emerson), 1836
History of the Conquest of Peru (Prescott), 1847
The Raven and Other Poems (Poe), 1845
Jane Eyre (Brontë), 1847
Evangeline (Longfellow), 1847
Sonnets (Mrs. Browning), 1847
Meliboeus-Hipponax: The Biglow Papers (Lowell), 1848
Vanity Fair (Thackeray), 1848

The History of England (Macaulay), 1849
In Memoriam (Tennyson), 1850
The Scarlet Letter (Hawthorne), 1850
The Stones of Venice (Ruskin), 1851
Uncle Tom's Cabin (Stowe), 1852
Men and Women (Browning), 1855
The Rise of the Dutch Republic (Motley), 1856
Adam Bede (Eliot), 1859
On the Origin of Species (Darwin), 1859
Rubáiyát of Omar Khayyám (FitzGerald), 1859
Apologia Pro Vita Sua (Newman), 1864
Essays in Criticism (Arnold), 1865
Snow-Bound (Whittier), 1866

One Hundred American Books Before 1900*

The Whole Booke of Psalmes, 1640
The Bloody Tenant, of Persecutions for cause of Conscience, London, 1644
A Platform of Church Discipline, 1649
The day of Doom (Wigglesworth), London, 1673
A True History of the Captivity & Restoration of Mrs. Mary Rowlandson (Mrs. Rowlandson), London, 1682
Magnalia Christi Americana (Mather), London, 1702
A Vindication of the Government of New England Churches (Wise), 1717
The New England Primer, 1727
A brief Narrative of the Case and Tryal of John Peter Zenger, 1736
Experiments and Observations on Electricity made at Philadelphia in America (Franklin), London, 1751
Supplemental Experiments and Observations . . . London, 1753
New Experiments and Observations . . . London, 1754
A Careful and Strict Enquiry into . . . *Freedom and Will* (Edwards), 1754

* Compiled by the Grolier Club, 1947.

THE

President's Address

TO THE

PEOPLE

OF THE

UNITED STATES,

ANNOUNCING HIS INTENTION OF

RETIRING FROM PUBLIC LIFE

AT THE EXPIRATION OF THE

PRESENT CONSTITUTIONAL TERM

OF

PRESIDENCY.

PHILADELPHIA:

PRINTED FOR *J. ORMROD*, No. 41, CHESNUT-STREET,

BY ORMROD AND CONRAD.

1796.

Noteworthy Americana

Poor Richard improved: Being an Almanack for . . . *1758* (Franklin), 1757
Letters from a Farmer in Pennsylvania . . . (Dickinson), 1768
Common Sense (Paine), 1776
A Declaration . . . *[of Independence]*, 1776
A Grammatical Institute, of the English Language . . . (Webster), 1783
An Ordinance for the Government of the Territory of the United States, North-West of the River Ohio, 1787
The United States Constitution, 1787
The Federalist (Hamilton and Madison), 1788
The Bill of Rights, 1789
Memoires de la Vie Privee . . . (Franklin), Paris, 1791
The Private Life of the late Benjamin Franklin, London, 1793
Works of the late Doctor Benjamin Franklin, London, 1793
The Farmer's Almanac . . . *for* . . . *1793* (Thomas), 1792
Charlotte, A Tale of Truth (Rowson), 1794
Farewell Address (Washington), 1796
The New American Practical Navigator (Bowditch), 1802
Marbury vs. Madison (Supreme Court opinion by Marshall), 1804
The Life of Washington the Great . . . (Weems), 1806
A History of New York . . . (Knickerbocker [Irving]), 1809
The History of Printing in America (Thomas), 1810
History of the Expedition . . . *to the Pacific Ocean* (Lewis and Clark), 1814
The Sketch Book (Crayon [Irving]), 1819–20
Poems (Bryant), 1821
The Monroe Doctrine (1823)
The Last of the Mohicans (Cooper), 1826
The Tales of Peter Parley About America (Parley [Goodrich]), 1827
An American Dictionary of the English Language (Webster), 1828
The Book of Mormon (Smith), 1830
Experiments and Observations on the Gastric Juice . . . (Beaumont), 1833
The Crockett Almanacks for 1835, 1836, 1837, 1838, 1839
The Yemassee (Simms), 1835

Elements of Botany (Gray), 1836
The Eclectic First Reader (McGuffey), 1836
An Oration . . . [The American Scholar Address] (Emerson), 1837
Twice-Told Tales (Hawthorne), 1837
The Birds of America (Audubon), 1840–44
Two Years Before the Mast (Dana), 1840
Essays (Emerson), 1841
Essays: Second Series, 1844
Ballads and Other Poems (Longfellow), 1842
*Report on an Exploration of the Country lying between the Missouri
   River and the Rocky Mountains* (Frémont), 1843
The Contagiousness of Puerperal Fever (Holmes), 1843
History of the Conquest of Mexico (Prescott), 1843
Poems (Moore), 1844
Rules of Proceeding and Debate in Deliberative Assemblies (Cush-
   ing), 1845
The Warwick Woodlands (Herbert [Forester]), 1845
Tales (Poe), 1845
The Raven and Other Poems (Poe), 1845
The Biglow Papers (Lowell), 1848
The California and Oregon Trail (Parkman), 1849
The Scarlet Letter (Hawthorne), 1850
Moby-Dick (Melville), 1851
Uncle Tom's Cabin (Stowe), 1852
Ten Nights in a Bar-Room (Arthur), 1854
Walden (Thoreau), 1854
Familiar Quotations (Bartlett), 1855
The Age of Fable (Bulfinch), 1855
The Song of Hiawatha (Longfellow), 1855
Leaves of Grass (Whitman), 1855
Dred Scott [Decision] (Taney et al.), 1857
The Autocrat of the Breakfast-Table (Holmes), 1858
Malaeska, The Indian Wife of the White Hunter (Stephens), 1860
Emancipation Proclamation (Lincoln), 1863
The Gettysburg Solemnities . . . (Lincoln), 1863
Snow-Bound (Whittier), 1866
Little Women (Alcott), 1868

Little Women, Part Second, 1869
Ragged Dick (Alger), 1868
The Luck of Roaring Camp (Harte), 1870
1st Mail Order Broadside (A. Montgomery Ward), 1872
1st Mail Order Pamphlet, 1874
Science and Health (Eddy), 1875
The Adventures of Tom Sawyer (Twain), 1876
The Leavenworth Case (Green), 1878
Progress and Poverty (George), 1879
Ben-Hur: A Tale of the Christ (Wallace), 1880
Uncle Remus: His Songs and His Sayings (Harris), 1881
The Common Law (Holmes), 1881
The Portrait of a Lady (James), 1881
Mrs. Lincoln's Boston Cook Book (Mrs. Lincoln), 1884
The Adventures of Huckleberry Finn (Twain), 1885
The Rise of Silas Lapham (Howells), 1885
Little Lord Fauntleroy (Burnett), 1886
Looking Backward: 2000–1887 (Bellamy), 1888
Poems (Dickinson), 1890
Poems, Second Series, 1891
Poems, Third Series, 1896
Principles of Psychology (James), 1890
The Influence of Sea Power upon History, 1660–1783 (Mahan),
    1890
Tales of Soldiers and Civilians (Bierce), 1891
Main-Travelled Roads (Garland), 1891
The Significance of the Frontier in American History (Turner),
    1894
The Care and Feeding of Children (Holt), 1894
The Red Badge of Courage (Crane), 1895
The Man with the Hoe (Markham), 1899
The Theory of the Leisure Class (Veblen), 1899

Some Notable Science Books Selected from
One Hundred Books Famous in Science*

De Ortu et Causis Subterraneorum . . . *De Natura Fossilium* (Agricola), 1546

De Re Metallica (Agricola), 1556

Théorie des Phénomènes Électro-dynamiques (Ampère), 1826

Experimenta circa Effectum Conflictus Electrici in Acum Magbeticam (Oersted), 1820

Two Bookes . . . *Of the proficience and advancement of Learning* (Bacon), 1605

Instauratio Magna (Bacon), 1620

Experiments and Observations on the Gastric Juice (Beaumont), 1833

Nouvelle Fonction du Foie (Bernard), 1853

Ars Conjectandi (Bernoulli), 1713

De Motu Animalum (Borelli), 1680–81

The Sceptical Chemist (Boyle), 1661

New Experiments Physico-Mechanical (Boyle), 1662

De Nova . . . *Stella* (Brahe), 1573

De Revolutionibus Orbium Coelestium (Copernicus), 1543

Dialogo . . . *sopra i due Massimi Sistemi del Mondo* (Galileo), 1632

Recherches sur les Substances Radioactives (Curie), 1903

Leçons d'Anatomie Comparée (Cuvier), 1800–5

Historique et Description des Procédés du Daguerréotype (Daguerre), 1839

A New System of Chemical Philosophy (Dalton), 1808–27

On the Tendency of Species to Form Varieties (Darwin), 1858

On the Origin of the Species (Darwin), 1859

Discours de la Méthode (Descartes), 1637

Encyclopédie, ou Dictionnaire Raisonné des Sciences, des Arts et des Métiers (Diderot), 1751–80

Zur Theorie . . . *in Normalspectrum* (Planck), 1900

Zur Electrodynamik bewegter Korper (Einstein), 1905

Die Grand lage der allgemeinen Relativitäts theorie, 1916

---

* Compiled by Harrison D. Horblit for the Grolier Club, 1964.

AN

INQUIRY

INTO

THE CAUSES AND EFFECTS

OF

THE VARIOLÆ VACCINÆ,

A DISEASE

DISCOVERED IN SOME OF THE WESTERN COUNTIES OF ENGLAND,

PARTICULARLY

GLOUCESTERSHIRE,

AND KNOWN BY THE NAME OF

THE COW POX.

———————

BY EDWARD JENNER, M.D. F.R.S. &c.

———————

———— QUID NOBIS CERTIUS IPSIS
SENSIBUS ESSE POTEST, QUO VERA AC FALSA NOTEMUS.

LUCRETIUS.

———————

London:

PRINTED, FOR THE AUTHOR,

BY SAMPSON LOW, Nº. 7, BERWICK STREET, SOHO:

AND SOLD BY LAW, AVE-MARIA LANE; AND MURRAY AND HIGHLEY, FLEET STREET.

———

1798.

An important science book

Experimental Researches in Electricity (Faraday), 1839–55
Experiments and Observations in Electricity (Franklin), 1751–54
Die Traumdertung (Freud), 1900
Herbarum Vivae Eicones (Brunfels), 1530–36
De Historia Stirpium (Fuchs), 1542
Siderus Nuncius (Galileo), 1610
Discorsi . . . a due nuove scienze (Galileo), 1638
De Viribus Electricitatis (Galvani), 1791
On the Electricity excited by . . . Substances of different kinds
    (Volta), 1800
Historiae Animalum (Gesner), 1551–87
On the Equilibrium of Heterogeneous Substances (Gibbs), 1874–78
De Magnete (Gilbert), 1600
The Principles of Mr. Harrison's Time-Keeper (Maskelyne and
    Harrison), 1767
Vegetable Staticks (Hales), 1727
Statical Essays: Containing Haemastaticks (Hales), 1733
De Motu Cordis et Sanguinis (Harvey), 1628
Essai d'une Théorie sur la Structure des Crystaux (Havy), 1784
Micrographia (Hooke), 1665
Horologium Oscillatorium (Huygens), 1673
Traité de la Lumière (Huygens), 1690
An Inquiry into the Causes and Effects of the Variolae Vaccinae
    (Jenner), 1798
Astronomia Nova (Kepler), 1609
Harmonices Mundi Libri V (Kepler), 1619
Zur Untersuchung von pathogenen Organismen (Koch), 1881
Mécanique Analitique (Lagrange), 1788
Photometria (Lambert), 1760
Traité de Mécanique Celeste (Laplace), 1802–27
Traité Élémentaire de Chimie (Lavoisier), 1789
Ontledingen en Ondekkingen . . . Brieven (Leeuwenhoek), 1686–
    1718
Nova Methodus pro Maximus et Minimis (Leibniz), 1684
Analysis Per Quantitatum Series, Fluxiones ac Differentias (New-
    ton), 1711
Systema Naturae (Linnaeus), 1735

Principles of Geology (Lyell), 1830–33
The Physical Geography of the Sea (Maury), 1855
Versuche über Pflanzen-Hybriden (Mendel), 1866
Die Mutationstheorie (De Vries), 1901–3
Mirifici Logarithmorum Canonis Descriptio (Napier), 1614
Mirifici Logarithmorum Canonis Constructio (Napier), 1619
Philosophiae Naturalis Principia Mathematica (Newton), 1687
Opticks (Newton), 1704
Memoire sur la Fermentation Appelée Lactique (Pasteur), 1857
Historia Naturalis (Plinius), 1469
Experiments and Observations on Different Kinds of Air (Priestley),
    1774–77
Cosmographia (Ptolemy), 1462
Historia Plantarum (Ray), 1686–1704
Über eine neue Art von Strahlen (Rontgen), 1896–97
Radioactivity (Rutherford), 1904
Mikroskopische Untersuchungen (Schwann), 1839
Grundzuge der Wissenschaftlichen Botanik (Schleiden), 1842–43
*De Solido intra Solidum Naturaliter Contento Dissertationis Pro-
    dromus* (Steno), 1669
De Humani Corporis Fabrica (Vesalius), 1543
Die Cellular pathologie (Virchow), 1858
Grundzuge der physiologischen Psychologie (Wundt), 1874
The Principles of Psychology (James), 1890

Selected Detective Fiction*

Edgar A. Poe
    The Murders in the Rue Morgue, 1843
    The Mystery of Marie Roget, 1842–43
Wilkie Collins
    The Woman in White, 1860
    The Moonstone, 1868
Charles Dickens

---

* Based on John Carter's essay "Detective Fiction" in *New Paths in Book-Collecting* and Jacques Barzun and W. E. Taylor, *A Catalogue of Crime*.

The Mystery of Edwin Drood, 1870
Emile Gaboriau
   The Steel Safe, or The Strains and Splendours of New York Life, 1868
   File 113, 1871
   The Mystery of Orcival, 1871
   The Widow Lerouge, 1873
Anna Katharine Green
   The Leavenworth Case, 1878
   Hand and Ring, 1883
   Behind Closed Doors, 1888
   The Filigree Ball, 1903
   The House of the Whispering Pines, 1910
   The Step on the Stair, 1923
Lawrence L. Lynch
   Shadowed by Three, 1879
   Madeline Payne, 1884
   The Diamond Coterie, 1885
   Dangerous Ground, 1885
Julian Hawthorne
   Section 558, 1888
   Another's Crime, 1888
Fergus W. Hume
   The Mystery of a Hansom Cab, 1887
   The Piccadilly Puzzle, 1889
   The Gentleman Who Vanished, 1890
   The Black Carnation, 1892
   The Chinese Jar, 1893
   A Midnight Mystery, 1894
   The Lone Inn, 1894
   The Lady from Nowhere, 1900
Sir Arthur Conan Doyle
   A Study in Scarlet, 1887
   The Adventures of Sherlock Holmes, 1892
   The Memoirs of Sherlock Holmes, 1894
   The Sign of the Four, 1890

The Hound of the Baskervilles, 1902
The Return of Sherlock Holmes, 1905
His Last Bow, 1917
Robert Louis Stevenson and Lloyd Osborne
The Wrong Box, 1889
Maarter Maartens
The Black Box Murder, 1889
Arthur Morrison
Martin Hewitt, Investigator, 1894
Chronicles of Martin Hewitt, 1895
The Adventures of Martin Hewitt, 1896
The Dorrington Deed Box, 1897
L. T. Meade and Clifford Halifax
Stories from the Diary of a Doctor, 1894
M. P. Shiel
Prince Zaleski, 1895
Louis Tracy
The Strange Disappearance of Lady Delia, 1901
The Silent House, 1911
The Case of Mortimer Fenley, 1915
Arnold Bennett
The Grand Babylon Hotel, 1904
Dr. R. Austin Freeman
The Red Thumb Mark, 1907
John Thorndyke's Cases, 1909
The Singing Bone, 1912
The Mystery of 31 New Inn, 1912
A Silent Witness, 1914
The Eye of Osiris, 1911
The Great Portrait Mystery, 1918
Baroness Orczy
The Scarlet Pimpernel (1905)
The Old Man in the Corner, 1918
G. K. Chesterton
The Innocence of Father Brown, 1911

H. C. Bailey
  Call Mr. Fortune, 1920
  Mr. Fortune's Practice, 1923
  Mr. Fortune's Trials, 1926
Ernest Bramah
  Max Carrados, 1920
  The Eyes of Max Carrados, 1923
  Max Carrados Mysteries, 1927
A. E. W. Mason
  At the Villa Rose, 1910
  The House of the Arrow, 1924
  The Prisoner in the Opal, 1929
E. C. Bentley
  Trent's Last Case, 1913
John Buchan
  The Thirty-Nine Steps, 1913
Agatha Christie
  The Mysterious Affair at Styles, 1920
Eden Phillpotts
  The Grey Room, 1921
A. A. Milne
  The Red House Mystery, 1922
Dorothy Sayers
  Whose Body?, 1923
  Lord Peter Views the Body, 1929
  Hangman's Holiday, 1933
  In the Teeth of the Evidence, 1933
G. D. H. Cole
  The Brooklyn Murders, 1923
Philip MacDonald
  The Rasp, 1924
Lynn Brock
  The Deduction of Colonel Gore, 1924
Ronald Knox
  The Viaduct Murder, 1925
Henry Wade
  The Verdict of You All, 1926

Dashiell Hammett
    The Dain Curse, 1929
    Red Harvest, 1929
    The Maltese Falcon, 1930
    The Glass Key, 1931
    The Thin Man, 1934
Raymond Chandler
    The Big Sleep, 1930
    Farewell, My Lovely, 1940
    The High Window, 1942
    The Lady in the Lake, 1943
    The Little Sister, 1949
    The Long Goodbye, 1954
    Playback, 1958
Erle Stanley Gardner
    The Case of the Velvet Claws, 1933
    The Case of the Perjured Parrot, 1939
    The Case of the Crooked Candle, 1944
    The Case of the Vagabond Virgin, 1948
Ellery Queen
    The Adventures of Ellery Queen, 1934
    The New Adventures of Ellery Queen, 1940
    The Case Book of Ellery Queen, 1945
    The Further Adventures of Ellery Queen, 1946
Ngaio Marsh
    A Man Lay Dead, 1934
    Enter a Murderer, 1935
    Death in Ecstasy, 1936
    Overture to Death, 1936
    Final Curtain, 1947
Rex Stout
    Black Orchids, 1942
    Three Doors to Death, 1949
    Three Men Out, 1954
    Three Witnesses, 1956
    And Four to Go, 1958
    Trio For Blunt Instruments, 1964

Georges Simenon
> *The Man Who Watched the Trains Go By,* 1946

Josephine Tey
> *A Shilling for Candles,* 1958/1936
> *The Franchise Affair,* 1948
> *The Daughter of Time,* 1952

Ross Macdonald
> *The Moving Target,* 1949
> *The Drowning Pool,* 1950
> *The Ivory Grin,* 1952
> *The Doomsters,* 1958
> *The Galton Case,* 1959
> *The Ferguson Affair,* 1960
> *The Far Side of the Dollar,* 1965

A SELECTED LIST OF CHILDREN'S BOOKS BY AMERICAN AUTHORS

The Tales of Peter Parley (Goodrich), 1827
A Wonder-Book for Girls and Boys (Hawthorne), 1852
Tanglewood Tales for Girls and Boys (Hawthorne), 1853
The Lamplighter (Cummins), 1854
The Age of Fable (Bulfinch), 1855
The Age of Chivalry (Bulfinch), 1859
The Seven Little Sisters (Andrews), 1861
The Man Without a Country (Hale), 1865
Ragged Dick (Alger), 1868
Tattered Tom (Alger), 1871
Little Women (Alcott), 1868
An Old-Fashioned Girl (Alcott), 1870
Little Men (Alcott), 1871
The Story of a Bad Boy (Aldrich), 1870
Jack Hazard and His Fortunes (Trowbridge), 1871
The Adventures of Tom Sawyer (Twain), 1876
The Adventures of Huckleberry Finn (Twain), 1884
The Peterkin Papers (Hale), 1880
Uncle Remus (Harris), 1881

Peck's Bad Boy and His Pa (Peck), 1883
The Hoosier School-Boy (Eggleston), 1883
Little Lord Fauntleroy (Burnett), 1886
A Story of the Golden Age (Baldwin), 1887
A Boy's Town (Howells), 1890
Betty Leicester (Jewett), 1890
Captain January (Richards), 1891
Cadet Days (King), 1894
The Little Colonel (Johnston), 1896
Wild Animals I Have Known (Seton), 1898
The Wonderful Wizard of Oz (Baum), 1900
Rebecca of Sunnybrook Farm (Wiggins), 1902
The Call of the Wild (London), 1903
White Fang (London), 1906
Pollyanna (Porter), 1913
Penrod (Tarkington), 1914
Tarzan of the Apes (Burroughs), 1914
The Story of Doctor Doolittle (Lofting), 1920
Daniel Boone (White), 1922
Smoky the Cowhorse (James), 1926
The Poor Little Rich Girl (Gates), 1912
Rootabaga Stories (Sandburg), 1922
Seven Dwarfs (Disney), 1938
Donald and Pluto (Disney), 1939
The World Is Round (Stein), 1939
The Gertrude Stein First Reader (Stein), 1949

A SELECTED LIST OF CHILDREN'S BOOKS BY ENGLISH AUTHORS

The King and Queen of Hearts (Lamb), 1809
Poetry for Children (Lamb), 1809
Beauty and the Beast (Lamb), 1811
Mrs. Leicester's School (Lamb), 1810
Tales from Shakespear (Lamb), 1816
The Book of Nonsense (Lear), 1846
A Christmas Carol (Dickens), 1843

The Cricket on the Hearth (Dickens), 1846
A Child's History of England (Dickens), 1852–53
Alice's Adventures in Wonderland (Carroll), 1865
Through the Looking-Glass (Carroll), 1872
Rhyme? And Reason? (Carroll), 1883
Alice's Adventures Underground (Carroll), 1886
Sylvie and Bruno (Carroll), 1889
Sylvie and Bruno Concluded (Carroll), 1893
Sing-Song (Rossetti), 1872
Goblin Market (Rossetti), 1893
Under the Window (Greenaway), 1878
Birthday Book for Children (Greenaway), 1880
Mother Goose or The Old Nursery Rhymes (Greenaway), 1881
Almanack for 1883 (Greenaway), 1882
Kate Greenaway's Alphabet (Greenaway) 1885 (?)
The Water Babies (Kingsley), 1885
The Happy Prince and Other Tales (Wilde), 1888
With Clive in India (Henty), 1884
Lion of the North (Henty), 1886
Stories of Adventure and Heroism (Henty), 1892
At Agincourt (Henty), 1896
Under Wellington's Command (Henty), 1899
Treasure Island (Stevenson), 1884
A Child's Garden of Verses (Stevenson), 1897
The Jungle Book (Kipling), 1894
The Second Jungle Book (Kipling), 1895
Captains Courageous (Kipling), 1897
When We Were Very Young (Milne), 1924
Winnie-the-Pooh (Milne), 1926
Now We Are Six (Milne), 1927
The House at Pooh Corner (Milne), 1928
The Magic Walking-Stick (Buchan), 1932

A Selected List of American Illustrators

Felix O. C. Darley
 Rip Van Winkle, 1848

  Irving's Sketch Book, 1848
  Knickerbocker's History of New York, 1850
Hammatt Billings
  Poems (Whittier), 1849
J. D. Woodward
  Ballads of New England (Whittier), 1870
  Snow-Bound (Whittier), 1881
E. W. Kemble
  Huckleberry Finn, 1885
A. B. Frost
  Out of the Hurly-Burly, 1874
  Story of a Bad Boy (Aldrich), 1870
Peter Newell
  The Hunting of the Snark, 1903
   (American editions)
Howard Pyle
  The Merry Adventures of Robin Hood, 1883
  Howard Pyle's Book of Pirates, 1921
  The Autocrat of the Breakfast-Table (Holmes), 1894
  The Man with the Hoe (Markham), 1900
Frederic Remington
  Pony Tracks, 1895
  Crooked Trails, 1898
  John Ermine of the Yellowstone, 1902
Joseph Pennell
  The Stream of Pleasure, 1891
  The Creoles of Louisiana, 1884
  English Hours (Henry James), 1905
  The Life of Whistler, 1908
Rockwell Kent
  Architectonics, the Tale of Tom Thumb, 1914
  Moby-Dick, 1930
  N by E, 1930
  Rockwellkentiana, 1933
  Canterbury Tales, 1934
Alexander King
  The Emperor Jones, 1928

The Hairy Ape, 1929
Anna Christie, 1930

A SELECTED LIST OF
ENGLISH ILLUSTRATORS

Thomas Rowlandson
   The Cries of London, 1784
   Tour of Dr. Syntax in Search of the Picturesque, 1812
   The Dance of Death, 1816
George and Issac Cruikshank
   Life in London . . . , 1821
George Cruikshank
   Fairy Tales (Grimm), 1823–26
   Barnaby Rudge, 1837
   Oliver Twist, 1838
   Jack Sheppard, 1839
Henry Alken
   The Life of a Sportsman, 1842
   Memoirs of the Life of the Late John Mytton, Esq., of Halston,
      1835
   Jaunts and Jollities . . . (Jorrock), 1843
   Analysis of the Hunting Field (Surtees), 1846
John Leech
   Handley Cross, 1854
   Mr. Sponge's Sporting Tour, 1853
   The Comic History of Rome, 1852
   The Comic Latin Grammar, 1840
Hablot K. Browne ("Phiz")
   Jaunts and Jollities . . . (Jorrock), 1843 (Co-illustrator)
   Mr. Facey Romford's Hounds, 1865
   Nicholas Nickleby, 1838–39
   A Tale of Two Cities, 1854
Sir John Tenniel
   Alice's Adventures in Wonderland, 1866
   Through the Looking-Glass, 1872

Walter Crane
 The Glittering Plain, 1891 (Kelmscott Press)
 Robin Hood, And the Men of the Greenwood, 1912
Aubrey Beardsley
 Le Morte d'Arthur, 1893
 The Yellow Book, 1894–97
Eric Gill
 The Canterbury Tales, 1929 (Golden Cockerel Press)
Max Beerbohm
 Caricatures, 1913
 Rossetti and His Circle, 1922
Arthur Rackham
 The Sketch-Book of Geoffrey Grayon, Gent., 1895
 Peter Pan in Kensington Gardens, 1906
 A Midsummer Night's Dream, 1908
 Gulliver's Travels, 1907
Kate Greenaway
 Under the Window: Pictures and Rhymes for Children, 1878
 A Apple Pie, 1886
 Almanacks, 1883–95, 1897
 Kate Greenaway's Alphabet, 1885 (?)
 Kate Greenaway's Birthday Book for Children, 1880
 Kate Greenaway's Book of Games, 1889
 Kate Greenaway's Pictures, 1921
 Marigold Garden, 1885
 Dame Wiggins of Lee and Her Seven Wonderful Cats, 1885
 A Day in a Child's Life, 1881
 Language of Flowers, 1884
 The "Little Folks," 1879
 Mother Goose or The Old Nursery Rhymes, 1881
 The Quiver of Love, 1876

12

Where to Find First and Rare Editions

The rarest and most interesting of books are sometimes found in quite improbable places. For instance, in 1867, Charles Edmunds, a London bookseller, was visiting Lamport Hall, the ancient residence of the Isham family in Northamptonshire, when he came upon a room where lumber and discarded furniture had been stored for many years.

He noticed some piles of books that were covered with dust, and as befitted a man of his profession, examined them curiously. After some time, and just at the moment when he was about to give up his investigation, he noticed what appeared to be an early edition of Shakespeare's *Venus and Adonis*. Fortunately for him and posterity, the volume was no ordinary edition of the poem, but the fourth edition, printed in 1599, whose existence had been unsuspected. Many years later, in 1919, despite the fact that this was not the first edition, Edmunds's *Venus and Adonis* was sold at Sotheby's of London for £15,000, nearly $75,000 at the time.

Strangely enough, the day after this sale, two young Englishmen decided to have an archery match on an old estate near Shrewsbury, but soon discovered that they were without a target. Searching among the buildings, one of the men found an old book which he decided would serve as a suitable target.

After the book had been positioned against a lower branch of a tree, the man, who had not looked at it closely, decided to adjust its position. He noticed that one of the words on the title page was "Venus." Upon closer examination, he discovered that this was another copy of the book that had been sold the day before at auction, and had achieved widespread publicity in the newspapers. Soon afterward the young men sold the book to Henry C. Folger of New York, the greatest collector of Shakespeare's works, for nearly fifty thousand dollars!

In the 1920s, the English poet and dramatist John Drinkwater, on a visit to America, discovered in an old bookshop on Fourth Avenue in Manhattan a copy of Melville's *Moby-Dick* in which Nathaniel Hawthorne had signed his name on the title page. It was not a first edition, but since the novel is dedicated to Hawthorne, it is not difficult to imagine Drinkwater's delight in discovering Hawthorne's own copy at a secondhand-book price!

Unfortunately, such discoveries as these come few and far between. Yet I can recall that in my own experience as a collector I have chanced upon smaller finds unexpectedly. One Sunday morning some years ago in Greenwich Village, I happened by a small store that had boxes of books outside that were being sold for the benefit of the building fund of a nearby church. After searching for nearly an hour among the dusty volumes, I noticed a green cover. It turned out to be a first edition of F. Scott Fitzgerald's *The Great Gatsby* (1925), one of my favorite novels. When I asked the clerk how much he wanted for it, he looked it over casually and asked for fifty cents. I literally ran out of the store with the book, anxious lest the other clerk notice the treasure I held in my hand. *Gatsby* is by no means as rare as Shakespeare or even *Moby-Dick*. Still, it is not an inexpensive book to acquire, and with the dust jacket would cost in the hundreds. I was justifiably elated with my bargain.

THE GREAT GATSBY

BY

F. SCOTT FITZGERALD

Then wear the gold hat, if that will move her;
  If you can bounce high, bounce for her too,
Till she cry "Lover, gold-hatted, high-bouncing lover,
  I must have you!"
        —THOMAS PARKE D'INVILLIERS.

NEW YORK
CHARLES SCRIBNER'S SONS
1925

First edition of a modern classic

Only recently I happened to pass two young children who were selling books "cheap," as their sign stated. The books were unprepossessingly displayed on orange-crates, yet I couldn't resist the temptation of looking at them. As it happened, I discovered a first edition of W. Somerset Maugham's *Of Human Bondage* (1915). When I asked the children where they had got their books, one replied that they all came from the library of an uncle, who had given them permission to sell them. Thus it was that for one dollar I obtained a first edition of another favorite novel of mine, one that at the time I was unable to afford from a dealer's shop.

My most joyous discovery occurred a number of years before either of these incidents, when I bought a large number of first editions of Henry James for virtually nothing. James, a supreme artist, rates high among collectors.

It so happened that I chanced into a secondhand bookshop on lower Fifth Avenue one winter day, and asked the proprietor if he had any old novels. He motioned toward a far wall and quietly returned to whatever business was at hand. To be sure, I could not believe my own eyes when I saw the rows of James's volumes. Of course, not every volume was a first edition, and for the most part, the volumes represented the first American editions of James's works. Still, I managed to carry away all the books my arms could hold, for fear that someone else would buy them if I did not.

It was then that I obtained many of the titles that now comprise my James collection. I had found the first American edition of *The Ambassadors* (1903), distinguished from its English issue, and of great interest to collectors since Chapters XXVIII and XXIX were somehow reversed during binding, and stood that way unnoticed for nearly fifty years. I acquired *The Wings of the Dove* (1902), *The Sacred Fount* (1901), *The Europeans*

(London, 1878), *In the Cage* (1898), *What Maisie Knew* (1897), one of 250 copies of *A Landscape Painter* (1919), *The Finer Grain* (1910), and *The Better Sort* (1903), which was issued simultaneously in New York and London, and contained the story "The Beast in the Jungle," a classic study of love and regret. Since that time, I have been offered many times the amount I paid for the books, yet I would not part with them. They are particularly valuable to me not only since James is the focal point of my collection, but because of the manner in which I found them, chance playing a major role.

Yet if collectors depended entirely upon chance and the possibility of finding their books at "bargain" prices, their collections would contain few books indeed. So it is that collectors invariably turn to the rare-book dealer and auction house for the books they want. What could be more logical? If one wants to buy a suit, one visits a clothier's shop. So it is with rare books and first editions. The people who are actively engaged in the business of antiquarian books are the best source for obtaining those books.

Of course, the beginning collector must not get the impression that as soon as he has decided upon the titles he wants, a mere shopping around in various dealers' shops will produce the desired volumes. More often than not, some dealer will have a copy of the desired title on his bookshelf, but not always, since many titles are becoming increasingly difficult to locate.

Now, since not all booksellers offer first and rare editions, the collector must seek the antiquarian bookseller who specializes in his particular field of interest. Specialties include first editions, manuscripts and incunabula, private press books, Americana, ships and the sea, natural history, science, hunting, fishing, children's literature, and fine bindings. What's more, the catalogues that most dealers periodically issue provide an invaluable source of knowledge to collectors.

Whatever the collector's interest, there is an antiquarian bookseller who can satisfy it. Of course, we should not discount the auction houses, but even though they will run auctions featuring a specialized aspect of book collecting, such as sporting books or nineteenth-century first editions, they are not inclined toward fulfilling the needs of individual collectors, as are the booksellers. A collector cannot approach the members of an auction house and ask them to obtain for him a copy of a particular work. Still, one should attend as many auctions as possible in the hope that an item one wants will be offered for sale.

For the benefit of collectors, I am reprinting with their permission the guide prepared by the Antiquarian Booksellers' Association of America which lists the various dealers and their specialties, as well as each dealer's location. While not every antiquarian bookseller in the country is listed, since not every dealer is a member of the ABAA, the collector would do well to consult one or more of these dealers. These specialists can prove extremely helpful to the collector in his or her quest for books. Good hunting!

13

How to Identify a First Edition

There are several methods by which the collector can attempt to identify a first edition. To begin with, he should be as familiar as possible with the dates and places of publication of the books he is seeking. Of course, it is highly improbable that the collector, whether a beginner or a past master, will be knowledgeable concerning all dates and initial places of publication. Yet you would be amazed to see how readily the dates of your favorite books can be absorbed through frequent reading of dealers' and auctioneers' catalogues, the *Oxford Companion* to American and English literature, the *Cambridge Bibliography of English Literature*, and the various author bibliographies, which will be discussed later in this chapter.

As to the methods, the easiest by far is to refer to the back or verso of the title page and look for the words "First Edition," "First Printing," or "First Impression." If one of these indications appears, it is reasonably safe to assume that the volume in hand is a first edition. If the words "Reprinted," "Second Printing," or "Second Impression" are on the verso, or such phrases as "Illustrated Edition," "New Edition," or "Revised Edition" appear on the title page's front or recto, the volume is not a first edition, though illustrated editions or revised editions are often of interest to collectors.

Should notice of the edition be omitted, as has been the practice of quite a number of publishers over the years, one should observe the date on the title page, if it is there, and compare it with the date noted on the verso, which is usually beneath the copyright notice. If both dates are the same, and there is no indication that the volume is the second or later impression or printing, the collector can assume that the book in question is a first edition.

When, however, the dates do not match, the collector should note if they are more than one year apart. Sometimes during the nineteenth century, and for that matter during our own, publishers issued books one year later than the date on which the copyright was secured. For instance, the first edition of Oliver Wendell Holmes's *The Professor at the Breakfast-Table* bears the date 1860 on its title page, but reads 1859 beneath the copyright notice on the verso. Similarly, Robert Louis Stevenson's *The Ebb-Tide*, written in collaboration with Lloyd Osbourne, presents confusion since the date on the title page of the American edition—which incidentally preceded the English edition—is 1894, while the year on the verso next to the copyright notice reads 1893.

Even more baffling is the practice by many publishers, especially in England, of not listing the date of publication on the title page of the first edition, listing instead the date of copyright on the verso, or even no date at all. This is particularly irritating to the collector since many times the presence or absence of the date from the title page determines the first edition. For example, when Harper's published Henry James's *The Awkward Age* in 1899, that date appeared on the title page of the first edition. Later printings, however, did not include the date on the title page.

And in the case of D. H. Lawrence's writings published in

England by Martin Secker, Ltd., there was no date on the title page, but on the verso, near the bottom of the page, the date could be found next to the publisher's name.

Some publishers do not print a copyright notice, but merely the phrase "All Rights Reserved," with or without a date, on the verso. Thus it can be seen that the practices of publishers in denoting first and later editions are various and numerous—too numerous, in fact, for the average collector, who has neither the time nor the inclination to memorize each and every publisher's practice.

Fortunately, however, there are two sources of consolation available. Henry Boutell, in *First Editions and How to Tell Them,* compiled from as many publishers as was possible their procedures for indicating first editions. No collector should fail to consult this book at least once, since the information included is truly invaluable.

We learn, for example, that when they first began publishing in 1928, the firm of Coward-McCann used to print a colophon in the shape of a torch on the right and left sides of the initials "C" and "M" on the copyright page of all first editions. Second and subsequent editions were printed without the torch. Their policy was to print the words "second" or "third printing" should a book be reprinted, but not note that a book was the first edition when it initially appeared on the market.

As valuable as Boutell's book is, most collectors are not likely to carry a copy of it in their pocket every time they enter a bookshop, or to become familiar with each and every publisher's practices. Also, some libraries do not possess a copy of this work. Yet what most libraries do possess is at least a random supply of author bibliographies, and reference to these volumes is almost required reading for any collector who pursues books seriously, however casually.

Bibliographies often represent many years of intensive and exhaustive scholarship. Each author bibliography will attempt to contain as complete a listing as possible of every item published by a particular author, with physical details described as accurately as possible. For instance, a volume will be analyzed in terms of size, color of covers, type and design of lettering on spine and covers, date on the title page, number of pages in the entire volume, presence or absence of advertisements, etc. In addition, bibliographies tell how many copies were initially printed, if and when a second edition appeared, in what country the first edition was published, and if there are any points or indications of difference between one issue of a first edition and another. The collector would do well to be at least vaguely familiar with the most reliable bibliography of his or her favorite author or field of interest in order to become acquainted with any unique characteristics of first editions he or she hopes to acquire.

Perhaps the most leisurely and enjoyable sources of information concerning the nature of first editions are the catalogues issued regularly by rare-book dealers throughout the world. These catalogues will frequently offer—in addition, of course, to listings of books one may want to acquire—descriptions of the characteristics that determine a book's priority as a first edition. The descriptions are as various as the dealers themselves. Some will note only a line or two, while other dealers describe their items in one or more paragraphs. In either case, collectors will find these catalogues an invaluable source of information.

Though dealers and auctioneers, even the most experienced and reliable ones, can and do err at times, for the most part, they are extremely reliable. As Vincent Starrett observed many years ago: "You must take their word for it. In time you will conduct your own inquiries, and your deductive faculties will become sharpened to the point where you will be able to check this against that."

Half the fun of book collecting rests with distinguishing a first edition without anyone's assistance. It is one thing to acquire a book through a dealer's catalogue or in the auction room, and another to be faced with deciding if the volume in hand, whether discovered in a secondhand bookshop, at a garage sale or a flea market or in an aunt's attic, is a first or not. Yet even though this sort of detective collecting is fun, you would do well to consult a reliable dealer or bibliography if the volume you are considering is priced higher than a few dollars.

14

The Issue of Points

It was once observed by the noted bibliographer John Carter that "books without points are like women without beauty—they pass unnoticed in the crowd. But books with points excite immediate interest and everybody, so to speak, turns to gaze at them."*

By definition a point is any peculiarity or eccentricity in type, textual content, color and design of covers or dust jacket, illustration, or any other number of internal or external variations that distinguish one issue of a first edition from another.

Many factors conspire to create a point in a book. The first issue of Edith Wharton's *Ethan Frome* (1911) is distinguished from other issues of the first edition by having perfect type on the last line of page 135. Later issues bear broken type, which apparently resulted from damage to the type plate sometime after the earliest copies were being printed, unnoticed by the printer. By virtue of this point, the first issue of this classic novel commands a much higher price than later issues of the same first edition.

Sometimes a printer's error in spelling leads to the creation of a point. In Ernest Hemingway's *The Sun Also Rises* (1926), the

---

* *Taste and Technique in Book Collecting,* page 102.

word "stopped" on page 181, line 26, was printed in the earliest issues as "stoppped." The error was ultimately caught, but not until several copies with the mistaken spelling were printed and bound. Collectors of Hemingway's novels naturally prefer the first state of the first edition, and are prepared to pay a higher price for it.

Not all points are the result of accidents or mistakes that occur in the printer's shop. When Mark Twain's *Life on the Mississippi* was first published in 1883, it contained an illustration on page 441 that depicted the author engulfed in flames. This so incensed Mrs. Twain that she asked that the illustration be deleted before further copies were ·printed. Collectors of Twain's works, to be sure, are partial to the issue with the suppressed plate, which in its turn becomes an indispensable point essential to the book being the "true" first edition.

On other occasions, the presence or absence of advertisements determines the first issue or state of a first edition. For instance, F. Scott Fitzgerald's *The Beautiful and the Damned* (1922), in order to be certified as the first issue, must not contain any advertisements at the back of the book, while H. G. Wells' *The Time Machine* (1895) must contain 16 pages of advertisements.

In other instances, the color of the cloth binding varies among issues of the first edition, as in T. S. Eliot's *Poems, 1909–1925*, which was issued initially in blue cloth and later in white linen. As for books issued with dust jackets, a variation among jackets often differentiates one issue of the first edition from another. For example, the first-state dust jacket of Thomas Wolfe's *Look Homeward, Angel* (1929) must include the author's photograph on the back.

At other times, points are the result of a difference in physical size between one issue and another. For instance, the first issue of Edgar Lee Masters's classic *Spoon River Anthology* (1915) must measure exactly seven-eighths of an inch across the top of the book.

The tremendous influence of points in determining the value and subsequent price to the collector of various first editions should never be underestimated. Thus, a number of notable points are listed below. Since it is impossible to include every work distinguished by the presence of one or more points, I strongly suggest that the collector become familiar with the most reliable bibliography available concerning his or her favorite author or particular field of interest in order to be fully aware of titles noted for their points. Yet before any aspiring collectors become frightened into believing that they must become scholars in order to collect books, let them be assured that most reputable dealers and auction houses note the issue or state of a title in their catalogues. But not always, and collectors should realize this fact also.

Some Notable Books and Their Points*

Little Women (Alcott), Boston, 1868–69. The spine of Volume 1 should not read "Part One." There should be no notice of "Little Women, Part First" on page iv of Volume 2 (1869).

Little Men (Alcott), Boston, 1871. The first issue includes an advertisement at the front of the book which lists *Pink and White Tyranny* as being almost ready.

The Story of a Bad Boy (Aldrich), Boston, 1870. The first issue reads "scattered" on page 14, line 20, and "abroad" on page 197, line 10.

Winesburg, Ohio (Anderson), New York, 1919. The first issue has an end paper map at the front, the top is stained yellow, page

---

* The following books have been chosen on the basis of their persistent interest to collectors and their availability.

86, line 5, reads "lay," and the type is broken in "the" on page 251, line 3.

Essays in Criticism (Arnold), London, 1865. First edition should contain one leaf of advertisement.

Poems (Barrett), London, 1844. First edition contains advertisements dated June 1 in Volume 1.

The Little Minister (Barrie), London, 1891. The first issue contains sixteen pages of advertisements in Volume 1 dated "5G.9.91."

The Wonderful Wizard of Oz (Baum), Chicago and New York, 1900. The first issue contains an eleven-line colophon on the back end paper.

Jane Eyre (Bell [Brontë]), London, 1847. The first issue must read "Edited by Currer Bell," not "By Currer Bell," and contain a thirty-six-page catalogue at the back of Volume 1 which is dated June and October; half titles; and a leaf advertising the *Calcutta Review*.

Shirley: A Tale (Bell), London, 1849. The first edition contains sixteen pages of advertisements dated October 1849.

Villette (Bell), London, 1853. The first edition contains twelve pages of advertisements at the end of Volume 1.

Tarzan of the Apes (Burroughs), Chicago, 1914. The first issue bears an acorn device at the foot of the spine.

The Corsair: A Tale (Byron), London, 1814. The first issue contains 100 pages.

Manfred: A Dramatic Poem (Byron), London, 1817. The first issue does not contain a quotation on the title page and bears the printer's imprint in two lines on the verso of the title page.

The French Revolution (Carlyle), London, 1837. Two pages of advertisements at the end of Volume 2.

Alexander's Bridge (Cather), Boston, 1912. The first issue reads "Willa S. Cather" on the spine.

Christabel: Kubla Khan, a Vision: The Pains of Sleep (Coleridge), London, 1816. Half title and four pages of advertisements dated February 1816 at the end.

The Moonstone (Collins), London, 1868. The first issue includes half titles, two pages of advertisements at the end of Volumes 2 and 3, and reads "treachesrouly" on page 129 of Volume 2.

The Woman in White (Collins), London, 1860. The first issue bears imprint of the woman in white on the spine.

Almayer's Folly (Conrad), London, 1895. The first issue contains a missing "e" in "generosity" on page 110, second line from bottom.

Tales of Unrest (Conrad), London, 1898. All edges untrimmed in first issue.

Typhoon (Conrad), New York, 1902. Four pages of advertisements.

Youth (Conrad), Edinburgh, 1902. Advertisements dated "10/02" at the end.

Nostromo (Conrad), London, 1904. The first issue contains seven preliminary leaves and 478 pages of text.

Under Western Eyes (Conrad), London, 1911. Advertisements dated September 1911.

'Twixt Land and Sea: Tales (Conrad), London, 1912. First issue bears misprint "Secret" for "Seven" on front cover.

The Shadow-Line (Conrad), London, n.d. (1917). Eighteen pages of advertisements at the end.

The Arrow of Gold (Conrad), Garden City, 1919. The first issue reads "credentials and apparently" on page 5, line 16.

The Red Badge of Courage (Crane), 1895. Perfect type in the last line of page 225.

The Posthumous Papers of the Pickwick Club (Dickens), London, 1837 (first book edition). The name "Tony Veller" is displayed on the signboard of engraved title page.

Oliver Twist (Dickens), London, 1838. The first issue has "Boz" on the title page.

A Christmas Carol (Dickens), London, 1843. The first issue reads "Stave I" on a red and blue title page. Also, the end papers are green.

The Life and Adventures of Martin Chuzzlewit (Dickens), London, 1844. In the first issue, the sign after the reward notice on the title page reads "100 £."

Pictures from Italy (Dickens), London, 1846. The first issue contains unnumbered pages 5 and 270, and two pages of advertisements.

The Personal History of David Copperfield (Dickens), London, 1850 (first book edition). Date engraved on title page.

Little Dorrit (Dickens), London, 1857. The first issue reads "Rigaud" instead of "Blandois" on pages 469, 470, 471, 472, and 473.

A Tale of Two Cities (Dickens), London, 1859. Page 213 is misnumbered 113.

Three Soldiers (Dos Passos), New York, n.d. (1921). "Signing" for "singing" on page 213, line 31.

A Study in Scarlet (Doyle), London, 1888. "Younger" spelled correctly in preface to first issue of first book edition.

The Sign of the Four (Doyle), London, 1890. The first issue reads "Spencer Blackett's Standard Library" on spine.

The Adventures of Sherlock Holmes (Doyle), London, 1892. Street sign lacks lettering on first binding.

An American Tragedy (Dreiser), New York, 1925. Boni and Liveright imprint on first issue.

Jennie Gerhardt (Dreiser), New York, 1911. First issue reads "is" instead of "it" on page 22, line 30.

Romola (George Eliot), London, 1863. Two pages of advertisements at the end of Volume 2.

Poems (T. S. Eliot), Richmond, England, 1919. First issue reads "capitaux" instead of "chapitaux" in line 12.

The Waste Land (Eliot), New York, 1922. "Mountain" spelled correctly on page 41, line 339.

The Classics and the Man of Letters (Eliot), London, 1942. First state contains "t" of "the" on title page correctly printed.

Four Quartets (Eliot), New York, n.d. (1943). First impression reads "First American edition" on copyright page.

Essays (Emerson), Boston, 1841. First binding does not read "First Series" on spine.

Poems (Emerson), London, 1847. First issue reads "Chapman Brothers" on spine and contains advertisements dated November 16, 1846.

Representative Men (Emerson), Boston, 1850. First issue bears hourglass design on front and back covers.

The Sound and the Fury (Faulkner), New York, n.d. (1929). First printing reads "First Published 1929" on copyright page.

As I Lay Dying (Faulkner), New York, n.d. (1930). First state contains dropped "I" on page 11.

This Side of Paradise (Fitzgerald), New York, 1920. First printing reads "Published April, 1920" and displays publisher's seal on copyright page.

Flappers and Philosophers (Fitzgerald), New York, 1920. First printing reads "Published September, 1920" and displays publisher's seal on copyright page.

The Beautiful and the Damned (Fitzgerald), New York, 1922. First issue reads "Published March, 1922" on copyright page and does not contain advertisements at the end.

Tales of the Jazz Age (Fitzgerald), New York, 1922. First printing reads "Published September, 1922" and displays publisher's seal on copyright page.

The Vegetable (Fitzgerald), New York, 1923. "Published April, 1923" and seal on copyright page.

The Great Gatsby (Fitzgerald), New York, 1925. First issue reads "sick in tired" on page 205, line 9.

All the Sad Young Men (Fitzgerald), New York, 1926. Publisher's seal on copyright page.

Tender Is the Night (Fitzgerald), New York, 1934. Scribner "A" must appear on copyright page.

Taps at Reveille (Fitzgerald), New York, 1935. Scribner "A" must appear on copyright page.

Where Angels Fear to Tread (Forster), Edinburgh, 1905. First issue does not contain this title in advertisements.

A Boy's Will (Frost), London, 1913. All edges are untrimmed in the first state.

North of Boston (Frost), London, n.d. (1914). First state includes blind-stamped rule around front cover, and gold lettering on cover and spine.

The Man of Property (Galsworthy), London, 1906. First issue contains broken bar of music on page 200.

The Vicar of Wakefield (Goldsmith), Salisbury, 1766. Page 159 incorrectly numbered 165 in Volume 2; the catchword "if" is omitted on page 213 of Volume 1, signature B4 is misprinted "D3" in Volume 2; on page 15, Volume 1, "husband" is omitted; catchwords "Within" misprinted for "Far" on page 71, Volume 1, "This" for "The" on page 75, Volume 1, "This" for "While" on page 77, Volume 1, "pre" for "a" on page 120, Volume 1. "Wake-field" variously misspelled on pages 95, 113, 133, 144, 168, 177, 192, 207, 210, 218, and 223.

Good-bye to All That (Graves), London, n.d. (1929). Poem by Siegfried Sassoon appears on pages 341–43 of first state.

The Thin Man (Hammett), New York, 1934. First issue contains misprint "seep" for "sleep" on page 209, line 17.

A Pair of Blue Eyes (Hardy), London, 1873. First issue contains dropped "c" from "clouds" on page 5, last line, of Volume 2.

Far from the Madding Crowd (Hardy), London, 1874. First issue contains "Sacrament" on page 2, line 1, of Volume 1.

The Hand of Ethelberta (Hardy), London, 1876. First issue reads "two or three individuals" instead of "five or six individuals" in caption facing page 146 of Volume 1.

A Group of Noble Dames (Hardy), n.p., n.d. (London, 1891). First issue bears yellow end papers.

Tess of the D'Urbervilles (Hardy), n.p., n.d. (London, 1891). First issue reads "Chapter XXV" for "Chapter XXXV," "horse-tracks" so spelled, Vol. II, page 206, "road" for "load" on page 198 of Volume III, "without" misspelled, Vol. III, page 257.

Jude the Obscure (Hardy), n.p., n.d. (London, 1896). First issue bears "Osgood" on spine and title page.

Uncle Remus (Harris), New York, 1881. First issue reads "presumptive" for "presumptuous" on page 9, last line, and this title is not listed in advertisements.

The Luck of Roaring Camp and Other Sketches (Harte), Boston, 1870. First issue does not contain short story "Brown of Calaveras."

Poems (Harte), Boston, 1871. "S. T. K." for "T. S. K." on page 136.

The Scarlet Letter (Hawthorne), Boston, 1850. First issue reads "reduplicate" on page 21, line 20, "characterss" on page 41, line 5, and "catechism" on page 132, line 29.

The Marble Faun (Hawthorne), Boston, 1860. Volume 2 ends on page 284 with no "Conclusion" at the end.

The Sun Also Rises (Hemingway), New York, 1926. "Stoppped" on page 181, line 26.

A Farewell to Arms (Hemingway), New York, 1929. Without disclaimer notice that "None of the characters in this book is a living person."

Death in the Afternoon (Hemingway), New York, 1932. First issue bears Scribner "A" on the copyright page.

Winner Take Nothing (Hemingway), New York, 1933. Scribner "A" on copyright page.

Green Hills of Africa (Hemingway), New York, 1935. Scribner "A" on copyright page.

To Have and Have Not (Hemingway), New York, 1937. Scribner "A" on copyright page.

The Fifth Column and the First Forty-nine Stories (Hemingway), New York, 1938. Scribner "A" on copyright page.

For Whom the Bell Tolls (Hemingway), New York, 1940. Scribner "A" on copyright page. First-state dust jacket does not bear photographer's name beneath the author's picture.

Across the River and into the Trees (Hemingway), New York, 1950. Scribner "A" on copyright page.

The Old Man and the Sea (Hemingway), New York, 1952. First book edition bears Scribner "A" on copyright page.

Cabbages and Kings (O. Henry), New York, 1904. First issue bears "McClure, Phillips & Co." on spine.

The Prisoner of Zenda (Hope), London, n.d. (1894). First issue contains a list of seventeen titles on page 311.

The Rise of Silas Lapham (Howells), Boston, 1885. First issue reads "Mr. Howells' Latest Works" in advertisement facing title page, and "sojourner" is printed in unbroken type on page 176.

Green Mansions (Hudson), London, 1904. First issue does not bear publisher's design on the back cover.

A Passionate Pilgrim (James), Boston, 1875. First binding reads "J. R. Osgood & Co." on spine.

Roderick Hudson (James), Boston, 1876. First binding bears "Osgood" imprint on spine.

The Europeans (James), London, 1878. Chapter V reads "IV" on pages 171–91. Catalogue dated June 1878 at the end, and on the verso of the title page appears the imprint "Bungay: Clay and Taylor, Printers."

Watch and Ward (James), Boston, 1878. First printing contains blank leaf after page 219.

An International Episode (James), New York, 1879. "Blue" in the first line of page 45.

Daisy Miller (James), New York, 1879. First issue lists seventy-nine titles in the "Harper Half-Hour Series" advertisements at the front of the book.

The American (James), Boston, 1877. Binding reads "J. R. Osgood & Co." on spine.

The Diary of a Man of Fifty and a Bundle of Letters (James), New York, 1880. Spine of first binding lettered with full title.

Washington Square (James), New York, 1881. First binding reads "H. James Jr."

Portraits of Places (James), London, 1883. "M" in Macmillan larger than other letters in first binding.

A Little Tour in France (James), Boston, 1885. No dots after "Mifflin" and "&" of spine imprint.

The Bostonians (James), London, 1886. No period after "Vol" on title page.

Embarrassments (James), London, 1896. First issue bears four irises on front cover.

The Wings of the Dove (James), New York, 1902. "Published, August, 1902" appears on copyright page.

The Better Sort (James), New York, 1903. "Published, February, 1903" appears on copyright page.

The Golden Bowl (James), New York, 1904. "Published, November, 1904" appears on copyright page.

A Small Boy and Others (James), New York, 1913. First issue contains eleven-line publisher's advertisement.

Deephaven (Jewett), Boston, 1877. First issue reads "was" on page 65, line 16.

A Dictionary of the English Language (Johnson), London, 1755. First issue bears title page printed in red and black.

From Here to Eternity (Jones), New York, 1951. Scribner "A" on copyright page.

Kim (Kipling), New York, 1901. First issue contains rhymed chapter headings for Chapters 8 and 13.

Sons and Lovers (Lawrence), London, n.d. (1913). First issue does not bear date on title page.

The Prussian Officer and Other Stories (Lawrence), London, n.d. (1914). First issue contains twenty-nine pages of advertisements at the end.

The Rainbow (Lawrence), London, n.d. (1915). Advertisements dated Autumn, 1914.

Amores (Lawrence), London, n.d. (1916). First issue contains sixteen pages of advertisements at the end.

Main Street (Lewis), New York, 1920. First issue contains perfect type on page 54.

Babbitt (Lewis), New York, 1922. "Purdy" on page 49, line 4.

Elmer Gantry (Lewis), New York, 1927. "G" on spine appears as "C."

The Call of the Wild (London), New York, 1903. First-issue binding cloth vertically ribbed.

The Sea-Wolf (London), New York, 1902. First issue bears gold lettering on spine.

John Barleycorn (London), New York, 1913. Blank leaf following page 243.

Letters from an Ocean Tramp (McFee), London, 1908. Foot of spine reads "Cassell & Co."

The Garden Party and Other Stories (Mansfield), London, n.d. (1922). First issue reads "sposition" on page 103, last line.

Spoon River Anthology (Masters), New York, 1915. First issue measures exactly ⅞ inch across top.

Of Human Bondage (Maugham), New York, n.d. (1915). First issue bears Doran imprint.

Moby-Dick (Melville), New York, 1851. First American edition with six blank leaves at front and back.

Renascence and Other Poems (Millay), New York, 1917. First issue printed on paper watermarked "Glaslan."

Gone With the Wind (Mitchell), New York, 1936. First issue notes "Published May, 1936" on copyright page.

Lolita (Nabokov), Paris, n.d. (1955). First issue notes price of 900 francs on back covers.

McTeague (Norris), New York, 1899. First issue contains "moment" as last word on page 106.

The Man Against the Sky (Robinson), New York, 1916. Top edges gilt.

Raise High the Roof Beam, Carpenters (Salinger), Boston, n.d. (1963). First issue does not include dedication page.

Cornhuskers (Sandburg), New York, 1918. Page 3 numbered in first state.

The Jungle (Sinclair), New York, 1906. First issue bears Doubleday imprint and "!" in perfect type on copyright page.

Paris, France (Stein), New York, 1940. Scribner "A" on copyright page.

The Grapes of Wrath (Steinbeck), New York, n.d. (1939). "First published in April, 1939" appears on copyright page, top edges are yellow, and a first-edition notice appears on front flap of the dust jacket.

Harmonium (Stevens), New York, n.d. (1923). First issue appeared in checked boards.

Treasure Island (Stevenson), London, 1883. Advertisements dated July 1883 in first state.

Kidnapped (Stevenson), n.p. (London), 1886. First issue appears in blue cloth and reads "business" on page 40, line 11.

The Strange Case of Dr. Jekyll and Mr. Hyde (Stevenson), London, 1886. First issue of first English edition bears date altered in ink on front cover from 1885 to 1886.

The Expedition of Humphry Clinker (Smollett), London, 1771. First issue bears date "MDCLXXI" instead of "MDCCXXI" on title page.

Poems and Ballads (Swinburne), London, 1866. First issue bears "E. Moxon" imprint.

In Memoriam (Tennyson), London, 1850. First issue reads "baseness" on page 198, line 3.

Maud, and Other Poems (Tennyson), London, 1855. Yellow end papers, eight pages of advertisements dated July 1855, and end leaf advertising Tennyson's works.

Idylls of the King (Tennyson), London, 1859. First issue contains blank verso of title page.

The Book of Snobs (Thackeray), London, 1848. First issue contains page 126 misnumbered "124."

Vanity Fair (Thackeray), London, 1848. First issue contains heading of page 1 in rustic type; portrait of Lord Steyne on page 336; and "Mr. Pitt" on page 453.

Adventures in the Skin Trade (Thomas), London, n.d. (1955). First issue reads "First published in Great Britain 1955" on verso of title page.

Portrait of the Artist as a Young Dog (Thomas), London, n.d. (1940). First issue reads "First published 1940" on verso of title page.

Under Milk Wood (Thomas), London, n.d. (1954). "First published 1954" appears on verso of title page.

Walden or, Life in the Woods (Thoreau), Boston, 1854. First edition reads "post" on page 24, "single spruce" on page 137, and "white spruce" on page 217.

Barchester Towers (Trollope), London, 1857. First binding is of brown cloth.

The Prince and the Pauper (Twain), London, 1881. First issue contains 32 pages of advertisements dated November, 1881.

Adventures of Huckleberry Finn (Twain), New York, 1885. First American edition, first issue reads "was" on page 57, line 23; final "5" in numbering page 155 left out; plate at page 283 tipped in; illustration called for on page 88 appears on page 87.

The Time Machine (Wells), London, 1895. First issue appears in cloth with purple stamping and contains 16 pages of advertisements at the end.

Ethan Frome (Wharton), New York, 1911. Type must be perfect in last line of page 135.

The Age of Innocence (Wharton), New York, 1920. Must quote from Burial Service on page 186, line 7, and not from Wedding Service.

Poems (Wilde), London, 1881. First issue reads "maid" on page 136, line 3, stanza 2.

The Picture of Dorian Gray (Wilde), London, n.d. (1891). Letter "a" missing from "and" on page 208, eight lines from bottom.

De Profundis (Wilde), London, n.d. (1905). First issue contains advertisements dated February, 1905.

The Cabala (Wilder), New York, 1926. First printing reads "conversation" on page 196, line 13.

American Blues (W. C. Williams), New York, n.d. (1948). First issue bears misspelled author's name on cover.

Look Homeward, Angel (Wolfe), New York, 1929. First issue bears Scribner seal on copyright page, and first-state dust jacket bears author's photograph on the back.

Orlando: A Biography (Woolf), n.p. (London), 1928. First issue of first English edition encased in brown cloth.

The Celtic Twilight (Yeats), London, 1893. Publisher's name appears on first binding in capital letters.

15

Foreign Books and
First Editions in English

A great many important works of literature, science, history, and art which may prove of interest to collectors are often published initially in languages other than English.

One need only recall such writers as Tolstoy, Flaubert, Dostoevsky, Ibsen, Balzac, Pasteur, Curie, Einstein, Sartre, Camus, Goethe, to name but a few, in order to realize that no collection of literature or science could be complete without at least one work representative of these masters' creative or scientific genius.

Strangely enough, while there are numerous collectors of Continental or European literature in England and America, the majority prefer to concentrate more heavily on works that first appeared in English. Nevertheless, there is still great demand for the first editions of Galileo, Tolstoy, Cervantes, and Proust, as well as scores of other writers. Yet the collector should be aware of the fact that there is a dual nature to the demand and value of foreign-language works.

To begin with, most collectors would assume—correctly—that there cannot be any first edition other than the work as it was originally published. However, since many great works have been translated into English at one time or another, and since that language is common to American and English collectors alike, a relative degree of value is often assigned to the first English-language edition of any work that originally appeared in a foreign language.

This is not to suggest that collectors prefer the English-language to the original editions. First is first, and no collector can deny that fact. I am merely attempting to point out that foreign-language books can be of interest in a number of ways other than as first editions. While this is true of all books (first illustrated edition, revised edition, children's edition, etc.), it is especially true of works originally published in a foreign language. The value, as always, is determined by the law of supply and demand.

For instance, the great popularity and stature of Leo Tolstoy's novel *War and Peace* no doubt accounts for the fact that the first edition in English of that work, translated by Clara Bell from the French edition in 1886 and published in New York in six volumes, brought four hundred dollars at auction in 1970. Also, at a recent auction held in London by the firm of Christie, Manson, & Woods, Ltd., the first English version of Galileo's seminal *Discorsi e Dimostrazioni Matematiche* (1638)—*Mathematical Discourses concerning Two New Sciences relating to Mechanicks and Local Motion*, translated by Thomas Weston in 1738—was estimated to bring up to two hundred pounds (over four hundred dollars at the time in U.S. dollars).

Quite often, a translator will specialize in one writer, or will translate many works of one language, as did Constance Garnett, who provided English versions of the stories, plays, and letters of Anton Chekhov from 1916 to 1926, and Gogol's various works from 1922 to 1928. Similarly, C. K. Scott-Moncrieff translated into English all but one of the seven volumes of Marcel Proust's *Remembrance of Things Past*, beginning in

1922 with *Swann's Way* (Stephen Hudson completed the final volume, *Time Regained,* in 1931). One important factor should always be borne in mind by the collector of translated works: individual volumes, though often of interest and value, are not nearly so greatly in demand as when they comprise an entire set. Many a collector of Proust or Chekhov will cease to rest content until he has acquired the translated editions of his favorite author's works in their entirety.

In other instances, works can acquire interest and value if they are translated by famous authors. For example, Remy de Gourmont's controversial *The Natural Philosophy of Love* was translated by Ezra Pound in 1922, and it is of interest to collectors of Pound's work even though the original thoughts are not Pound's, since the rendering of de Gourmont's ideas into English certainly is the result of Pound's efforts and genius.

Similarly, collectors of the novels and stories of D. H. Lawrence and of Italian literature may be interested in acquiring Lawrence's translation of Giovanni Verga's classic *Cavalleria Rusticana and Other Stories* (1928). Collectors of the writings of Virginia Woolf might be surprised to learn that she assisted in the translation of Dostoevsky's *Stavrogin's Confession* in 1922; and it may interest others to know that mystery writer Dorothy Sayers translated Dante's *Inferno* in 1949. Needless to say, this was not the first translation of this classic work into English; still, to collectors of Dante's works or of Sayers's, this item may be of intense interest. Though foreign works translated by renowned authors need not be the first English translation to be of value to collectors, when translated works do in fact represent the first English-language editions, and the translator is widely renowned, and his or her works are usually in demand by collectors, such volumes acquire dual interest, and sometimes dual value.

16

The Care and Protection of Rare Books

It is only natural for anyone who collects first and rare editions of books—or any books upon which they place especial value—to want to protect them from general wear and tear, soil, dust, and possible damage by fire and flood. Quite a number of options are available to the collector with respect to protecting valuable books.

Since most collectors enjoy displaying their treasured volumes not only for their own pleasure, but for anyone else who may be interested, the bookcase is indispensable. While it is true that glass-enclosed bookcases are attractive and perhaps one of the best means of protecting books from dust, an open wooden or even plastic bookcase will generally offer sufficient protection from soil and abuse.

Unless the books in question are extremely valuable, and cannot be placed high enough on the shelves in order to afford protection from the crayons and paints of children too young to understand their value, the collector need not feel the need to purchase an expensive glass-fronted bookcase. In most instances, a shelf in a china closet will suffice.

As an additional protection for cherished books, many collectors provide leather slipcases. While enclosed in the slipcase, on whose spine can be printed the book's title, author, and date of publication, as well as any other information the collector deems necessary—such as that the volume is a presentation copy—it is virtually impossible for that book to become soiled or damaged —barring, of course, fire or flood or other unforeseen catastrophe.

One problem does arise with the use of slipcases: in general, they are rather expensive. Ironically enough, on some occasions, and dependent on the choice and quality of the leather, the slipcase may prove more costly than the book it is designed to protect!

Cardboard and cloth slipcases are available, but they are hardly ever as attractive as the leather ones. For this reason, I am offering the collector another method of protecting his books that is nearly as functional as slipcases, but far less expensive. In any store that sells art or office supplies, there are available in various thicknesses and sizes clear sheets of acetate plastic. By merely cutting the sheets to fit around the volume much in the same manner as a dust jacket, the owner can provide adequate protection from dust and soil for books of almost any size or thickness.

The best way to store your books on a bookshelf is upright. Many a collector unconsciously abuses his books by packing the volumes too closely together. Never store your books so tightly together that the volume literally cannot breathe; leave a slight space between volumes. And always avoid removing a book by grasping the top or bottom of the spine, since many a volume has thereby received unnecessary fraying or wear. Remove a book from the shelf by placing your thumb and index finger around its middle. Needless to say, exceptionally tall or large volumes may be placed on their sides, yet should not be weighed down excessively with other large volumes.

For all its warmth and beauty, sunlight is quite detrimental to a book's condition. The value and desirability of many a volume has been depreciated as a result of sun spots on the covers, or faded spines. The collector should place his bookcase either in a shaded area of his living room or library, or at a safe distance from direct sunlight. Sunlight should never be permitted to shine on the backs or spines of treasured books, else there will be a sharp discrepancy between the color tone of the spine and the front and back covers of the book or dust jacket.

Also, books should not be placed in rooms that are humid or very dry, since either of these conditions can warp the shape of a volume, or cause its pages to become so brittle as to virtually crumble into dust at the slightest provocation or abuse. Better a cool room than a hot one, and preferably a room in which the temperature is relatively consistent, or can be regulated as the seasons change.

In the case of books that cost a small fortune, or are of extreme rarity and delicacy, the collector might consider placing them in a bank safety-deposit box, for which there is a modest annual fee. Many a collector who has found that insurance would prove too costly for any number of treasured books has perhaps slept soundly in the thought that his or her books were safe from fire, flood, or theft for just a fraction of the cost of an insurance premium.

Some collectors, to be sure, may discover that a fireproof file cabinet is preferable to a bank safety-deposit box, for then their books will be in easy reach, and they won't have to trouble to visit the bank every time they want to add an item to their collection or show someone their books. Most collectors, I suspect, would choose to deposit their most valuable volumes in a bank vault, simply because they do not care to go to the expense of buying a file cabinet, or do not have room for it in their home.

It should never be forgotten that valuable books should not be left lying about on sofas, desk chairs, coffee tables, or any other place where they might unnecessarily come to harm. Further, open bookends hardly ever provide adequate protection, for they do not enclose the books.

Last but far from least, never entrust a cherished volume to the hands of someone who does not appreciate the value of your book collection in general, or is inexperienced in handling rare volumes, or has little interest in book collecting and regards a book as being just that and no more. In this way, the collector will avoid experiencing the pain sadly related years ago by a collector who carelessly left a recently acquired and long-sought volume on top of a neighbor's coffee table, only to look up in horror at the sight of his neighbor placing a dripping cup of coffee on top of the volume so that the tabletop would not be damaged. Alas, the volume was damaged beyond hope, to the despair of the unfortunate collector. Take care of your books!

III

SAGE ADVICE
AND
TIMELESS ANECDOTES

17

Buying and Selling

BY REGINALD BREWER

Now I would tell you something about the easiest part of collecting first editions and other book rarities. It is buying them. Not, mind you, paying for them, but merely the process of acquiring these desirable volumes.

The obvious method is to notify various rare-book dealers, both in this country and abroad, that you will be delighted to receive their catalogues—or, better yet, to advise them of the specific authors, subjects, or items in which you are interested. Then, as they offer in their catalogues, or by private advice, the books you would like to see on your shelves, the transfer of ownership is easily accomplished by ordering the desired item or items. Really very simple!

Of course, in following this procedure you will pay the current retail value of the books you acquire. It is quite unlikely you will make many "buys" by this method for the simple reason that book *values* are the book dealer's business. Once in a great while the dealer will overlook a book's true value—but only once in a while. I have already mentioned the one happy time in a dozen years of book collecting this happened to me—securing a copy of the rare trial binding of Katherine Mansfield's *The Garden Party* when I had ordered only a regular first edition.

No, do not, I warn you, expect to discover some perfectly priceless book by merely paying close attention to the stock of the regular rare-book dealer.

Nor can I highly recommend the secondhand bookshop as a fertile field of search. Personally I am inclined to listen with open suspicion to the many stories of "Yes, sir, he found it in an old, secondhand bookstore, and it was worth over five hundred dollars!" In my travels around the country I have visited scores of secondhand book establishments. Some were in the large metropolitan centers, others in the small towns. I have enjoyed every hour spent in their musty atmosphere, but let me confess that, other than a few average items, I obtained little except a pair of dirty hands. For some time the failure to find even a few of the better known collectible books was, in a sense, baffling. Surely out of all the thousands of volumes gravitating to these secondhand bookmen, some should be by the "collected" authors. Where were the Longfellows, the Lowells, the Bret Hartes, the Cranes, *ad infinitum?* People certainly had bought and read these books. Why were they not just as likely to find their way to the secondhand dealer as the abundance of cheap novels? Moreover, the individuals operating these businesses rarely give the impression of bookish knowledge. Some, especially in the large cities, are hardly able to speak the English language. But be not deceived. Behind the apparent ignorance is a shrewd and competent experience in rare books. One proprietor such as I have just mentioned—a man who can only talk in broken English— operating a small, general secondhand bookstore, is as posted on book values as the most ardent collector. Quite by accident I discovered in the rear of his shop a sizable collection of rare-book catalogues. Later I learned he regularly attended the Chicago book auctions. Since that time I have entered the secondhand store with a new attitude. No longer do I look endlessly for some real rarity. I have learned that these bookmen are, by and large, well informed. Should a really valuable item come into their hands they know it. They have their outlets for these books. How many collectors step into these establishments feeling very superior in their knowledge of book rarities and values! That they rarely find anything is set down as "just bad luck." Nothing of the sort. The really scarce and valuable books never get on the shelves!

However, the secondhand bookstore offers two genuine possibilities for the collector. First, as a source of acquiring a goodly number of the less valuable items. I speak of first editions that would ordinarily cost from two to five dollars if purchased from a regular rare-book dealer. The secondhand man knows full well they are collectible "firsts," but the problem and trouble of disposing of them is too involved to make the effort profitable. He is content to let those wanting such books buy them at his usual price—probably between fifty cents and a dollar. The other suggestion is to take the secondhand bookman into your confidence. Instead of assuming an unmerited ignorance on his part, tell him frankly you are a collector. Frequently he will have something tucked away or will watch for your wants. And you will benefit, for he will dispose of it at what might be termed a "wholesale" price—the amount some rare-book dealer would pay him.

But there is a far more likely hunting ground than the secondhand bookstore. In nearly every community one can find a "rummage shop"—usually operated in the interest of some church or charity. To these shops come the cast-off articles of families—old clothes, unwanted furniture, Victrola records, and frequently the books they have read. The quality of these volumes is frequently higher than average, for many of them come from the homes of better than ordinary means. Rather than be bothered to sell surplus books to a secondhand dealer, these people are glad to give them to some organization for the benefit of the poor. Moreover, those charged with operating these "rummage shops"—or occasional sales—are totally unconcerned with the matter of book values. Thus, there is every hope and opportunity for the collector of finding many a desirable item—especially at the occasional rummage bazaars held by church organizations.

Another source is the books sold as part of the possessions of private homes. A careful and consistent watch of the classified advertising in your local newspaper will frequently disclose people having books for sale. Naturally many of the trips you make will be a complete disappointment. But there is always the chance you may run across some genuinely important items. In any event the chase is always exciting.

Every collector cherishes the hope that some day he will chance upon some untouched source of "first editions"—such as a long established bookstore still blessed, or damned, with the remains of many years of book buying. If such should be your good fortune, I pray you do not commit the same sad error as did one young man of my acquaintance.

In the course of his collecting he recalled the principal bookseller of the upstate town from which he came. At the first opportunity he paid him a visit, innocently inquiring if he had any old books. "Yes, we have some upstairs," replied the aged proprietor, and conducted his customer to the upper regions. Piled high, in dusty confusion, were hundreds of books purchased from departed families. A veritable collector's gold mine! After picking over a fair-sized pile, my young collector friend held up a volume, with the simple query, "How much?"

"Twenty-five cents," came the reply, and the transaction was completed. With the book safely tucked under his arm he started for the door; but bad judgment overtook him. He couldn't resist pausing long enough to say, "I don't suppose you know what you sold me?"

"No, I guess not," answered the old bookseller with casual indifference.

"Just a first edition of *Uncle Tom's Cabin*—that's all. Only worth about three hundred dollars or so." And with this parting remark, my friend walked out.

Then and there the old bookseller decided to "take stock." Others came, including myself, in the hope of making similar finds. To one and all, he politely explained that his upstairs stock was being "rearranged"—perhaps next month it would be ready. Smartness had been out-smarted.

The last buying method I want to discuss is through the auction room—a battle ground fraught with danger for the private collector. If certain books you desire are to be put up at auction, let a recognized dealer represent you. He can operate far more satisfactorily than a private collector. In the first place, he *knows* what the book is worth. He is familiar with the psychology of the auction room and is not stampeded into paying a fancy price. To be sure, he will charge you a commission for executing your bid—but it will be well worth it. Except on rare occasions, or purely for the fun or experience, it is far wiser to let professional book dealers act for you at auction than to attempt competition against them.

I am beset with a faint suspicion that some of my readers, especially those already collecting, may express a slight disdain at a few of the foregoing suggestions on book buying. The idea of pawing over the dust-laden volumes of the ordinary second-hand store, of entering all sorts of private homes to scan the contents of bookcases, may not conform to their conception of the bibliophile. To be sure, it is much more dignified and pleasant to be received in one of the fine establishments devoted to rare books or to make your selections in the quiet of your library from a tastefully printed catalogue. I know, for the vast majority of first editions I own have been acquired in this very manner. But, personally, I have spent just as many and equally enjoyable hours poking in odd spots—always in the hope of finding a book treasure. A little dirt is not objectionable, nor do I mind hying here and there on usually fruitless quests. And, were I ever to find a genuine first issue of Walt Whitman's *Leaves of Grass,* it would not seem any less desirable to me should it have come out of a "rummage sale," a poor home, or a junk shop. As a matter of fact, I know full well I should take more pride in having found it under any one of these circumstances than if I had quietly written my check in favor of the most exclusive book dealer. Frankly I enjoy prospecting for books. There is an element of adventure akin to the treasure hunt, and to those willing to put on their old clothes and fare forth into the world I promise an extra measure of enjoyment as book collectors.

Let me now talk a bit about the sale of books. Selling, as you might imagine, is far more difficult than buying. I am sure that one of the great disappointments to the new book collector will come when he desires to dispose of one or more books he believes possess definite value. Probably he has seen this or that item quoted in dealers' catalogues with fair frequency at, let us say, $30. Now, he has a copy he would like to sell. Should he offer it to any of these dealers, the chances are they will insist on a quoted price. Or, if they make an offer, it will be only a fraction of the current retail value.

It is perfectly obvious that the book dealer makes a profit, and a pretty good one, on every book he sells. It is not possible to go into the questions of "overhead," "selling costs," and other factors determining his margin of profit. That they do affect the price he can pay for a book—and the price he must get for it—is obvious.

To the dealer, all *good* books are salable. It makes not a great deal of difference, as a general rule, *what* books he buys. They all go on the shelves, are listed in the catalogues and are ultimately sold. Therefore, he attempts to buy everything as cheaply as possible. It is his prerogative.

The only exception to this rule is where he has a very urgent request for a specific item, and even then he will hold off buying it until he has found the cheapest possible copy.

The best source of sale, if you can possibly find it (and I freely admit the difficulty), is a private collector desiring the items you have for sale. By naming a price slightly under the regular book dealer's quotation you can frequently make a decidedly profitable transaction. Of course, I do not mean that books cannot be sold to dealers at a profit. If you have paid a relatively small price for the book in the first place and it has subsequently jumped to many times that amount, you can still get a nice profit out of it. But you will not get nor are you entitled to its full current value.

Finally, we come to selling at auction. If you will stop and think of the auction business, you will readily see that it is operated on a percentage basis. This means that the auctioneer and the auction house are far more interested in selling a thousand-dollar item than a ten-dollar item. For the same amount of talking the auctioneer makes one hundred times the commission on the thousand-dollar book that he does on the ten-dollar book. Consequently, if you have a number of books which, let us say, are only moderately valuable and offer them to one of the leading auction houses, the chances are that they will not be especially interested in handling the sale. There is too little in it for them. An examination of auction catalogues will reveal the fact that moderately priced items are frequently bundled together in "lots" in order to make the unit sale of fair size.

Moreover, in addition to the commission charged, there is also the cost of listing the item in the catalogue of the sale. This is priced at so much per line, with a minimum charge. There have been instances where, after paying the selling commission plus the charge for listing, nothing was left for the unfortunate seller.

Selling at auction is always a gamble. One never knows what a book will bring. It depends on who happens to be bidding and how much demand there exists at the moment. Except in the case of genuinely important books, values mean nothing. Possibly you may see your book bring an all-time high price, or it may be quickly knocked down for only a pitiful fraction of its true worth.

Book auction sales are held during the fall and winter seasons, with the principal sales occurring in New York and Chicago. Those desiring to dispose of valuable volumes may deal directly with the auction houses or proceed through a dealer who will act as agent and protect items, if so instructed, by bidding them in if the current interest lacks sufficient impetus to realize a fair value. Obviously the latter procedure is only feasible in the case of a sizable sale—for example, a complete collection of quite valuable books. Naturally, for this service the agent-dealer must be recompensed.

The problem of selling should be really of little concern to the true collector. Once you have acquired a book it becomes much more than a mere first edition—it is a part of your own personal collection. You will discover that even though the necessity arises you will be loath to part with it. I well remember, during the more active book-buying days of 1928–29, having a book that had cost me very little but which was selling for better than $300. Many of my friends asked why I did not sell this book if I could get that much for it, and take a really handsome profit. On the face of it, this seemed a good idea. Think how many more books I could have bought with the proceeds—and one or more of them might ultimately rise to a similar value. But I could not part with it. The very fact that it had become so scarce and was in such great demand, clothed it with a desirability far greater than the temptings of a handsome profit. Nor did the dire circumstances of the depression separate me from many a volume that surely would have helped the sad state of my finances. I believe, however, that there are books every collector is bound to acquire, which sooner or later should be sold. Everyone attempting a new venture is certain to make mistakes. In the case of a book collector they are the purchase of books by authors who ultimately fail to interest him, the pursuit of subjects which later prove unwanted. Under these circumstances, I believe such books should be sold at an early opportunity—even at a considerable loss, if necessary. First, because they are constant reminders of unfortunate mistakes or bad judgment, and so detract from one's collection. Second, because it is good business to unload undesirable items and put the money into other things having better possibilities. By this method you will be constantly improving your collection even though you are forced to accept occasional financial losses. And not only will your collection benefit but you, too, will feel the better for it.

In either buying or selling, a knowledge of values is obviously essential. Experience will provide you with this knowledge—especially about the books in your own collection and those you hope to acquire. The constant study of dealers' catalogues will contribute to your familiarity with current prices. But once in a while you may encounter an item outside the regular channels of book buying about which you lack any definite information. There are two sources of information which may help you. Both are to be found in practically every public library. One is "Book Prices Current," which gives a detailed record of all books sold at auction in London, England, for the year it is dated. The other is "American Book Prices Current," supplying the same information for books sold at auction in this country. There is, of course, no assurance that you will be able to find a sales record of the particular book claiming your attention. On the other hand, you may find several sales listed giving a range of prices. In considering them, be sure to note any special circumstances responsible for an abnormally high price or vice versa. Likewise, take into account the time elapsed since the last recorded sale. If it is a matter of years, there is every likelihood that a reasonable increase in value has occurred. Sometimes, as we have all learned, the reverse is true—book values fall as well as rise. Remember that such prices are merely a guide, and if the book is of considerable value it will be wise to consult some authority before either buying or selling. The safe procedure is to take nothing for granted. Check—check constantly, and you will have few regrets on either side of your book buying or selling ledger.

18

Dealers and Dealer Psychology

by Barton Currie

For some curious reason that I am unable to elucidate, collectors have ever been timid in writing about dealers. In a few instances it may be because they are greatly in their debt; in other and more numerous cases it may be because they fear that the offended dealers might expose them to their wives by inviting the terrible ladies around to their shops and opening their books to their inquiring gaze. Take such a hypothetical case as this:

"I have asked you here, Mrs. Brown," begins Dealer Hawkins, with his customary gentle suavity, "in order to reveal to you how much money your husband is spending on his hobby. Rumors have percolated to me that Mr. Brown is not so liberal to you and your children as a man of his ample means should be—that he holds you down to one footman instead of the three your social position demands and that he manifests at various times great irascibility over your household, wardrobe, and beauty-parlor bills. I hear also that he is never altogether candid with you concerning the books and manuscripts he buys and the prices he pays for them. This may very well be, for he has us send all bills to his office and he has hinted to me that he slips into the house with his treasures carefully concealed under his coat and tucks them away, when no one is watching, on some obscure shelf in the library.

"I know, very naturally, that I risk the displeasure of your husband in telling you the amount of money he has spent in this establishment during the past year, but I rely upon your discretion not to betray us. It should be a simple matter for you to put him at your mercy by some offhand reference to the values of rare books—including certain items which an inspection of our records will show you he owns. For he will hardly resist the temptation to boast of his acumen (and thereby unwittingly give himself away) in those cases where the books he bought have greatly enhanced in value."

What follows in this imaginary drama you can guess. All collectors are somewhat in the same perilous predicament as Mr. Brown, so far as their pet dealers are concerned, nor will I exempt the multimillionaires. I have seen men with very impressive incomes cringe before their wives as some obtuse friend disclosed that they had paid a spectacular sum for some treasure furtively acquired. And I have met scores of important dealers round about the world who chuckled about this almost universal foible of their married customers—their reluctance to allow it to be known at home how much they squander on their collections.

Happy, but frightfully rare, the collector who can go about with a great bundle of bills in his pocket, paying as he goes and paying on the nail! Happy, also the bachelor or the widower collector, who has no accounting to make for any of his insanities or extravagances. There are probably no more than a corporal's guard of them, and they do not seem to be of the writing sort.

The most important facts for all manner of collectors to have fixed in their minds are these:

That the market for rare books and manuscripts is a blind market; that the merchandise bought and sold in this market is hopelessly unstandardized, for no two objects dealt in are ever absolutely alike; and that the spread between what the dealer pays for a given rarity and what he may demand is just as likely to represent a ten thousand percent profit as a ten percent profit.

The same, of course, may be said of all dealers in antiques. The buyer will find much the same situation, whether he is collecting Titians and Rembrandts or Caxtons and the scarcest of incunables. Also old silver, old china, old pewter, old glass, ancient tapestries, ancient furniture, scarabs and cartouches, stamps, coins, engravings and etchings, prints, sculptures, pottery, rugs and carpets, birds' nests, butterflies, eggs, stuffed birds and mounted fishes, heads and antlers of game, antique kitchen utensils, stagecoaches and outmoded sedans, fans, laces and embroideries, old cutlery, daggers, poignards, and stilettos of the Dark and Middle Ages, hoary battle-axes, armor and artillery, church paraphernalia from the beginnings of religious worship (pagan, Christian, and Moslem), Tanagra figurines, Mycenean goblets, Stone Age flints and artifacts, and fossil trilobites.

The great junk market, in short, that mankind has dabbled in almost from the time he ceased to be a troglodyte—a market dominated by a few experts and patronized by a multitude of amateurs. (For the purposes of this chapter I am dubbing all experts as dealers and all collectors as amateurs. Once in a purple moon an amateur evolves into an expert, but never into a topnotcher. He can never shake off the defects of his early amateurishness.) The safest of all dealers to do business with is the dealer who began as a dealer and has not reformed either his worst or his best habits.

His best habit is, in the American vernacular, to know his stuff; his worst habit is, also in the American vernacular, to charge the very ultimate that the traffic will bear. But possess yourself of some early edition (some *cheap* early edition) of Blackstone's *Commentaries,* tear out the chapter on Caveat

Emptor, and learn it by heart before dealing with your man.

If you are a beginning collector, he will size you up at a glance. You are in the first and worst stage of bibliomania, an assimilator. Way back in the primordial civilization of the Sumerians some keen and prosperous junk dealer recognized three degrees of collectors, three stages of their evolution—first the *assimilators*, second the *discriminators*, and lastly the *integrators*.

In your initial madness you want about everything and you will buy indiscriminately. You are the most luscious of fruit, ripe for plucking by all manner of dealers, big and little. They lick their lips on your approach and will turn you over to their head clerk to practice on. It is the head clerk's job to work off on you the surplus stock, the slow-moving merchandise that neither the discriminator nor the integrator ever buys. The titbits that will entice the more seasoned and experienced victims are tucked away on the shelves of the little back room or are locked up in the safe.

Elsewhere I have dealt at some length with the subject of collecting by plan, but whatever your plan may be at the beginning or whatever modification it may undergo, you may never pass beyond the first stage of your mania. You can assimilate thousands of items of incunabula without exercising any marked discernment, and you can do the same with bindings, with illustrated books, with science books, with theological works, with children's books, with works on typography, with fifteenth- and sixteenth-century woodcuts, with poetry, with history, with biography. There is not one of the special-plan divisions named in which you could not bring tens of thousands of specimens together and in the end have practically nothing of any extraordinary value.

It is recognized in the book trade everywhere that there are five hundred assimilators to one discriminator and fifty discriminators to one integrator. To attain that lofty place in dealer esteem which marks you as an integrator, to whom it is needless to show anything save the veriest rarissima, should be the goal of every bibliomaniac.

But this will never come to pass. A miracle that would transform all the assimilators into integrators would bring universal bankruptcy to dealers in its train. Many dealers will tell you that the ignorance and futility of most of their customers pain them to desperation; that dealing with discriminators and integrators is their chief joy and delight. Some of them believe that they are sincere when they say this. Most verily, they are not; assimilators are the customers they cherish and adore.

I can never be convinced to the contrary until such a day as Rosenbach or the Maggs brothers in London refuse to sell me a ten thousand dollar item on veterinary surgery on the ground that it would not fit into my collection of eighteenth-century novelists and poets. And on that day an infant will lean from its perambulator at the Place de la Concorde in Paris and knock the obelisk over with a feather.

Whenever a dealer offers you something that is wholly outside your field, he shifts his line of persuasion to an appeal to your cupidity: "Here is something you should buy as an investment. It is of extraordinary rarity. So far as I can ascertain there are only seven copies known, and this is the only one that has turned up in three years."

We are back on the subject of sordid considerations—a subject that the gentleman amateur is supposed to abhor. In discussing the writings of A. Edward Newton, I have agreed with him that in the minds of those collectors who are men of common sense there must be at least some figment of an idea of investment values.

Back in the days of chivalry, throughout the Renaissance, and during most of the seventeenth century, there were monarchs and nobles who created splendid libraries, yet never for a moment gave a thought to such considerations. Many of them loved books, were notably men of culture and refined taste (for their times); they fostered the art of making magnificent books and bindings. But they were not in the least quixotic; as overlords of the world, they had no need to weigh the commercial aspect of their acquisitions. They bought with the idea of passing their wealth in every form along to their descendants. In their notion there was no limit to the land, the castles, the jewels, statuary, paintings, furniture, and bric-a-brac that they might rake in for themselves and the first-born scions who would follow after.

The social disturbances that have come in the brief span of two centuries have practically wiped out this class of collectors. . . . How many fill their libraries today without considering the investment value of their purchases? Possibly two; probably one; most likely none.

I hold that it is greatly to their credit that such is the case. A great many of them have proved that they knew more about investment values than the shrewdest of dealers from whom they bought. Sagacity in this respect has killed off the trade in a score of unsound fads that were associated with book collecting in the earlier days, particularly that shoddy craze for ornate and jeweled bindings. It has also killed off the vogue for the elaborate printing and illumination of books that were of themselves devoid of merit. It has killed off the vogue for unwieldy folios, the vogue for overillustrated books and for fore-edge painting, also the vogue for the tiny minuscules which no human eye could read but which at one time found great favor among amateur gentlemen collectors.

Bookmakers and book dealers through the centuries promoted and bolstered up all of these now outdated fads; and great prices, for those days, were paid for what is the veriest trash today. I have visited private libraries on the Continent which were chock-full of such meretricious curios and which could be bought for a few thousand dollars today, though the total cost to their collectors must have run into hundreds of thousands. I visited one library of one hundred and sixty thousand books on an island in the Mediterranean which was offered for sale at eight thousand dollars but went begging even so. The collection was just so much waste paper; to ship it to a paper mill would cost more than its worth as junk.

Such are some of the monuments left behind by the gentlemen amateurs of earlier days who scorned to consider the factor of investment value. Rare-book dealers are disinclined to talk about these tragedies of collecting to their customers, though among themselves I imagine they may discuss this topic with relish. But they will call your attention to the commentaries of John Hill Burton on the subject of the pure in spirit as it applies to book hunters. The following titbit, for instance:

> The mercenary spirit must not be admitted to a share in the enjoyments of the book-hunter. If, after he has taken his last survey of his treasures, and spent his last hour in that quiet library, where he has ever found his chief solace against the wear and worry of the world, the book-hunter has been re-moved to his final place of rest, and it is then discovered that the circumstances of the family require his treasures to be dispersed,—if then the result should take the unexpected shape that his pursuit has not been so ruinously costly after all—nay, that his expenditure has actually fructified—it is well.
>
> But if the book-hunter allow money-making—even for those he is to leave behind—to be combined with his pursuit, it loses its fresh relish, its exhilarating influence, and becomes the source of wretched cares and paltry anxieties. Where money is

the object, let a man speculate or become a miser—a very enviable condition to him who has the saving grace to achieve it, if we hold to Byron that the accumulation of money is the only passion that never cloys.

Let not the collector, therefore, ever, unless in some urgent and necessary circumstances, part with any of his treasures. Let him not even have recourse to that practice called barter, which political philosophers tell us is the universal resource of mankind preparatory to the invention of money as a circulating medium and means of exchange. Let him confine all his transactions in the market to purchasing only. No good ever comes of gentlemen amateurs buying or selling. They will either be systematic losers, or they will acquire shabby, questionable habits, from which the professional dealers—on whom, perhaps, they look down—are exempt.

There are two trades renowned for the quackery and the imposition with which they are habitually stained—the trade in horses and the trade in old pictures; and these have, I verily believe, earned their evil reputation chiefly from this, that they are trades in which gentlemen of independent fortune and considerable position are in the habit of embarking.

The result is not as unaccountable as it might seem. The professional dealer, however smart he may be, takes a sounder estimate of any individual transaction than the amateur. It is his object, not so much to do any single stroke of trade very successfully, as to deal acceptably with the public, and make his money in the long-run. Hence he does not place an undue estimate on the special article he is to dispose of, but will let it go at a loss, if that is likely to prove the most beneficial course for his trade at large. He has no special attachment to any of the articles in which he deals, and no blindly exaggerated appreciation of their merits and value. They come and go in an equable stream, and the cargo of yesterday is sent abroad to the world with the same methodical indifference with which that of to-day is unshipped.

It is otherwise with the amateur. He feels towards the article he is to part with all the prejudiced attachment, and all the consequent over-estimate, of a possessor. Hence he and the market take incompatible views as to value, and he is apt to become unscrupulous in his efforts to do justice to himself. Let the single-minded and zealous collector then turn the natural propensity to over-estimate one's own into its proper and legitimate channel. Let him guard his treasures as things too sacred for commerce, and say, *Procul, o procul este, profani,* to all who may attempt by bribery and corruption to drag them from their legitimate shelves.

It would be difficult to find a dealer anywhere who disagreed with this credo of Doctor Burton's for the amateur gentleman collector. Indeed, there is much old-fashioned Anglo-Saxon common sense in what he says that is as applicable now as it was when he uttered it seventy years ago. His strictures on the gentleman jobber in horses, pictures, and books are everlastingly true. That nauseous pest should be, but probably never will be, outlawed from polite society. He is more often than not a cheat and a liar, and proud of it. He preys on both the gullibility and the good nature of his friends. Luckily his dealings are confined chiefly to the downy fledglings who are sowing their wild oats and buying their little yardsticks of experience.

Really, Doctor Burton was very gentle in his comment on this species. He could have resorted to the most savage abuse and had my approval. But I do not hold with him that the mercenary spirit must not be admitted to a share in the enjoyments of the book hunter. The collector who is utterly without it is all and vastly more than the designation bibliomaniac implies. He should have a committee appointed to administer his affairs and this committee should put him on a parsimonious allowance for book buying. Thus safeguarded, let him go forth in his simple

and rhapsodic pursuit as Doctor Burton suggests. What he buys
and what he spends need never be of painful concern to anyone.

All collectors should possess at least a modicum of mercenary
spirit. I am not sure that those who have the least of it are a bit
happier in the pursuit of their hobby than those who have the
most of it.

True, too many American collectors boast overmuch about
the money value of their treasures. You will hear it said, in
contrast, that the greatest Continental and English collectors
scorn to allude to mercenary worth when they discuss their
books and manuscripts. I swallowed this assertion—until I
began meeting these gentlemen amateurs of the eastern hemisphere, when I swiftly revised my impression. For I found that
the commercial factor was just as preponderant with them as
with the barbarians on our side of the Atlantic.

Indeed, what appeared uppermost in their minds was the regret that American collectors did not go in for the same types of
rarities—fine bindings, illustrated books, incunabula, and manuscript books—that are sought after in Europe. Our peculiar
penchant for what we call old English and American books
(more or less modern trash, from the general European view-
point) puzzles and depresses them. A Swiss collector I talked to
in Geneva almost sobbed as he referred to an item in the London *Times* which stated that Doctor Rosenbach had paid four
thousand pounds for a first edition of Fanny Burney's *Evelina*.

"A book," he said, "of absolutely no importance in the
world's literature, and not yet two hundred years old. And to
think that I could not get a tenth as much for manuscript works,
more than a thousand years old, that are of supreme significance
as literary relics! Why, I doubt if many of the finest Aldine
books would bring such a price at auction in either London or

Paris. To me it is all quite unaccountable. Is there no likelihood that the American taste may change?"

I could offer him no encouragement on that score. As I saw it, the sentimental interest of American collectors in items that in any way relate to American history, to American printing, or to what we like to regard as American literature was growing rather than diminishing—catching up rapidly on the predilection for English classics, in fact. American appreciation of ancient foreign literature was confined largely to a small group of scholars. Nor was this condition likely to change for several generations.

But could not the influence of our more important dealers serve to divert the interest of American collectors to the ancient lines? No, I thought not. Not even Rosenbach could alter the taste of American collectors by and large. He might serve as mentor to a few extremely rich men, but despite his acknowledged skill as a salesman and his extraordinary foresight in anticipating new demands, it did not seem to be within the range of his genius to create a general market for items that have little or no place in the average American collector's consciousness.

There is occasional speculation overseas concerning the possibility of inducing American rare-book dealers to band together in an effort to market the unwanted ancient literary treasures of Europe. We have formed associations to promote the sale of divers sorts of merchandise; why not rare books and manuscripts? Because, as I interpret the dealer of today, he is not of the clubby get-together type. He prefers to play the lone wolf, be the tendency in other trades and industries what it may. Occasionally you will find rare-book dealers on friendly terms, saying kind words of one another; more often you will hear them disparaging their rivals and warning you to avoid them as sharks and robbers.

A dealer is never so pleased as when he can continue to keep a good customer away from the other fellow's shop. The collector who gets about too much may make invidious comparisons.

In the early days of my collecting I confined most of my purchases to two dealers, neither of whom seemed to have the least use for the other. I was warned by both that if I patronized the rival I would pay through the nose for whatever I bought or I would get something of doubtful authenticity. On one occasion I asked B for a certain book, to be told he did not have it in stock. A few days later I journeyed to the city where the hated rival, Dealer A, had his headquarters. I inquired of Dealer A for this certain book.

"Too bad," he said. "I sold a copy of that book just yesterday —a very fine copy, by the way—for two hundred dollars." He described the copy in some detail but did not name the buyer. Later I returned to Dealer B, who greeted me with: "I found that book for you. I had to pay a stiff price for it. I'll let you have it, at a very slight advance, for two hundred and fifty dollars."

I looked at the book. Unquestionably it was the one I had heard about at Dealer A's. I asked B where he got it; he lied very sweetly. I declined the book—the price was too high. I did not mention my talk with Dealer A but I did say casually that I had just spent a few days in Dealer A's town. Rather pleased with myself for my cunning (for had I not conveyed to B that I was not quite so green as he imagined?), I resolved to keep on looking around, in hopes of finding a better copy of that book for two hundred dollars or even less.

It would be flattering to my vanity to record that I had done so. I did not. I paid eighty pounds for the copy I picked up in London a year later. While it is true that first editions of this same book bring three hundred pounds nowadays, there is nevertheless a little sting of regret in the back of my mind for not having closed with Dealer B, despite his surreptitious traffic with a confrère I was supposed to believe he detested and despite the fifty-dollar rake-off he hoped to collect.

I had another amusing experience in London, and in this instance likewise the acerb rivalry of two dealers seemed not to disturb their commercial relationships behind the scenes. I had been hunting, unsuccessfully, for a three-volume early Victorian novel—nothing of great rarity but one of those books that occasionally disappear from the shelves of most shops.

There was one important dealer I had rarely been to, chiefly because of what I had heard about him from other dealers in both London and New York. Also many collectors seemed to agree with the dealers in doubting his business ethics and the integrity of his stock. In the shop of Mr. X, not far from Old Bond Street, where I was well acquainted, the important rival (let us call him Mr. Y) was a subject of frequent discussion but of infrequent favorable mention.

Mr. X, I found, had no copy of the book I was after, so I asked if it would not be well for my to try at Y's. Mr. X discouraged the idea. Y might have the book, *but*— That was all, but— I could draw my own conclusions. The obvious inference was that there would be something wrong with the copy or the price.

Nevertheless, a few days later I dropped in on Y. Did he have the book?

"Yes," he said, "I have three fairly good copies of it. If you had come in day before yesterday, I would have had fourteen copies to show you. I had them all in one package, gathering dust for heaven knows how many years. I don't suppose they cost me more than a few shillings each when I began to buy them. I am one of the few, though, who has always had faith that the three-volume Victorian novel would come into its own, and I have continued to gather them in for thirty years or more. Day before yesterday Mr. X's man dropped in and asked if I had a copy of the book you want. I showed him my fourteen specimens and he bought eleven of them. I kept the three best copies of the lot."

I bought the choicest of the three. On my next visit to Mr. X he announced that they had found two very good copies of this book. I could have one at a very reasonable price (not quite twice what I had paid Mr. Y for the pick of his original stock). Nothing was said of the nine additional duplicates. Naturally I did not buy; nor did I mention my dealings with Mr. Y.

Perhaps I missed my cue. I should have enjoyed Mr. X's explanation of how he came to buy eleven copies at a whack from a rival whose stock was questionable and whose methods of doing business were best referred to by the hanging conjunction *but*. Certainly Y had made no bones about his part in the transaction. Indeed, he had gloated over it, had conveyed to me with evident great satisfaction that the rivals who abused him most were compelled to come to him to replenish their stocks; and he had added that when they did he made them pay the piper. It required very little wit to derive from this remark that it would be economical for the collector to deal with Mr. Y as a party of the first part; otherwise he would be paying two profits instead of one.

No, Mr. Y didn't appear to be concerned in the least as to whether or not I revealed to X that I knew all about those eleven first editions. But for some reason I cannot quite analyze, I could not bring myself to open up on X. Possibly it was because I did not want to see him writhe. There are some men and more women who delight in putting on the screws; whether for better or for worse, I am not built that way. There is a greater personal satisfaction in treasuring up these little secrets and turning them over in my mind philosophically, examining my inner consciousness to learn whether I might not have followed the same devious course had I been placed in a similar situation. I found, also, that to keep my own counsel helped sharpen my perception of the machinations of various dealers; it served, furthermore, to put me on my guard, to reduce if not to extinguish my gullibility.

The vanity of all collectors is inordinate and therein lies their chief vulnerability. The man who is daft about Dickens, for instance, prides himself on his acumen as the prices of Dickens items mount. The dealer feeds the flame, flatters him at every opportunity—and marks up the prices of his Dickens items for his special benefit. The only salvation for the wise specialist is to wander far afield and never to surrender himself to the tender mercies of any one dealer or even of any one group. He should always have in the back of his mind that the most bitter business rivals can get together to pluck a particularly fat goose; and there can be no more succulent goose than a bibliomaniac in the full flight of his hobby.

Probably the easiest of all easy marks is the collector who seeks not only first editions, letters, manuscripts, and authentic association items of a given author, but who is avid to gather to his bookshelves everything that in any way relates to that author. Here is a description of one of this ilk which I found in an old scrapbook:

> The Waltonian library of the Rev. Dr. D—— reveals the predilective passion of a practical piscatorist. [This latter word is likely intended as a synonym for angler but it is not in any of my dictionaries. The new Oxford dictionary calls him a piscatorialist] During the darker seasons of the year, when forbidden the actual use of his rod, our friend [the Rev. Dr. D——] has occupied himself with excursions through sales catalogues, fishing out from their dingy pages whatever tends to honor his

favorite author or favorite art, so that his spoils now number nearly five hundred volumes, of all sizes and dates. Pains have been taken to have not only copies of the works included in the list, but also the several editions; and when it is of a work mentioned by Walton, an edition which the good old man might have seen. Thus the collection has all the editions of Walton, Cotton, and Venables in existence, and, with few exceptions, all the works referred to by Walton, or which tend to illustrate his favorite rambles by the Lea or the Dove. Every scrap of Walton's writing, and every compliment paid to him, have been carefully gathered and garnered up, with prints and autographs and some precious manuscripts. Nor does the department end here, but embraces most of the older and many of the modern writers on ichthyology and angling.

Now, such a collector as the Reverend Doctor D—— might well be termed a lone-lamb collector. He would associate very little with the general run of bibliophiles; he would not talk their language or understand their patter. Should he become attracted to any one dealer he would undoubtedly never be weaned away; for where is the dealer who would not find it worth his while to coddle such a customer?

I heard of a case in Boston where a small-fry dealer lived happily all the latter years of his life on one such customer, whose sole interest was in the *New England Primer*. He wanted every edition of the *New England Primer* going and everything he could get hold of that was ever written or published about this celebrated work. The dealer devoted himself assiduously to the job and in the course of time found thousands of items, among them a superb first edition which he obtained for a few dollars on one of his rambles through the countryside. This he sold to his voracious customer at a very slight advance. Today it is worth several times as much as the customer paid out for all the rubbish he accumulated—though, alas! neither customer nor dealer lived long enough to have that satisfying knowledge.

Now and then you will meet an old-time dealer who is altogether philosophical about the tricks of his trade and also about the idiosyncrasies of his customers. I met one long, lean Caledonian in Edinburgh who discoursed amiably on the subject of fishers of books and the dealer's attitude toward them.

You hear much nowadays [he said] of the scandalous prices being paid for certain rare books and manuscripts and of the wicked profits that accrue to dealers. It is very amusing, most of this talk, and it generally falls from the lips of the superficially informed. Of course, from time to time there are wicked profits in the sale of rare books, just as there are in the sale of old paintings, old silver, old china, old glass, and old everything which has no fixed value as merchandise and must be distributed at haphazard to a special group of buyers who are noted for their erratic likes and dislikes.

It is true that our profits will vary from five percent to one thousand percent, that we will take every last farthing we can get for an article, no matter how little we paid for it. No man can criticize us for that provided we have not misrepresented the article we sell. We have devoted our lives to learning how to buy and what to buy in a market in which there are many pitfalls. We are brought into contact with frauds and cheats, with forgers and imitators, and in some cases with manufacturers of spurious wares. We must protect ourselves and our customers from an infinite variety of deceits. If we are wisely honest, if we exercise proper forethought in building up good will, we never pass on to our customers any of the doubtful items that the shrewdest of us sometimes buy. Instead, we pocket our losses and hope to make them up in the course of time.

We extend credit with great liberality and for long terms, we have our debtors who never pay and who fail to return the goods purchased. We are supposed to deal for the most part with men of wealth, and that is largely true. But as every merchant who dispenses luxuries knows, a man of large wealth does not always make the most satisfactory customer. He is apt to neglect or forget about his bills; now and then he will return a costly article after having had it in his possession for a year or more, saying merely that he has changed his mind. If you should attempt to charge interest in such a case you would incur his bitter enmity—would, indeed, risk having him denounce you in his clubs as a swindler and an extortionist.

Since you sold that article you may have had inquiries from several other customers who would have paid as much or more for it; but when you get it back those customers have disappeared, have obtained another copy elsewhere, or have spent their money on something else.

That we charge varying prices for the same article within a very brief span of time is often held against us. To the shallow thinker, I grant you, this seems all wrong. But suppose a seller came to me tomorrow and offered me a fine first edition of *The Vicar of Wakefield* for one hundred pounds. I would buy it, of course, and, knowing that it has been selling for from three hundred pounds to five hundred pounds, would notify some likely buyer that he could have it for two hundred and fifty pounds. Suppose, further, that he accepts my offer and that a few days later I have an opportunity to buy two first editions of *The Vicar of Wakefield* for one hundred and fifty pounds. I should buy them, to be sure, and as my method of doing business is to turn my money over without too much delay, I should gladly accept one hundred and seventy-five pounds for one of those two copies and two hundred pounds a little later for the other. Most likely I should offer one of the two to some fellow dealer with whom I was on friendly terms, whereupon he could add on whatever profit the exigencies of his business demanded. If I were one of the great dealers in London or New York I would probably put away my two bargain copies of *The Vicar* for a few years and then take the ultimate profit that its increased scarcity made it possible to obtain.

We little dealers continually undersell the big dealers, but not always. There are times when the big fellows want cash very badly for some large venture and hence are willing to sell some of their stock at a loss in the expectation of making up that loss, and a great deal more besides, through the immediate use of a large sum of cash. If the book hunter could only happen around during some of these pinches he would acquire some pretty bargains. Generally, however, the big dealer will prefer to protect market prices by selling low only to other dealers; exceptions will occur when he has a pet customer who must be coddled from time to time by getting some little treasure at a much smaller figure than he could hope to obtain elsewhere.

Can you discern anything that is iniquitous in these little tricks of the trade? The book hunter who is not aware of them should straightway abandon his hobby for some other fad. He might try hunting, photography, fishing, phrenology, spiritualism, socialism, communism; he might become a publicist or a pacifist, or adopt foundlings. If there be the dimmest glow of the mercenary spark within his breast, however, I should point out to him that though they may cost as much if not more than his book hunting, these pursuits lead to the acquisition of nothing of marketable value.

By sticking to his books he is pretty sure to leave a little fortune, and to have had his fun besides. And so, to be fair, would it be in the case of certain other hobbies. I am reminded of the celebrated Quaker collector of paintings who was chided in meeting for his frivolous indulgence. The Friends were particularly curious as to what he had paid for a certain bauble—a painting by Goya—mentioned in the papers.

"About one thousand pounds," replied the worldly one.

"Is not that an outrageous wasting of the substance on vanities?"

"Not in my judgment," he answered. "I was offered five thousand pounds for it only two days gone. If any Friend will point out a better way to obtain a four hundred percent profit in so short a space of time I shall willingly abandon this objectionable frivolity of mine."

Another specious indictment laid at the door of the dealer by unreasoning amateurs and critics has to do with bidding. Now whenever any staggeringly high price is offered at auction for a book or manuscript you may count it a ninety-nine to one certainty that no dealer is putting up that sum at his own sole risk, but is bidding for a temperamental customer with an uncontrollable itch to possess that particular item. And when you witness determined duels between two dealers that drive the bidding skyward, it is safe to assume that there are two customers in the background. The winning dealer collects ten percent on the final price; when he has a virtually unlimited bid, can you blame him for carrying out instructions?

It was here suggested to this outspoken Scotsman that some of the duels which made romantic reading in the dailies might have been "framed"—that Dealer Cross, who had received carte blanche from Sir Reginald Midas, the coughdrop millionaire, could cook up a star-tickling bidding party with Dealer Double Cross, who would supposedly represent a mythical South American ham baron. After the glorious item had been knocked down to Dealer Cross for twenty thousand pounds, the mysterious unknown patron of the losing contender could melt away into the dim background. Would Sir Reginald not be unlikely to pursue an inquiry that could only heap ridicule upon his gilded head and invite a bear attack in the stock market upon his coughdrop shares?

True, indeed [replied my Caledonian friend]. Such mock duels have undoubtedly occurred. But no dealer who wished to maintain his standing and increase his importance and prosperity would undertake such shady ventures. Sensational chicanery is difficult to keep hidden for any length of time. For one thing, your partner in crime can never be wholly relied upon. Even though you may think him a loyal and loving brother, he is a potential blackmailer. You must split your profits with him at the outset; and thereafter he may come early and often to borrow and to bleed.

Some may assume that being a *particeps criminis*, he is inhibited, to save his own skin, from showing you up, but scant reliance can be placed upon this factor of safety. Small-fry accessories to crime can very readily be made to talk by promising immunity, when the law spreads its net for the bigger fish. There is an infinity of precedent for this which the cautious do well to remember.

All in all, I should say that collectors have little to fear on that score. Apart from the fact that the possibility of rigging the sale in such a way is practically negligible, there are not a baker's dozen collectors the world around who would give any dealer an absolutely free hand at an auction.

Now and then a lone-wolf collector—I might better say a lone sheep—will drop into an auction, bid crazily for something that he has set his heart on having, and thus start the fireworks going. A few experts may tease up the bids for their own secret satisfaction, relying upon their skill to drop out at exactly the right time. Once in so often, though, the playful dealer becomes the victim of his own little game and finds himself with a doubtful treasure bought at a very high price. He is better off, of course, than the collector so victimized; for he need only wait, if he is that sort of dealer, for some greenhorn to come along. He will then produce the auction record (without revealing that he was the one responsible for setting the price) and clinch the sale by launching forth on the alluring selling talk that so many amateurs love to listen to.

To return to generalities, let me say that we dealers in rare books and manuscripts are much as other merchants. There are some crooks among us and no angels. We strive to earn the wherewithal to live and as much to spare as our individual ambitions demand. Some of us are endowed with great adroitness and sagacity, more of us are just middling shrewd.

We are uniquely fortunate in having, as customers, a charming lot of folk. Among them are many great aristocrats, scholars, statesmen, bankers, manufacturers; others are just plain rich men who have inherited the means to enjoy a gentle, unobtrusive, luxurious obscurity. Some few are bounders who take up the hobby simply because it seems the thing to do, and there is an inevitable sprinkling of amateur speculators who have none other than a pounds-sterling or dollars-and-cents interest in what they buy.

19

Have You a Tamerlane in Your Attic?

BY VINCENT STARRETT

Deep down at the bottom of his erring, optimistic heart, every book collector in Christendom probably believes that the day will come. There is nothing cryptic in the phrase. He means that some day, sooner or later, standing beside the ten-cent basket, before an obscure little bookstall, idly pawing over the miscellany of worthless bibelots offered at that reckless sum, he will turn up a little pamphlet in tea-colored wrappers, upon whose title page he will read the legend, *Tamerlane and Other Poems. By a Bostonian.* Paradoxically, the reason he believes this is that only six copies of the work are known to exist.*

An Oriental monarch, decrepit and dying, pours into the ears of an attending friar—in whose incongruity an author's note acquiesces—the tale of his early peasant life, his passion for a lovely maiden, his ambition to win power for her sake, his unexplained desertion of the enchantress, his adventures and conquests culminating in his assumption of the role of Khan of

---

* Only four had been found when this chapter was first published, in the *Saturday Evening Post.* As a result of that publication, a fifth copy came to light in a Worcester (Mass.) attic, and I managed to lose it, through my own procrastination and the impatience of the frantic possessor. It was sold for $10,000 and immediately resold at a handsome profit. Since that time, the sixth copy has turned up, but information about it is not available.

Tartary, his return to his native valley to take possession of his love, and his discovery of the heartbroken lady's grave. She had been dead, alas, for many a year. . . .

> What was there left for me now? despair—
> A kingdom for a broken heart.

That, to misquote Oscar Wegelin, is what the collector of rare books will read if he finds the volume, or rather, what he will find if he reads it. A stupid tale of a stupid monarch, expecting his light o' love to sit and smile through seven years of desertion, keeping her beauty untarnished for him, if he should happen to return to her. Obviously, the literary and philosophic content of the scarce pamphlet is not the lure that attracts our snooping Autolycus of the bookstalls. What then? There is no secret about it. Everybody knows what I am talking about. The trifle was the first published performance of Edgar Allan Poe, and the most recent recorded price paid for a copy was $10,000.

Well, they do turn up. Six of them have turned up since 1860, when Henry Stevens, of Vermont, sent the first discovered copy to the British Museum; and, in 1867, the machinery of the museum at length having reached the grimy little pamphlet with its outer covers gone, received for it a shilling. But how often they do not turn up! Frankly, I have stopped looking for the thing. I no more than glance at a volume whose appearance remotely suggests it. Since adopting this sane attitude of renunciation, I have been happier and have slept better o' nights. I now smile whimsically and tolerantly at poor Will Douglass, who has been looking for a *Tamerlane* for forty-five years, and is still looking. I take a great deal more pleasure out of living, and in watching others hunt. It has been my happiness to start many earnest searchers on the endless trail, and it is my boast that I have disrupted more homes than all the divorce courts in the land.

That is not perhaps strictly true; but my victims, if laid end to end, would reach from Nevada to the Golden Gate. Poor, eager, amiable, fatuous idiots! They even thank me for the tip.

Seriously, there is nothing more certain to break up a gathering of whatever nature than a brief statement of the rarity and value of a copy of *Tamerlane*. Bridge parties disintegrate before the magic of that name and the resounding sum for which it stands. Nearly every person to whom I have told the tale is certain that there is a copy in his attic; usually a relic of his grandfather's library. He has seen it; he recognizes it by every descriptive point furnished him; he *knows* it is there. The only thing he professes not to have known is that the author of the opus was Poe. If I will guarantee the price, he will guarantee the book. He earnestly collects his wife and children and rushes home. Days are spent rummaging in the attic. Trunks are overhauled and cedar chests are all but pulled to pieces. Frantic letters are dispatched to Aunt Lou and Uncle Dan. Nothing, of course, ever comes of it. Indubitable first editions of *Snow-Bound* and *The Vision of Sir Launfal*—even of the Rev. E. P. Roe—come to light in the chaotic resurrection; but *Tamerlane* remains always in concealment. It existed only in the heated imagination of the searcher.

It must have happened often, much as I have described it. Third parties, listening in, catch the purport of the communication and quietly disappear. I always know where they have gone. They have gone home to turn the attic inside out. I am a bit ashamed of myself about it all; but on the foundation of what the mischievous trick has taught me of human nature, of greed, of envy, of ignorance, of cunning, even of superstition, I could build, I am sure, a new and devastating philosophy. Only once have I been fooled by a victim's earnestness. She was so very positive that I had no choice but to believe her. The incident began at a card party to which, unwillingly, I had been dragged. It was an objectionable affair, conducted by imbeciles for other imbeciles. I doubt if any member of the group had read a book through since childhood, or had heard of Edgar Poe to remember the name. Crossword puzzles had not then come along, to make necessary a knowledge of three-letter words. The conversation was moronic and the air stifling, when into the unhappy situation I dropped the bombshell of *Tamerlane*. It was difficult to bring the conversation to that point, but I managed it.

"Ever hear of it?" I casually inquired.

One or two of the men grunted, whether in assent or negation I could not say.

"It's really quite a rare book," I continued, not too enthusiastically.

"Yeh?" inquired somebody.

"Yes, indeed," I said. "It's worth anything from ten thousand up."

A glassy silence fell upon that company. Immediately everybody in the room was looking at me. In the glances were disbelief, amazement, stupefaction and something like horror.

Finally a man said, "What are you giving us?"

I retorted by giving them the story, and after that the inquiries fell thick and fast. Suddenly everybody was desperately interested in the first published volume of Edgar Allan Poe. At once several of the women clearly remembered having seen the book in their father's or their grandfather's library:

"He was a great one for books, you know. I suppose he had—well, hundreds of them!"

At a neighboring table, a stout dowager in creased satin appeared to be having an apoplectic seizure. She was red and gasping. In her eyes were little covetous points of steel. In a cataract of bungled pronouns, the seizure came out.

She had the very book at home in her own bookcase at that moment!

Surprising as was the intelligence that the lady had a bookcase, I passed the point and deprecatingly smiled. The torrent of words continued. Was it a little thing about so big? Was it in paper covers? Did it have Poe's name on the wrapper? No? *She knew it!* At every point the ten-thousand-dollar rarity checked with the copy in her bookcase. It had been her grandfather's, then her father's, and now it was hers. She was going home to get it!

The rest of the company was as excited as she, and a vague doubt was gnawing at my heart. A doubt of myself, of my cynical and infallible self. After all, she might have the thing! With one arm in a sleeve of her jacket, she wheeled about. Could she depend upon my figures? Would I undertake to get her ten thousand dollars for the book? I swallowed hard and nodded.

Then, as an idea struck me, I said, "I'll give you five thousand dollars myself for it and risk getting the rest of it from a dealer. Whatever I get over five thousand I shall keep as my profit."

If she did have the item, I saw no reason why I should not be paid for my knowledge and for the information.

She considered this sporting proposition only for an instant. Then, "I'll sell it myself," she announced, and got her second arm into its corresponding sleeve. "Perhaps," she added, "you would like to come with me. I'd like to have you see it, you know. You'll see that I'm right. I can see it now. About so big, paper covers, and no name of the author. Why, I even remember the name—*Tamerlane!*"

By this time I was almost as excited as the lady herself. My enthusiasm, running amuck, had carried me past all my own danger signals.

"Come on!" I said, and hurried out to call a taxi.

Half an hour later, with audibly pumping hearts, we entered her apartment and plunged for the bookcase. With a shout of triumph, the stout lady snatched a volume from an upper shelf and started to hand it to me. Then her jaw dropped and her eyes pushed out. Her huge body seemed to sag at all points. She was a ludicrous and pathetic figure. Silently I took the volume from her hand. It was twice as large as the item she had earlier indicated; it was bound in dull green cloth with gold lettering; it was beyond a question of doubt an early American edition of Tennyson's *Locksley Hall*.

I have never since been fooled.* However earnestly the tale is told, I grin, and know that the volume my victim is talking about is *Locksley Hall*, or *Enoch Arden*, or the *Tales of a Wayside Inn*.

All this, of course, is mean and malicious; but I feel mean and malicious toward the sort of person whom I make my victim. An intelligent booklover, or a cultured citizen, learning that only six copies of the brochure had turned up in more than sixty years, would refuse to become excited. He would realize the odds against him, even with his grandfather's library to draw upon. For the rest, I am content to drive them to the attics of the world.

But what mad times those were, back in the days when I still believed that some day *I* should find a *Tamerlane*, under a heap of government reports, in a dusty barrow, or bound up with other odds and ends in one of those queer, calf-raimented galaxies, or miscellanies, our forefathers liked to compile. The days I have spent in ancient bookshops, browsing among forgotten volumes, not specifically looking for a *Tamerlane*, but not for a moment forgetting the possibility of its resurrection. The day

---

* See previous note.

Ben Hecht and I went ferreting, at the sardonic direction of a mysterious and ghostly "Mr. Wilson." We were cubs, then, on the old *Chicago Daily News*, and we spent our luncheon money and our luncheon periods in the lurking-spots of literary treasure. Ben, for some reason that he has forgotten and will deny, became interested in the manifestations of *Ouija*, and brought his board to the office. We worked at the thing after hours.

"What is the rarest book in the world?" he asked, one day.

"*Tamerlane*," said I, promptly; although probably it wasn't, and isn't.

"What's it worth?" pertinently continued my fellow-mystic.

I told him. He drew a long breath, and whistled a little tune. Then he bent lower over the varnished board, as if to coax it to his mood.

"Let's see if 'Mr. Wilson' knows where there is a copy," said he.

And "Mr. Wilson" knew!

He spelled it out very cleverly for us, answering all our eager questionings as we would have had them answered. There was a copy of *Tamerlane*, it appeared, at Jansky's bookshop, a miniature *libreria* conducted in a hole in the wall in Adams Street, once occupied by a bootblack. Did Jansky know it was there? we asked; and waited breathlessly for the board to move. He did not! A final question: just where was the book? A pause, and then we had our answer: the book was in the ten-cent case in front of the shop!

We pushed the board away, ungratefully, and stood up.

"Does he have a ten-cent case, out in front?" asked Ben doubtfully. But I assured him that that much was true.

"Then come on!" he breathed.

I shall not further embarrass this distinguished novelist by a recital of his subsequent burrowings and breathings, his groanings and squirmings, sometimes on hands and knees, as we ran-sacked the ten-cent container of Mr. Anton Jansky. It is suffi-cient to record that "Mr. Wilson" was an obliging liar, and that from that moment we lost faith in him.

And poor Will Douglass is still looking for *his* copy. He is as optimistic as ever, although his hair has turned white since he began his search. Perhaps he is a bit *more* optimistic than ever. He now believes that when Calvin F. S. Thomas, who published the volume, back in 1827, moved westward with his family he boxed up the remainder of the edition and brought it west with him. Douglass expects, sooner or later, to find the missing box. If he does, he will not, however, flood the market with the priceless works. He will hide them away very carefully, and "discover" one every two or three years, until he is comfortably well off. It is a good scheme; I have often heard it outlined.

As to the real *Tamerlane*, there is little enough that can be told. Calvin F. S. Thomas published it in Boston, in 1827. He died, it is believed, in Springfield, Missouri, in 1876. No other volume with his imprint is known to collectors. It is possible that he never found out who his eccentric and penniless customer was. What became of the bulk of the edition is the merest con-jecture. Certainly something drastic occurred to make the tiny volume the rarest of its kind. The story goes that less than a dozen copies were sold when the edition was placed on the mar-ket, and that Poe, in a rage, called in and destroyed the rest. It is a plausible tale, but I believe it to be apocryphal. And there is a legend of a Boston bookseller who, late in his career, vaguely recalled having destroyed a publisher's "remainder" of a small volume in wrappers, long years before. He rather thought it *might* have been the *Tamerlanes*! But that, too, is only a story. Of the six copies known to exist, one, as stated, is in the British Museum, and the others are in the libraries of wealthy collectors.

That other copies exist somewhere seems more than likely; but only heaven knows where. Meanwhile the devoted collector still dreams of the day that will mark the crowning achievement of his dubious career. When it arrives, he will see a tiny pamphlet measuring six and three-eighths by four and one-eighth inches, in tea-colored wrappers, the title page of which will read, *Tamerlane and Other Poems. By a Bostonian. Boston: Calvin F. S. Thomas, Printer. 1827.* And between the "Bostonian" and "Boston" two lines quoted from Cowper. There are forty pages all told, and the item is distinguished chiefly by its insignificance.

It is worth ten thousand dollars!

Perhaps there is one in your attic!

20

Mighty Women Book Hunters

BY A. S. W. ROSENBACH

"Is it possible for a woman to be a bibliophile?"

This is a question that was argued, over a century ago, at the breakfast table of the famous collector Guilbert de Pixérécourt. I can imagine his friends, other collectors and scholars, looking down their long French noses, knitting their brows, and exclaiming, "*C'est impossible, monsieur!*" Would that I might have been present to refute such masculine slander!

Women, someone wittily said, have always been collectors. From the earliest time they have gathered, somewhat mysteriously, the store of the world's luxuries. It was a very modern young lady who aptly voiced the wisdom of her sex, when she said, "Kissing your hand may make you feel very very good, but a diamond and sapphire bracelet lasts forever." But in contrast to this, the jewels of the mind have appealed more strongly to some of her wiser sisters.

Today, when women excel in sports, in golf, tennis, swimming, flying, it often amazes me that they do not attempt something equally thrilling and even more adventurous. I suppose that the greatest game of all, the art of love, which women played before the dawn of history, is, and always will be, their own charming province. After love—I say, *after* love—book collecting is the most exhilarating sport of all.

To glean something of the history of women book collectors we must travel back five hundred years, to France of the magnificent châteaux, with gay lights o' love, with mistresses of kings, whose naughty flame-colored stockings were once termed blue. What women! They added, not only to the flamboyancy and gaiety of life in the fifteenth and sixteenth centuries, but dared to thumb their pretty noses at Savonarola and Martin Luther, who tried quite unsuccessfully to rob these fair imps of the many pretty ways that so well became them.

Who are they? Their musical names are familiar. Diane de Poitiers, Gabrielle d'Estrées—beloved of Henry IV—Catherine de Medici, Madame de Pompadour, and many others who made French history glittering. While these bewitching creatures dutifully carried exquisitely illuminated breviaries on the Sabbath, and took pride in owning little prayer books penned by some noted calligrapher, such as Bourdichon or Nicholas Jarry, it was in their boudoirs, in some intimate corner, seductively arranged, that they kept the choicest morsels of Anacreon, of Aristophanes, beautifully bound copies of Ovid, and bejeweled examples of the *Heptameron* of the Reine Margot. In those happy days, as you will see, love and book collecting went hand in hand.

It speaks rather well, I think, for the kings of France that they chose for friends beautiful ladies who loved beautiful books. What romantic stories must be hidden in these treasures of binding and print. When I behold a royal binding with the interlaced initials of King Henry II and the fair Diane de Poitiers, or come upon a lovely romance of chivalry with the devices of the Great Louis and the crests of Madame de Montespan, I begin at once to ponder on the hidden motive for this regal love of books.

When Henry, second of that name, wooed Diane, did he present to her a jeweled crown, executed by Benvenuto Cellini, or

at the height of his infatuation, the Château d'Anet? Your true
bibliophile thinks otherwise. He loves to amuse himself with the
thought that the most persuasive of the King's gifts was a book.
Some glorious volume, with superb illustrations, that would
make the frail recipient murmur ecstatically, "This is *too* much!"
The true collector dreams, as he sits in his library, of the golden
days when women could be wooed and won by a book! I know
several bibliophiles who wish they would soon return!

Women first began to preen themselves as book collectors in
the years immediately preceding the invention of printing. Then
the writing of books was such a costly affair that the production
was extremely limited. The early libraries consisted almost entirely of hand-written, decorated breviaries, books of hours, mis-
sals, lives of the saints, and works by the fathers of the Church.
Today these manuscripts are regarded with the greatest affection
by the bibliophile, and he considers nothing this side of heaven
more beautiful. The first time he sees the prayer book of the
Duchesse de Berri, with its magnificent miniatures, or the brevi-
ary of the Duchesse de Lorraine, a feeling of faintness mixed
with envy must come over him. Alas, that such masterpieces are
nearly all unattainable, locked away in great national libraries.

Louise de Savoie, Duchesse d'Angoulême, twice regent under
her son, Francis I, was one of the first French women to form
an important collection of books. Born in 1476, just twenty years
after the invention of printing, and six years after the first press
was established in Paris, this distinguished mother of the first
Francis did much to encourage the new art and to make it flour-
ish in France. Among the volumes gathered by Louise de Savoie
were the *Life of Saint Jerome*, the *Triumphs of Virtue*, Boccaccio's *Lives of Noble Ladies*, and a curious work, the *Epistles of
Ovid, or Examples of Letters Suitable for a Lady to Write to Her
Husband*. Among her possessions was also a lovely manuscript

with twenty-one large miniatures depicting Penelope, Phyllis, Hermione, and Hero, in costumes of the sixteenth century. Twenty-five years ago this precious volume was one of the glories of the Hermitage in St. Petersburg. Where is it, I wonder, today?

Another famous bibliophile was the beautiful and willful Marguerite d'Angoulème, Queen of Navarre, sister of Francis. Born the year this country was discovered, she lives forever in the praises of Brantôme, Calvin, and Melanchthon. Rabelais wrote his greatest eulogy, when he dedicated his immortal work to "L'Esprit de la reine de Navarre." All scholars are conversant with this amazing queen's own literary works, her chansons, poems, her mysteries. Her most renowned work, the *Heptameron*, did not appear in print until 1558, nine years after her death, although the manuscript was in circulation during her lifetime. These seventy stories were first issued under the title *Histoire des Amans Fortunez*. Where is Marguerite's own autograph manuscript of the *Heptameron*? Many a collector would like to know. Did it ever exist?

The Queen of Navarre had the human qualities necessary to every great collector. To begin with, she was a true daughter of the Renaissance, imaginative, generous. A patroness of poets and of beggars, the companion of courtly ladies and gallant gentlemen, and the delight, too, of precious vagabonds. Book lovers venerate her memory, not only for her charm and erudition, but because of her position among the women bibliophiles of France.

Diane de Poitiers, Duchesse de Valentinois, to whom I have already alluded, was a lady whose pictures reveal a charming mouth, a noble expression, and burning eyes. She became the beloved of Henry II. Born the daughter of a bibliophile, Jean de Poitiers, she was reared from the day of her birth, in 1499, in an atmosphere of scholarship and the sacred traditions of a library. Married at the age of sixteen to Louis de Brézé, grand seneschal of Normandy, her career is the subject of many legendary histories. Ancient chroniclers relate that in order to save her father, who was implicated in the conspiracy of the Constable of Bourbon, she had to sacrifice her honor to Francis I. But bibliophiles have always chosen to disbelieve this somewhat sordid if dramatic story. Considering the literary tastes of both Francis and Diane, we prefer the more reasonable theory that some rare volume was the chief allure. The real problem for the bibliophile is—which one?

In the annals of bibliomania the reign of Henry II has always been considered of enormous importance. It was in 1558 that an ordinance was passed (presumably at Diane's instigation) to the effect that every publisher should present to the libraries of Blois and Fontainebleau a copy of each book he issued. This copy-tax soon added nearly eight hundred volumes to the national collection. All of Diane's books are marked with an ambiguous cipher, cleverly arranged to represent what might be taken for the initials of Henry and his queen, Catherine de Medici, or Henry and his mistress. This was very far-sighted of Diane, who wished to avoid offending this powerful de Medici, a most distinguished collector herself.

The origin of the devices on the covers of Diane de Poitiers' books is interesting. When first a widow, she ordered each volume stamped with a laurel springing from a tomb, and the motto "I live alone in grief." But later, when Henry offered his consolation, she suppressed both the tomb and the legend. Her famous crescent shone not only on her books, but on the palace walls of France, in the Louvre, at Fontainebleau and Anet. Her initials, so conspicuous on her breviaries, were not absent either from that little treasury of books which she and Henry II assembled in the Château d'Anet. Her boudoir was renowned, not only for its luxurious size, its fine furniture, exquisite paintings, and gorgeous tapestries designed by Bernard Van Orley, but for a cabinet of delightful volumes. Oddly enough, this literary trove was not discovered until long after the owners ceased to be. The bedchamber did not relinquish its secret, and the cache remained unnoticed until the death of the Princess de Condé in 1723.

One of the most beautiful volumes from her library was sold in the collection of the Marquess of Lothian in 1932. It was her own copy of Boccaccio's *de la louenge et vertu des nobles et clares dames*, printed in Paris by Anthoine Vérard in 1493. Bound in dark olive morocco, the back and sides decorated with gilt arabesque borders, with the interlaced initials of Diane, and her bows, quivers, and crescents, it sold for ninety-four hundred dollars to a New York collector.

The vivacious Diane lives in the pages of Clément Marot, Ronsard, Du Bellay, and other poets. Her château at Anet was justly celebrated, combining the great talents of such famous French artists as Philippe Delorme, who built it, Jean Goujon, who carved it, and Jean Cousin, who made the mirrors. Leonard Limousin furnished the enamels, and Bernard de Palissy supplied the furnishings. Let wealthy collectors yearn for the gorgeous trappings by Goujon, Limousin, and the rest—give me the contents of Diane's little cabinet!

For Americans it is interesting to note that among the Bibles, psalm books, discourses on sibyls, and other items in Diane de Poitiers' library, were two books relating to this country, Serveto's edition of Ptolemy's Geography, published at Lyons in 1541, and *Singularitez de la France Antarctique,* printed by Christopher Plantin at Antwerp in 1558. And so a woman has the distinction of being one of the earliest collectors of Americana.

Queen Isabella of Spain, the patroness of Columbus, was an ardent book lover. I longed for years to own a volume from her library and that of her neglected husband, Ferdinand. Nearly all of them were locked up in the national libraries of Spain. I knew of one, however, in England. It was in the great collection formed by Sir Thomas Phillipps at Thirlestaone House, Cheltenham. I spent several days in that noble library, with Sir Thomas's learned grandson, Mr. T. FitzRoy Fenwick. I asked if he had a book belonging to Ferdinand and Isabella. "Yes," he replied, and opened a safe, taking from it a large volume bound in old green velvet.

What a book and what a provenance! It was a world-famous manuscript, *Le Livre de La Chasse*, by Gaston de Foix, surnamed Phébus, written in the year 1387! It contained eighty-eight superb miniatures in gold and colors by an artist of superior merit, in my estimation, to the celebrated Jean Fouquet, to whom it was once attributed. Its frontispiece was a masterpiece, containing the device of Ferdinand and Isabella, with the arms of Castile and Aragon exquisitely emblazoned. It had been given to the "Reyes Catolicos" by the King of France. It was beyond question the finest sporting book in the world!

When Mr. Fenwick placed it in my hands my blood pressure must have gone up fifty points. That was in 1926. The following year I went again to see my beloved manuscript. I could not keep my mind off its charm. In 1928 I went to Cheltenham determined to possess it. I succeeded at length. The price, though high, was really low, as its value could not be measured in pounds sterling. I asked Mr. Fenwick when his grandfather had purchased it. He told me the exact date in 1828. It was precisely one hundred years, *to a day*, from the time Sir Thomas Phillipps had bought it!

Queen Isabella was not only a bibliophile, but was extremely

fond of the chase. It is this happy combination—books and sport
—that makes this wonderful volume from her library doubly
entrancing. Isabella was one of the "women of all time." This
great manuscript is surely in the same category.

Catherine de Medici, although twenty years younger than
Diane, was equally eager in her search for books. It was her
good fortune to inherit the splendid tastes of her famous fore-
bears, and she came to France bringing "with her from Urbino a
number of manuscripts that had belonged to the Eastern Em-
perors, and had been purchased by Cosimo de Medici." Catherine was not so meticulous in her dealings where a book was
concerned as was Cosimo. If she could secure a volume in no
other way, she did not hesitate to steal it. When the Marshal
Strozzi, one of her kinsmen, died in the French service, she
immediately seized upon his noble library. She made no secret of
the fact that she had awaited his death with anticipation, knowing that she would then be able to pounce upon the Strozzi
treasures. Let us forgive her! She was a genuine bibliophile.
Brantôme, in giving an account of the transaction, says most
generously that the Queen purchased the books—but forgot to
pay for them. She seems never to have been afraid of the natural
enemies of all collectors—creditors!

A beautiful specimen from her library was sold in the Rahir
sale in Paris in 1930, and brought 322,000 francs! Entitled *La
Cyropédie de Xenophon*, printed at Lyons by Jean de Tournes
in 1555, it was superbly bound in citron morocco, delicately
tooled in silver and gold, with the arms and devices of Catherine. In the catalogue of the sale it was described as one of the
most remarkable specimens of the binder's art of the French
Renaissance.

Catherine's daughter, Marguerite de Valois, Queen of Navarre, emulated the example of her distinguished mother. Nour-

ished on books, she soon became the most learned lady of her time. Scaliger said she was liberal and studious, that she had more kingly virtues than the King. As the wife of Henry IV she collected a large library. Nearly all her books are magnificently bound and stamped with daisies, which give the volumes from her library an air of purity. Clovis Eve is said to have bound them from the Queen's own designs. Her books were systematically clad, science and philosophy in citron morocco, the poets in green, history and theology in red, Aretino in spotless white.

Anne of Austria, daughter of Philip of Spain, and wife of Louis XIII, is renowned in the kingdom of books. She was patroness of that eminent binder Le Gascon, and the lacy gilt borders executed by him on the royal volumes are famous. Anne's library included many devotional treatises, sermons, and histories of the Church, which were no doubt recommended to her by her ecclesiastical friend, Cardinal Mazarin. The Cardinal himself was an illustrious collector, and his books have always been highly esteemed. His device, with the cardinal's hat, is frequently seen on old volumes. Anne, on the death of her husband, became Queen Mother, and for some years ruled the destinies of France. When Louis XIV reached his majority, Anne gracefully retired to the shelter of her library, where she consoled herself with her books and Mazarin.

Madame de Pompadour in her forty-three years influenced her epoch more than any other person, the King not excepted. Poets, including the great Voltaire, painters, sculptors, designers, all were indebted to her patronage. The porcelain factory at Sèvres owes its existence to her. Boucher, Fragonard, Falconnet, Cochin, each one, received from her the inspiration for his greatest works. Dérôme, one of the most skillful binders, executed his choicest coverings for her books. She was fortunate to live during an epoch in which some of the most famous illustrated volumes were issued. Madame de Pompadour was herself an illustrator and etched a set of sixty-two plates, which she presented to her friends. Her most famous work was her etched frontispiece, after Boucher, for Corneille's *Rodogune*, published in 1760. Amateurs with a curious perversity prefer the rather naughty volumes of Madame de Pompadour to the austere books of Madame de Maintenon.

Madame de Montespan's love for Louis XIV is well known, but her love of books is seldom dwelt upon by historians. She became the beloved of the King in 1668, and lived during a period that saw the rise of Corneille and Molière, and the development of book illustration with copperplate engravings. But a few works from her library remain; one of them, a copy of the Psalms of David, in seven volumes, was printed especially for her use. Luckily, an extremely interesting volume survives, the Marquise de Montespan's own copy of the *Works of an Author Aged Seven* (her son, the young Duc de Maine), published under the direction of his governess, Madame de Maintenon, in 1678.

This leads me to her successor in royal favor, none other than the poor governess Frances, afterward the Marquise de Maintenon, second wife of Louis XIV. The Grand Monarch insisted, with pleasing propriety, that all the ladies surrounding him should be lovers of books. While Madame de Maintenon's name is also a household word, few have even peeped into her library at Saint-Cyr. The bindings are magnificent, and the gold is in profusion, but the contents of the volumes are decidedly ordinary, dull works of theology, philosophy, sermons, concordances. The more mundane volumes of that period are conspicuously absent.

The Queen Marie Antoinette was also a book collector, and the volumes from her library are all highly treasured. I had the good fortune to own her own copy of *Les Baisers* of Dorat, one of the most beautiful books of the eighteenth century. It is in green morocco, with the Queen's arms in gold on the sides. It is now in the collection of Mr. Joseph Widener.

The most touching relic of this unfortunate lady is her own prayer book. When she entered the Prison of the Conciergerie for the last time, she clasped tightly in her white hands the *Office de la Divine Providence*, by Pierre Préault, 1757. A few hours before her execution, in deepest anguish she wrote on the flyleaf:

> 16 October (1793). Half past four o'clock in the morning. My God, have pity on me! My eyes have no more tears to shed for you, my poor children. Adieu. Adieu.
>
> Marie-Antoinette

This tender volume, an ever-living memorial of the Revolution, was long in the possession of M. Garinet, who left his splendid library to his native city, Châlons-sur-Marne.

When I purchased *en bloc* the Roederer library in Paris in 1923, there was one little volume that I particularly desired. It was Moreau's catalogue of Marie Antoinette's own library, entitled, *Bibliothèque de Madame la Dauphine*, printed in 1770. It has a gracious frontispiece, exquisitely engraved by Eisen, representing Marie Antoinette as Dauphine being crowned by the Graces. What made this charming volume so enticing was that it was bound in old red morocco with the arms of her husband, later to become Louis XVI.

The world, I am told, has become tired of kings and of royalty, so perhaps you are wearying of a too vigorous flow of purple blood. I must therefore turn to a woman who was a genuine collector, with just enough spice in her nature to make her eternally attractive. Madame de Verrue was born in 1670, and at thirteen years of age espoused the Comte de Verrue, a noble of considerable wealth. She was a person of charm, of beauty, and of distinction, as can be perceived from her portrait by Largillière. Her husband died in 1703, and whatever emotions she may have felt for him she now directed to book collecting. Indeed, almost overnight she sprouted as a real collector. Some contemporary said of her that, fearing to take a chance on heaven, Madame de Verrue determined to have a good time here below. Her epitaph is famous:

> Here lies in sleep secure a dame inclined to mirth
> Who, by way of making sure, chose her Paradise on earth.

She had countless love affairs, famous in her time, and gathered many books even more renowned, and, a woman of rare judgment, she chose to collect the masterpieces of the world's literature. French collectors, with their debonair manner, now prefer among her volumes the trifles that bear such names as *Gallant Adventures at the Court of France,* the *Love-Affairs of the Grand Monarch with Mademoiselle du Tron,* the *Parnasse Satyrique,* and many other choice *morceaux,* which are really tame in comparison with some of the novels of today. Madame de Verrue had her own librarian, and left for the edification of posterity an inventory of all her property. Her taste was sure, exquisite, unfailing. She possessed the finest pictures by Van Dyke, Rubens, Rembrandt, and Nattier. Everything she had was according to the best canons of all time. Her snuffboxes in gold, in tortoise shell, in porcelain, in lacquer, in jasper, defied computation. Among the most interesting things in the inventory is the catalogue of snuffs, more than sixty-five in number, which filled these delicate boxes, so prettily carried by Madame de Verrue. The snuff goes by vintages. For instance, there is a special cask dated 1734, a box marked 1736, another given her by the Cardinal de Rohan in 1740. There were five boxes of "Messalina finissima," which was kept in a leaden jar, and probably considered in the Corona-Corona class. I must reluctantly leave Madame de Verrue in the fragrant odor of the sweetest tobacco.

In Paris not long ago, Baroness James de Rothschild passed away at the age of eighty-three. The owner of the finest private library in France, she was the dean of modern women book collectors.

France is naturally proud of her lady book lovers. They created a noble history, extending from the early part of the fifteenth century, which encompassed all the grace, the *esprit*, the elegance of times long past. I may perhaps have treated them too openly. I would not, if I could, paint them as saints. They would be the first to rebuke me. We love them for their many-sided characters, their enchanting ways, their charming wit, and above all for their love of books.

Quentin Bauchart has written a delightful treatise entitled *Les Femmes Bibliophiles de France* (1886), and Andrew Lang has a charming essay on the same subject.

No country in the world has had so many great collectors as England. Her heritage is a glorious one. Henry VII, the founder of the house of Tudor, became a collector of printed books and manuscripts, though his taste was apparently not shared by his wife, Elizabeth, eldest daughter of Edward IV. His son Henry VIII inherited his father's tastes, and at least three of his wives were able to share his enthusiasms and collected their own libraries, having their books specially bound for them. Books from the libraries of Catherine of Aragon, Anne Boleyn, and Katherine Parr, with their arms impressed on the bindings, are all to be found in the old Royal Library in the British Museum.

Both the Tudor princesses, daughters of King Henry VIII,

were book collectors, and the library of the unhappy woman known to posterity as "Bloody Mary" was deposited in the British Museum in 1757. It is a notable collection, the books for the most part having been bound for the Queen by Thomas Berthelet, the royal binder.

One of the most outstanding book collectors of Queen Elizabeth's day was a woman as celebrated as Elizabeth herself, but alas, far less fortunate. I refer to her tragic kinswoman, Mary Queen of Scots. This romantic princess, famous for her beauty and her talent as well as for her misfortunes, was a great bibliophile. Her love of books may have been inherited from her father, James V, whose library was sacked by English invaders. It was certainly encouraged in France, where she lived at a time when the examples of Catherine de Medici and Diane de Poitiers had made the possession of a library fashionable.

Mary's taste was by no means narrow and her son James VI, when he inherited her library at Holyrood, found books to delight the heart of any collector. The works of Rabelais, Marguerite de Navarre, and most of the great French poets; romances of chivalry; tales of voyage and discovery; religious books, including books of hours; manuscripts on vellum; books in Greek and Latin—and of these it may be mentioned to her credit that she wished to bequeath them to the University of Saint Andrews; all these and many more testified to the literary discrimination of one of the loveliest and most tragic figures in the history of the world.

The bindings of her books show in part her sad and pitiful history. Many of them are black and have black edges—a mark of mourning for her first husband, the Dauphin of France, who shortly after their marriage became King Francis II, but who died after only two years of married life. These books have impressed in the sides a cipher—M and F—for Marie and François, with the crown of France and the motto "Sa vertu M'atire," an anagram on the name Marie Stuarte.

Queen Elizabeth, too, loved books. As a young princess exiled from court, she amused herself by embroidering bindings for her own volumes, on blue silk with gold and silver thread, in the style made famous a few years later by the nuns of Little Gidding. After she became the mighty Queen, she established her own library at Whitehall, and in her day this must have been the finest cabinet of presentation books in the universe. Unhappily many of them are lost, but it takes only a slight effort of the imagination to see the manuscripts of Sir Philip Sidney, of Sir Walter Raleigh, and of the unfortunate Earl of Leicester, all presented to her by their noble authors. The *Tales of Hemetes the Heremyte*, 1576, by George Gascoigne, has an engraving of the author, meekly kneeling upon his knees, presenting a copy of his book to his royal patroness.

Edmund Spenser dedicated to Queen Elizabeth *The Faerie Queene*, with the finest lines ever prefaced to a work:

> To the most high, mightie, and magnificent Emperesse, renouned for pietie, vertue, and all gracious government: Elizabeth by the Grace of God, Queene of England, France, and Ireland, and of Virginia, Defender of the Faith &c. Her most humble Servaunt, Edmund Spenser, doth in all humilitie dedicate, present, and consecrate these his labours, to live with the eternitie of her Fame.

Perhaps William Shakespeare gave her the manuscript with a dutiful dedication of his Sonnets, or his most popular play, *Romeo and Juliet*, which she doubtless read with much enjoyment. In the British Museum, in the Bodleian, and in the Pierpont Morgan Library some of the treasures of the great Queen can still be seen, the royal arms emblazoned in gold on their luxurious liveries. Queen Elizabeth not only collected the rare and splendid books of her immortal contemporaries, but she gathered about her person the great poets and dramatists themselves, and by her encouragement and inspiration fostered an era whose brilliance has never been equaled.

The poets of England, however, had a patroness whom they loved far more than the imperious Elizabeth. The Countess of Pembroke, "Sidney's Sister, Pembroke's Mother," had in some respects a much stronger hold upon the literary imagination of her time. She was the Urania of Spenser's *Colin Clout,* and she suggested the composition of her brother's *Arcadia,* which she edited and augmented. In fact, Sir Philip Sidney called his celebrated romance, not *The Arcadia,* but *The Countess of Pembroke's Arcadia.*

Her own copy of this great work, which she gave to her daughter, the Countess of Montgomery, is one of the treasures in the library at Harvard College. A neat story hangs upon this precious volume. I had always known of its existence. Even in my youthful days I coveted it in the library of Mr. Clarence S. Bement, of Philadelphia, one of the most fastidious collectors of his time. My mouth used to water as I tenderly took it in my hands, to admire one of the finest bindings of the Elizabethan period. In contemporary red morocco, the back and sides are powdered with small hearts and flames impressed in gold; in the center are the initials of the houses of Sidney and Montgomery. The inscription, signed by the Earl of Ancram, is written on the title page: "This was the Countess of Pembroke's own book given me by the Countess of Montgomery her daughter, 1625."

Some years later, with the book hunter's proverbial luck, I acquired this magnificent volume. I showed it to poor Harry Widener, then just beginning to form his great collection. Tears came to his eyes when he first saw it. "Take it," I said. "It belongs to you of right." "No," he said firmly but sorrowfully, "I cannot afford it now, and I must always be able to pay for any book I buy." I reluctantly sold it to someone else.

After five more years the bibliophile's god decreed that the book should once again come into my possession. I wrapped it carefully and rushed with it to Mr. Widener. Before I had a chance to open my package he said, "I know what you have brought me. It is the Countess of Pembroke's own *Arcadia*." It is now in his library in the Harry Elkins Widener Memorial, at Harvard.

By a happy coincidence, the library of the greatest of all American women collectors rests in the same building. Miss Amy Lowell was an inspired bibliophile with a restless imagination, great courage, and untiring zeal, those disquieting qualities of the astute book lover. I have known her to travel miles just to see a fine book.

I remember as though it were yesterday one day years ago when Miss Lowell, accompanied by her dear friend Mrs. Ada Russell, the noted actress, visited me in Philadelphia. Miss Lowell was eager to see the original draft of one of Keats's poems. That evening we sat down to rather. a formal dinner at eight o'clock. But at ten minutes after eight all formality had entirely disappeared. I recall Eddie Newton was in particularly good form that evening. Between courses, in which Miss Lowell indulged in large fat cigars, for she was as fond of tobacco as Madame Verrue, we had a lively discussion as to which was the first draft of Keats's beautiful sonnet "On First Looking into Chapman's Homer," her own, or the one in the Pierpont Morgan Library.

Miss Lowell had her own way, as usual. Then she really started something. She stated that there was a vital quality in modern verse found lacking in the old. She donned her war paint and prepared for the fray. For opponent she had that veteran of many battles, Joseph Pennell. He, naturally, championed the other side, and the battle raged eloquent and heated for hours. The timid ones were speechless, while others tried unsuccessfully to interpose a few feeble blows. The food had long since been cleared away, the wineglasses alone remaining upon the table. Suddenly Miss Lowell exclaimed: "I'm dying of hunger. It's four-thirty—time for something to eat!" I routed out the cook, who sleepily but adequately fed the famished book lovers, most of them for the first time in their lives breakfasting by the light of the rising sun. I can yet recall Miss Lowell, going down the stairs on the way to her hotel, still arguing with Joseph Pennell.

Miss Lowell had a well-defined plan in the formation of her library. She wanted unpublished Keats material first and foremost, and the Keats manuscripts in her collection speak more eloquently of her successful endeavors than anything I can say of her. If she desired a particular item, she would not rest until she secured it. It was not unusual for her to call me from Boston at any hour of the night to learn if I had purchased something for her at one of the auction sales. The cost was nothing, the book everything.

Another great woman collector of books lived in Brooklyn, New York, which has the proud distinction of having had more distinguished bibliophiles than any other city of its size in the world. I refer to the late Mrs. Norton Quincy Pope, who gathered together in a short time a magnificent collection. Among her treasures she possessed probably the finest Caxton in the world, a dream of a book, the only perfect copy in existence of Malory's *Morte d'Arthur*, printed at Westminster in 1485. At her death it passed first to Robert Hoe, and then into the Pierpont Morgan Library.

This reference to the Morgan collection must inevitably bring up the name of its distinguished director, Miss Belle da Costa Greene, who has reached a height in the world of books that no other woman has ever attained. Miss Greene, besides possessing a genuine love of books, has a knowledge of customs and manners in the medieval period excelled by few scholars.

It is sometimes dangerous for women to possess rare volumes —they might for that very reason receive offers of marriage! This sounds fantastic, but it is true. I can only quote the celebrated case of a great feminine amateur at the beginning of the nineteenth century. Miss Richardson Currer owned a valuable library containing over fifteen thousand volumes, including a beautiful copy printed on vellum of the *Book of St. Albans,* 1496, written by the first woman sports writer, Dame Juliana Berners. Richard Heber, probably the most enthusiastic book collector who ever lived, tried to wheedle it out of her by hook or crook. Not succeeding by nefarious ways, he took the honorable method of proposing marriage. The lady, not caring to share the volume with a husband, indignantly refused. Good for her!

A charming American lady has recently acquired the superb Pembroke copy of the first edition of the *Book of St. Albans,* as the *Book of Hawking and Hunting* is usually termed, printed in 1486. It is ten years earlier than the romantic copy that belonged to Miss Currer. I would rather have the first issue of this famous book than the one on which Mr. Heber looked with such longing eyes, even if it were printed on vellum. It is particularly fitting that this famous volume, written by a woman, should grace the shelves of a distinguished feminine collector.

There have been two women who by their bookish gifts are enshrined in the hearts of all bibliophiles. In 1892 a widow, unknown to fame but not to fortune, walked into a bookstore in

London and stated almost casually that she would like to buy the finest private library then in existence, the renowned collection of Lord Spencer, at Althorp. The bookseller stood aghast. After he recovered from the shock, he replied that Earl Spencer would never part with his precious library. The lady, nothing daunted, walked into another shop. Here she was more warmly received and, although the dealer had not the slightest reason to know that the Earl would sell his library, he politely informed her that he would write to his lordship. The negotiations were successful and the lady drew a check for over two hundred thousand pounds in payment, the largest sum, up to that time, that had been given for a collection of books and manuscripts. Who was this courageous lady? It was none other than Mrs. John Rylands, of Manchester, England, who presented the Spencer library to that city as a memorial to her husband. This gift placed Manchester at once on the map as a center for learning and scholarship. This, in the annals of book collecting, is one of the finest gifts made by man or woman.

The other lady to whom I referred above happily lives in America. Mrs. Edward S. Harkness has made extraordinary gifts to American institutions, and when she presented the Melk copy of the Gutenberg Bible to Yale University she made a sensation on two continents.

The West is now rivaling the East in feminine activities in the "City of Books," to use a phrase of Anatole France. Mrs. Edward L. Doheny in Los Angeles has beautiful specimens of typography and many exquisite bindings and manuscripts. Some literary treasures of the highest importance are in the library of Mrs. W. H. Stark, of Orange, Texas. Mrs. F. M. P. Taylor has just presented a Fine Arts Center to Colorado Springs, and her collections contain beautiful specimens of some of the rarest English books.

I have always thought it rather strange that no wife of a President of the United States has been a book collector. A few were interested in books to read, but not to collect. It is a sad commentary.

There have been mighty women book hunters. There will be many more in the future, for the quest has everything that appeals to woman—mystery, charm, subtlety, sweet companionship. It has just enough spice in it to make it eternally attractive. Ladies, why leave the triumphs of this sport to Men?

Glossary

all edges gilt—outer edges of leaves of book cut smooth and gilded with gold leaf

Americana—books or pamphlets on America, its development, history, and peoples

armorial binding—binding stamped with a coat of arms

association copy—book once owned by someone associated with the author of a particular work, or by the author himself

authorized edition—legitimate or nonpirated edition

backstrip—the spine of a book

binding copy—book in such a poor state that it is fit only for rebinding

blank leaves—usually at the beginning or end of a book, and noted in collation of a work, since they represent an integral part of the book

blind stamp—impression made in the paper, often to indicate ownership

block book—volume printed from wooden blocks

blocked in blind (gilt)—marked with an impression in the binding, often for decorative purposes

boards—covers made of cardboard and covered with paper only. Usually the spine has a paper label printed with the title and perhaps the author's name. Although the practice of issuing books in boards flourished primarily between the mid eighteenth century and approximately 1830, when publishers began to use cloth bindings, a number of books through the years have appeared in boards.

bookplate—paper label, usually pasted on the front inside cover to denote ownership

broadside—sheet of paper printed on one side only for declarations or ballads

calf—smooth leather used for binding purposes

cancel—leaf or slip of paper pasted over or tipped in to conceal or indicate printed errors

catchword—first word on the following page printed at the lower-right-hand corner of the preceding page, in order that the pages may be properly collated

cathedral bindings—bindings, usually of leather, with pictures of churches blocked in

chain lines—watermarks of widely spaced lines appearing on laid paper

chapbooks—"cheapbooks," sold by chapmen in the streets in the nineteenth century. The content was often sensational, or pertained to folk tales, and the quality of the printing was often poor.

cloth boards—boards covered with cloth

collation—verification of a book's completeness, in which the binding and format is compared with that of the original edition

colophon—reference at the end of a book, sometimes including a printer's device, indicating place and date of publication

conjugate leaves—leaves connected to each other to form a single piece of paper

contemporary—binding, plates, inscriptions made near the date of a book's publication

cover—front or back of binding

deckle edges—uncut edges

dedication copy—book inscribed by the author to the person to whom it is dedicated

device—printer's mark or design

disbound—without a binding

drop title—title placed at the head of the first page of the text *dropped letter*—missing printed letter

duodecimo (12mo)—small book, approximately 5 by 7½ inches

dust wrapper (jacket)—paper cover enclosing a book to protect it from dirt. Jackets these days also serve to make books attractive to buyers.

editio princeps—Latin for "first edition"

embroidered binding—needlework binding

end papers—sheets of paper at the very beginning and end of a book, with one half pasted to the inside cover and the other half free

engraving—illustration or design

errata—errors in the printed text

errata slip—used to cover or denote errors; usually pasted in

ex library—denoting a book that originally belonged to a library or other public lending institution

ex libris—bookplate

extra-illustrated—book with additional plates or illustrations pasted in

facsimile—copy of the original

first edition—initial appearance of a work in book format

first separate edition—first appearance of a work that previously appeared included with other material

first trade edition—first edition of a work that may have appeared initially in a limited edition or privately printed format

flyleaf—front free end paper

folio—relatively large book, approximately 12 by 15 inches

fore-edge painting—painting that appears on the front outer edge of a book when it is fanned out

foxed—brown discoloration on plates and sheets

frontispiece—illustration that usually is placed opposite the title page

galleys—earliest proofs, usually printed on very long sheets of paper

gathering—section (quire) of sheets

grangerized—augmented with extra illustrations not in original edition

guard—paper or muslin strip bound in book to which a plate or sheet can be glued

half title—sheet that precedes the title page and bears the title, often in abbreviated form *hinge*—inside or outside joint of the binding

horae—book of hours; manuscripts or books of prayers

hornbook—tablet made of leather, wood, or metal on which were printed alphabets, prayers, etc., intended to be read by children

impression—one of a number of printings made at different times from the same set of type

incunabula—books printed during the early days of printing (fifteenth century)

inscribed copy—book with an inscription written by the author

inscription—comment or phrase inscribed in a book, not necessarily by the author

inserted leaves—sheets tipped in after binding has been completed

issue—copy of the first edition of a book which somehow differs, either internally or externally, from other copies

Japon vellum—smooth, glossy stiff paper with smooth glossy surface, most often pale yellow in color, used for deluxe editions

label—usually made of leather or paper; leather labels have been used since the late 17th century; paper labels from late 18th century, and used on spines of paper-covered boarded books.

laid paper—usually hand-made, with parallel lines watermarked in, and visible when the paper is held up to light

Levant—highly polished morocco leather

limited edition—special edition limited to a given number of copies, sometimes signed by the author or illustrator, and constituting either the first edition or that which follows the first trade edition, or both issued simultaneously

made-up or sophisticated copy—imperfect copy perfected by adding missing leaves or plates

marbled paper—end paper colored to appear like marble

mint copy—book in perfect condition

misbound—book with a plate or gathering erroneously bound in

morocco—leather used for binding

octavo—book measuring approximately 6 by 9 inches

part issues—novel's first appearance in weekly or monthly parts issued in a magazine or in separate wrappers

pictorial cloth—cloth bindings that contain pictures

pirated edition—illegitimate or unauthorized edition

point—internal or external characteristic that is often used to determine priority of issue

presentation copy—book that is presented as a gift, sometimes by the author, at other times by the publisher

provenance—history of a book's ownership

quarto—book measuring approximately 9 by 12 inches

reading copy—usually one that is more suitable for reading than collecting due to its poor condition

rebacked—given a new spine

recased—book removed from and then replaced in its covers to preserve its condition after it has become loosened. Glue, resewing and sometimes new end papers are often involved when a book is recased.

recto—front of a page

remainder binding—unsold copies of a book sold en masse by the publisher to wholesalers or individual booksellers. Sometimes the new owner has the books rebound in a binding unlike the original.

review copy—copy sent to a critic or reviewer, and sometimes constituting the earliest issue

rubbed—scuffed (binding)

shaken—loose between its covers

signatures—letters or numbers printed on the first sheet of a gathering to ensure that the gatherings are bound in the correct order

slipcase—box into which a book can be slipped for protection

spine—backstrip

three-decker—usually a novel written in the nineteenth century and published in three volumes

tipped in—(plate or slip of paper) glued into a book

trimmed—having sheet edges that were roughly cut by the binder

uncut—having sheet edges that were not trimmed

unopened—having sheets that have not been opened or separated

variant—differentiation in text, color of cloth binding, etc., between copies of the same edition upon which rests no priority of issue

verso—back of a page

wove paper—usually machine-made, and distinguishable from laid
    paper in that no chain lines are visible when the paper is held
    up to light

wrappers—paper covers as opposed to hard cloth covers

Abbreviations

ABA	Antiquarian Booksellers' Association
ABAA	Antiquarian Booksellers' Association of America
a.e.g.	all edges gilt
a.l.s.	autographed letter, signed
BAR	*Book Auction Records*
BMC	*British Museum Catalogue*
BPC	*Book Prices Current*
ca.	circa
CBEL	*Cambridge Bibliography of English Literature*
cf.	calf
comp.	compiled
cont.	contemporary
cr. 8vo	crown octave size
dec.	decorated
d.s.	document, signed
d.w.	dust wrappers
ed.	edited
edn.	edition
engr.	engraved (engraving)
e.p.	end paper
ex lib.	ex library
facs.	facsimile

fol.	folio size
frontis.	frontispiece
g.e.	gilt edges
g.l.	gothic letter
gt.	gilt
hf. bd.	half-bound
illus.	illustrated
impft.	imperfect
inscr.	inscription (inscribed)
lge.	large
lith.	lithograph
l.p.	large paper
l.s.	letter, signed
ltd. edn.	limited edition
m.e.	marbled edges
mor.	morocco leather
MS(S).	manuscript(s)
n.d.	no date
n.p.	no place
ob.	oblong
oct.	octavo size
o.p.	out of print
orig.	original
pict.	pictorial
pl(s).	plate(s)
pol.	polished
port.	portrait
pp.	pages
p.p.	privately printed
prelims.	preliminary leaves
pres.	presentation copy
pt.	part
ptd.	printed
pub(d).	published
qto.	quarto size
rev.	revised
sgd.	signed

sm.	small
spr.	sprinkled
STC	*Short Title Catalogue*
swd.	sewed
t.e.g.	top edges gilt
thk.	thick
t.l.s.	typed letter, signed
t.p.	title page
transl.	translated
unbd.	unbound
v.d.	various dates
v.g.	very good (copy)
vol(s).	volume(s)
v.p.	various places
wrs.	wrappers
y.e.	yellow edges

Bibliography

GENERAL REFERENCE

Bateson, F. W. *Cambridge Bibliography of English Literature.* 5 vols. Cambridge: Cambridge University Press, 1940–57.

Blanck, Jacob. *Bibliography of American Literature.* 6 vols. New Haven and London: Yale University Press, 1955–73.

Hart, James D. *The Oxford Companion to American Literature.* 4th ed. New York: Oxford University Press, 1965.

Harvey, Sir Paul. *The Oxford Companion to English Literature.* Oxford: Clarendon Press, 1973.

Harvey, Sir Paul, and J. E. Heseltine. *The Oxford Companion to French Literature.* Oxford: Clarendon Press, 1959.

BOOK COLLECTING

Brewer, Reginald. *The Delightful Diversion.* New York: Macmillan, 1935.

Carter, John. *ABC For Book-Collectors.* 1952. 5th ed., rev. London: Rupert Hart-Davis, 1972.

———. *New Paths in Book-Collecting.* 1934. Freeport, N.Y.: Books for Libraries Press, 1967.

———. *Taste and Technique in Book Collecting.* 1948. London: Private Libraries Association, 1970.

Curle, Richard. *Collecting American First Editions.* Indianapolis: Bobbs-Merrill, 1930.

Currie, Barton. *Fishers of Books*. Boston: Little, Brown, 1931.

Haller, Margaret. *The Book Collector's Fact Book*. New York: Arco, 1976.

Muir, Percy. *Book Collecting as a Hobby*. London and Chesham: Gramol Publications, 1944.

Newton, A. Edward. *The Amenities of Book-Collecting and Kindred Affections*. 1918. Port Washington, N.Y.: Kennikat Press, 1969.

———. *End Papers*. 1933. Port Washington, N.Y., Kennikat Press, 1969.

———. *The Greatest Book in the World*. 1925. Port Washington, N.Y., Kennikat Press, 1969.

———. *A Magnificent Farce*. 1921. Freeport, N.Y.: Books for Libraries Press, 1970.

———. *This Book-Collecting Game*. Boston: Little, Brown, 1928.

Quayle, Eric. *The Collector's Book of Books*. New York: Clarkson N. Potter/Crown, 1971.

Rosenbach, A. S. W. *A Book Hunter's Holiday*. Boston and New York: Houghton Mifflin, 1936.

———. *Books and Bidders*. Boston: Little, Brown, 1927.

Starrett, Vincent. *Penny Wise and Book Foolish*. New York: Covici Friede, 1929.

Stewart, Seumas. *Book Collecting: A Beginner's Guide*. Newton Abbot, David and Charles, 1972.

West, Herbert. *Modern Book Collecting for the Impecunious Amateur*. Boston: Little, Brown, and Co., 1936.

Winterich, John T., and David Randall. *A Primer of Book Collecting*. 1927. 3rd rev. ed. New York: Crown, 1966.

EARLY PRINTED BOOKS

Pollard, A. W., and G. R. Redgrave. *Short-Title Catalogue of English Books 1475–1640*. London: Bibliographical Society, 1946.

Stillwell, Margaret Bingham. *Incunabula and Americana*. New York: Columbia University Press, 1931.

Wing, Donald. *Short-Title Catalogue of Books 1641–1700*. 3 vols. New York: Index Society, 1945–55.

PRIVATE PRESS BOOKS

Cave, Roderick. *The Private Press*. London: Faber & Faber, 1971.
Ransom, Will. *Private Presses and Their Books*. New York: R. R. Bowker, 1929.
———. *Selective Check Lists of Press Books*. New York: Philip C. Duschnes, 1945.
Ridler, William. *British Modern Press Books*. London: Covent Garden Press Ltd., 1971.

ILLUSTRATED BOOKS

Illustrators of Children's Books: 1744–1945. Boston: The Horn Book, Inc., 1947.
Bland, David. *A History of Book Illustration*. Cleveland and New York: The World Publishing Co., 1958.
The Artist and the Book. Boston: Museum of Fine Arts and Harvard College Library, 1961.

CHILDREN'S BOOKS

Blanck, Jacob. *Peter Parley to Penrod*. 1938. Reprint. Cambridge, Mass.: Research Classics, 1961.
Meigs, Cornelia, et al. *A Critical History of Children's Literature*. New York: Macmillan, 1953.
Muir, Percy. *English Children's Books 1600–1900*. New York: Praeger, 1954.
Quayle, Eric. *The Collector's Book of Children's Books*. New York: Clarkson N. Potter, 1971.
Rosenbach, A. S. W. *Early American Children's Books*. Portland, Maine: Southworth Press, 1933.
Targ, William. *Bibliophile in the Nursery*. Cleveland: World Publishing, 1957.

FIRST EDITIONS

Blanck, Jacob. *Merle Johnson's American First Editions*. Waltham, Mass.: Mark Press, 1965.
Boutell, Henry. *First Editions and How to Tell Them*. 1928. Rev. ed. Philadelphia and London: Lippincott, 1937.

Brussel, I. R. *Anglo-American First Editions*. New York: R. R. Bowker, 1935–36.

Sawyer, Charles J., and F. J. Harvey Darton. *English Books 1475–1900: A Signpost for Collectors*. New York: E. P. Dutton, 1927.

Tannen, Jack. *How to Identify and Collect American First Editions: A Guidebook*. New York: Arco, 1976.

GOTHIC FICTION

Summers, Montague. *A Gothic Bibliography*. New York: Russell & Russell, 1964.

DETECTIVE FICTION

Barzun, Jacques, and Wendell Herty Taylor. *A Catalogue of Crime*. New York: Harper & Row, 1971.

BIOGRAPHIES

Randall, David. *Dukedom Large Enough*. New York: Random House, 1969.

Wolf, Edwin, and John Fleming. *Rosenbach*. Cleveland: World Publishing, 1960.

MAGAZINES AND JOURNALS

The Colophon. New York: 1930–50.

The Book Collector. London: 1952–   . The Collector Ltd. 58 Frith Street.

American Book Collector. 1434 So. Yale Avenue, Arlington Heights, Ill. 61312

Antiquarian Book Monthly Review. London.

The Dolphin. 4 vols. New York: Limited Editions Club, 1933–41.

The Fleuron. 7 vols. Cambridge: Cambridge Univ. Press, 1923–30.

Signature. London: Curwen Press, 1935–52.

AUCTION RECORDS

Book Auction Records. 1902–   . Kent, England: Wm. Dawson & Sons, Ltd.

American Book Prices Current. 1895–   New York: Bancroft-Parkman, Inc.

Author Bibliographies

Too numerous to mention here, reliable author bibliographies are available in the reference section of most big libraries. The collector would do well to choose the most modern and complete bibliography of individual authors or subjects of interest available in order to secure accuracy of description.

Book Prices

Bradley, Van Allen. *The Book Collector's Handbook of Values.* Rev. ed. New York: G. P. Putnam, 1975.*

---

* The prices indicated in this work are by no means standard among dealers since they reflect the value of a particular title in a given year and presumably in fine condition. As condition varies among copies of the same title, and prices reflect the rise and fall of inflation in bad and good economic times, the collector must realize that the prices are subject to change.

ABAA Membership List

ABRAMS, HARVEY DAN
  2637 Peachtree Road, N.E., Atlanta, Georgia 30305
  Georgia, Southern and Confederate Americana, Maps & Prints

ACRES OF BOOKS, INC.
  633 Main Street, Cincinnati, Ohio 45202   (513) 721-4214
  Out of Print, Fiction, Nonfiction

ADELSON, RICHARD H., ANTIQUARIAN BOOK-SELLER
  North Pomfret, Vermont 05053   (802) 457-2608
  *Voyages, Americana, Western Americana, Maps & Atlases, Rare
  Natural History*

ALBATROSS BOOK COMPANY
  166 Eddy Street, San Francisco, Calif. 94102   (415) 885-6501
  Large general stock of Antiquarian Books

ALDREDGE BOOK STORE
  2506 Cedar Springs, Dallas, Tex. 75201   (214) 823-2800
  Texas, Southwest, Fine Bindings, General Nonfiction

ALLEN, D. C.
  Box 3, 503 North Elm Street, Three Oaks, Mich. 49128
  (616) 756-9218
  *Social History, Commerce & Industry, Midwest, American 19th-
  century Literature*

Antiquarian Booksellers' Association of America, Inc.
630 Fifth Avenue, Shop 2 Concourse, New York, New York 10020

ALLENSON, ALEC R., INC.
635 East Ogden Avenue, Naperville, Ill. 60540   (312) 355-2595
Theology, Religion

ALTA CALIFORNIA BOOKSTORE
1407 Solano Avenue, Albany, Calif. 94706   (415) 527-7711
Old Books, General Stock

422 North Coast Highway, Shop 2, Laguna Beach, Calif. 92651
(714) 494-5252
Antiquarian Ephemera, Broadsides & Pamphlets, Photographica, Printing & Bibliography, Literature, Americana, Mexicana

AMTMANN, BERNARD, INC.
1529 Sherbrooke Street West, Montreal, P.Q., Canada H3G IL7
(514) 935-2262
Canadiana

ANGLER'S & SHOOTER'S BOOKSHELF
Route 63, Goshen, Conn. 06756   (203) 491-2500 (By appointment)
Angling, Art (Sporting), Hunting, Shooting, Sporting Books

APPELFELD GALLERY
1372 York Avenue, New York, N.Y. 10021   (212) 988-7835
Appraisals, Fine Bindings, Rare Books, Standard Sets, English & American Literature, Autographs

APPEL, PAUL P.
119 Library Lane, Mamaroneck, N.Y. 10543   (914) 698-8115
Out-of-Print Scholarly in the Humanities, 20th-century Editions

ARGONAUT BOOK SHOP
792 Sutter Street, San Francisco, Calif. 94109   (415) 474-9067
Americana, California, Primitive Art, Western Prints, Manuscripts

ARGOSY BOOK STORES, INC.
116 East 59th Street, New York, N.Y. 10022   (212) 753-4455
Old Medical Books, Americana, First Editions, Old Maps, Old Prints

ARGUS BOOKS
2741 Riverside Boulevard, Sacramento, Calif. 95818
(916) 442-2223
California & the Far West, Out-of-print Social Science, Broadsides, Maps, Pamphlets

ARNOLD'S OF MICHIGAN
  511 South Union Street, Traverse City, Mich. 49684
  (616) 946-9212
  Literature, History, Children's Books, Hunting & Fishing

ATLANTIS BOOKS
  6513 Hollywood Boulevard, Hollywood, Calif. 90028, and Box
  38202, Hollywood, Calif. 90038   (213) 461-4491
  General Antiquarian, Political, Social & Economic History

BARKER, CONWAY, AUTOGRAPH DEALER
  1231 Sunset Lane, P.O. Box 35, La Marque, Texas 77568
  (714) 935-2810
  Autographs, Historical Manuscripts

BARNETTE'S BOOKS
  22727 Adams Road, South Bend, Ind. 46628   (219) 272-9880
  Americana, American Revolution

BARTFIELD, J. N.
  45 West 57th Street, New York, N.Y. 10019   (212) 753-1830
  Color Plate Books

BEAVER BOOK STORE
  1027 S.W. 5th Avenue, Portland, Oregon 97204   (503) 223-7959
  General, Western Americana, Victorian & Modern Fiction, American & English Literature, Illustrated Books

BEIL, DOROTHY—BOOKS
  2712-9th St., North, P.O. Box 7045, St. Petersburg, Fla. 33734
  (813) 822-3278
  First Editions, Fine Press Books, Americana, Floridiana, General Out of Print

BENELL BOOKSHOP
  P.O. Box 351, Cooper Station, New York, N.Y. 10003
  (212) 662-7928
  Education, Latin America, Out of Print

BENJAMIN, WALTER R., AUTOGRAPHS, INC.
  P.O. Box 255, Scribner Hollow Road, Hunter, N.Y. 12442
  (518) 263-4133
  Autographs, Letters & Manuscripts; History, Music Science

BENNETT & MARSHALL RARE BOOKS
  8214 Melrose Avenue, Los Angeles, Calif. 90046   (213) 653-7040

Americana, Travels & Voyages, First Editions, Early Maps, Prints, Manuscripts, Literature

BERLIAWSKY, LILLIAN—BOOKS
23 Bay View Street, Camden, Maine 04843   (207) 236-3903
General Americana & European History, Biography, Literature, Music & the Arts

BERNETT, F. A., INC.
2001 Palmer Avenue, Larchmont, N.Y. 10538   (914) 834-3026
Fine Arts, Archeology, Architecture, Bibliography

BEST BOOKS
P.O. Box 701, Folkston, Ga. 31537   (912) 496-2193
Americana, Biography, English & American Literature, Military: World Wars I & II, 19th-century Prints

BIBBY, G. A.—BOOKS
714 Pleasant Street, Roseville, Calif. 95678   (916) 783-3270
Gardening, Horticulture, Natural History

BIBLION, INC.
P.O. Box 9, Forest Hills, N.Y. 11375   (212) 263-3910
Scientific Periodicals, History of Science, Medicine (Early)

BLACK SUN BOOKS
667 Madison Avenue, Suite 1005, New York, N.Y. 10021
(212) 688-6622
19th- & 20th-century First Editions, Press Books, Fine Printing, Manuscripts, Letters

BLEDSOE, WILLIAM, BOOKSELLER
P.O. Box 763, San Carlos, Calif. 94070   (415) 593-6878
Business & Economics, Industrial & Labor Relations, Political Theory and Practice, Government, Foreign Affairs

BOND, NELSON
4724 Easthill Drive, Sugarloaf Farms, Roanoke, Va. 24018
(703) 774-2674
Literature, Association Copies, Virginiana

BOOK CHEST
19 Oxford Place, Rockville Centre, N.Y. 11570   (516) 766-6105
Natural History, Birds, Botany, Orchids, Zoology

BOOK GALLERY
512 Mamaroneck Avenue, White Plains, N.Y. 10605
(914) 949-5406

Architecture, Fine & Applied Arts, Rare Books, Fine Printing, Search Service

BOOK STALL
126 North Church Street, Rockford, Ill. 61101   (815) 963-1671; 398-2113
Americana, Scholarly Books, General Out of Print, Illinoisiana

BOOKS FOR COLLECTORS
60 Urgan Street, Stamford, Conn. 06905   (203) 323-1726
Americana, Nautical, Limited Editions, Fine Bindings, Books about Books

BOOKS-ON-FILE
7014 Park Avenue, Guttenberg, N.J. 07093   (201) 869-8786
Search Service, General

BOOKED Up INC.
1214 31st St., N.W., Washington, D.C. 20007   (202) 965-3244
English & American Literature, Modern First Editions, Travel & Exploration, Belles Lettres

THE BOOKPRESS, LTD.
P.O. Box K.P. 420 Prince George Street, Williamsburg, Va. 23185
Rare Books, Old Prints, Maps

BOSWELL, ROY V.
P.O. Box 278, Gilroy, Calif. 95020   (408) 842-9702
Antiquarian Books & Maps, History of Cartography, Discovery & Exploration

BRADLEY, VAN ALLEN, INC.
P.O. Box 578, Lake Zurich, Ill. 60010 (Barrington, Ill.) (312) 381-4299
Literary First Editions, Historical Americana, Rare & Fine Books, Autographs & Manuscripts

BRATTLE BOOK SHOP
5 West Street, Boston, Mass. 02111   (617) 542-0210
General, Economics, Sociology, Political, Fiction

BRENTANO'S, INC.
586 Fifth Avenue, New York, N.Y. 10036   (212) 757-8600
Rare Books, First Editions, Fine Bindings, Sporting Books, Color Plate Books, Autographs

BREWER, HARVEY W.
270 Herbert Avenue, Closter, N.J. 07624   (201) 768-4414

Fine & Applied Arts, Color Plate Books, Photography, Architecture, Textiles

BRICK ROW BOOK SHOP
251 Post Street, San Francisco, Calif. 94108   (415) 398-0414
English & American Literature, Bibliography, Texas, Mexico & Latin America

BROUDE BROTHERS, LTD.
56 West 45th Street, New York, N.Y. 10036
Early Books on Music, Fine Facsimile Reprints of Music, Music Books & Music Literature

BROWN, ROBERT K., ART & BOOKS
120 East 86th Street, New York, N.Y. 10028   (212) 427-4014
20th-century Fine & Applied Art, Illustrated Books & Original Posters

BUCCANEER BOOK CO.
P.O. Box 1881, St. Augustine, Fla. 32084   (904) 824-4617

BURGER & EVANS
3421 Geary Boulevard, San Francisco, Calif. 94118
(415) 752-8582
Autographs & Historical Manuscripts on Early America, Early West & California, Prints, Paintings

BURSTEIN, HAROLD M.
16 Park Place, Waltham, Mass. 02154   (617) 893-7974
Reference, Bibliography, Scholarly Journals, Americana, American Literature

BUSCK, HARRY, BOOKSELLER
710 North Humphrey Avenue, Oak Park, Ill. 60302
(312) 848-2850
General, Old, Rare, Out of Print

ROGER BUTTERFIELD, INC., ANTIQUARIAN BOOKSELLERS
White House, Hartwick, N.Y. 13348

CALER, JOHN W., PUBLICATIONS CORP.
7506 Clybourn Avenue, Sun Valley, Calif. 91352
(213) 877-1664; (213) 765-1210
Aeronautics, Military History, Science Fiction, General

CANTERBURY BOOKSHOP
29 East Congress Parkway, Chicago, Ill. 60605   (312) 939-2923

Literary Biography & Criticism, English & American Literature, Books on Books, the Arts, Chicago, Hunting, Fishing

CARAVAN BOOK STORE
605 South Grand Avenue, Los Angeles, Calif. 90017
(213) 626-9944
Western Americana, Military History, Railroads, Early Travel & Exploration, Antiques & Rare Books

CARAVAN—MARITIME BOOKS
87-06 168th Place, Jamaica, N.Y. 11432   (212) 526-1380
Arctica, Early Steamships, Logs, Modeling, Naval History, Shipbuilding, Americana

CARLOS BOOK STALL
1115 San Carlos Avenue, San Carlos, Calif. 94070
(415) 593-3392
California, Fore Edge Painted Books, 17th- and 18th-century Bindings, Rare and General

CARRY BACK BOOKS
Franconia, N.H. 03580   (603) 823-8892
Vermont, White Mountains, Literature, Americana, Hemingway

THE CARTOGRAPHER
168 Governor Street, Providence, R.I. 02906
Maps

CASSIDY, WILLIAM J.
109 East 65th Street, Kansas City, Mo. 64113   (816) 361-4271
Economics, Political Science, Sociology, Dance

CELLAR BOOK SHOP
18090 Wyoming, P.O. Box 6, College Park Station, Detroit, Mich. 48221   (313) 861-1776
Orientalia, Philippines, Pacific Islands, Africa, City Planning

CELMER'S BOOK STORE
4433 North Broadway, Chicago, Ill. 60640   (312) 334-9237
Bibliography, Books about Books, Americana, Rare Books & Prints, Early Comic Books & Art

CHEROKEE BOOKSHOP, INC.
6607 Hollywood Boulevard, Hollywood, Calif. 90028
(213) 463-6090
Americana, Biography, Business, Education, Folklore, Hispanic, Literature, Indians, Military

CHILTON'S INC.
938-944 Conti Street, Mobile, Ala. 36604   (205) 432-3036
Old Prints, Natural History, Old Maps, Americana

CHISWICK BOOK SHOP, INC.
Walnut Tree Hill Road, Sandy Hook, Conn. 06482
(203) 426-3220
Rare Books, First Editions, Private Presses, Illustrated Books, Typography & Calligraphy

CLARE, ROY W.—ANTIQUARIAN AND UNCOMMON BOOKS
47 Woodshire South, Getzville, N.Y. 14068   (716) 688-8723
Incunabula, 16th and 17th centuries (all subjects), Early Books in English, Witchcraft

CLARK'S, TAYLOR, INC.
2623 Government Street, Baton Rouge, La. 70806
(504) 342-4929
Natural History Color Plate Books, Audubon Prints, Louisiana

COGITATOR BOOKSTORE
919 Foster Avenue, Evanston, Ill. 60201   (312) 869-7783
English & American Literature, Literary Criticism & Biography, Performing Arts

COLEMAN, LUCILE—A-Z BOOK SERVICE
P.O. Box 610813, North Miami, Fla. 33161
19th & 20th-century Biography, Poetry, Juveniles, Fiction, Search Service

CORNER BOOK SHOP
102 Fourth Avenue, New York, N.Y. 10003   (212) 254-7714
Food & Drink (Old), Cinema, Drama, Textiles, Herbals (Old)

COUNTRY LANE BOOKS
Box 47, Collinsville, Conn. 06022   (203) 693-2245
Arctic, Travel, Children's Books, Americana, Sporting & First Editions

COUTANT, GRACE H.
R.D. 4, Box 342, Amsterdam Road, Scotia, N.Y. 12302
(518) 372-1916
Back Number Magazines, Dolls, Needlework

COWAN, NATHANIEL L.
2196 Stoll Road, Saugerties, N.Y. 12477   (914) 679-6475

English Literature, American Literature, Medieval Literature, Art, American History

CURRENT COMPANY
12 Howe Street, Bristol, R.I. 02809 (401) 253-7824
Americana, Literature, First & Rare Editions of Important Books, Travel Marine

CURREY, L. W., INC.
18 Church Street, Elizabethtown, N.Y. 12932 (518) 873-6477
19th-century American Literature & History, Modern First Editions, Fantasy & Science Fiction, Fine Printing

DABNEY, Q. M. & Co.
Box 31061 (4894 Stamp Road), Washington, D.C. 20031
(301) 423-9077
History, Social Sciences, Government Publications, Literary Criticism, Search Service

DALY, CHARLES, COLLECTION
36 Golf Lane, Ridgefield, Conn. 06877 (203) 448-6790
Angling, Art, Sporting, Guns, Hunting

DAME, NATHANIEL & Co.
127–133 Walden Street, Cambridge, Mass. 02140
(617) 876-6846
Fiction & Juveniles, New & Remainders

DAUBER & PINE, INC.
66 Fifth Avenue, New York, N.Y. 10011 (212) 675-6340
Americana, American & English Literature, Art, History

DAVIES, OWEN—BOOKSELLER
1214 North La Salle Street, Chicago, Ill. 60610 (312) 642-6697
Travels & Voyages, Naval History, Shipping, Railroads, Aeronautics

DAWSON'S BOOK SHOP
535 North Larchmont Boulevard, Los Angeles, Calif. 90004
(213) 469-2186
Western Americana Books about Books, Sets, Printing, Miniature Books, Rare Books

DECKER, PETER
45 West 57th Street, New York, N.Y. 10019 (212) 755-8945
Americana, Western Americana, Western Canadiana; Voyages & Explorations, Travel in America

DREW'S BOOK SHOP
P.O. Box 163, Santa Barbara, Calif. 93101   (805) 966-6083
Americana, Literature, Literary Criticism, Prints

DRISCOLL, EMILY
P.O. Box 834, Shepherdstown, West Va. 25443   (304) 876-2202
Autographs, Manuscripts, Drawings, Illustrations, Association Books

DUNAWAY, R., BOOKSELLER
6138 Delmar Boulevard, St. Louis, Mo. 63112   (314) 725-1581
*Bibliography, Biography (Literary), First Editions, Literary Criticism,
Out of Print*

DUSCHNES, PHILIP C.
699 Madison Avenue, New York, N.Y. 10021   (212) 838-2635
*Rare Bibles, Bindings, Fine Printing & Press Books, First Editions,
Manuscripts*

DWYER'S BOOKSTORE, INC.
P.O. Box 646, 44 Main Street, Northampton, Mass. 01060

DYKES, JEFF—WESTERN BOOKS
Box 38, College Park, Md. 20740   (301) 864-0666
*Range Livestock, Western Illustrators, Outlaws, Rangers, County
Histories, J. Frank Dobie*

EAST AND WEST SHOP, INC.
4 Appleblossom Lane, Newton, Conn. 06470   (203) 426-0661
*Orientalia, Oriental History, Oriental Philosophy, Oriental Litera-
ture, Oriental Topography*

EBENSTEN, HANNS & COMPANY
55 West 42nd Street, New York, N.Y. 10036

EBERSTADT, EDWARD, & SONS
70 Park Street, Montclair, N.J. 07042   (201) 783-6675
Western Americana, Rare Books, Manuscripts, Paintings

EDGEWATER BOOK STORE
5941½ North Broadway, Chicago, Ill. 60660   (312) 271-4657
General, Used, Search Service, Out of Print

EDMUNDS, LARRY
6658 Hollywood Boulevard, Hollywood, Calif. 90028
(213) 463-3273
Cinema, Theatre, Art, Used Books

EMDIN, JACOB L.
11 Euclid Avenue, Summit, N.J. 07901
American & English Literature, New Jersiana

ERIE BOOK STORE
717 French Street, Erie, Pa. 16501   (814) 452-3354
Western Pennsylvania, General Used Books, Early Pennsylvania Oil, Great Lakes

ESTATE BOOK SALES
1724 H St., N.W., Washington, D.C. 20006   (202) 298-7355

FALES, EDWARD C.
P.O. Box 56, Salisbury, N.H. 03268   (603) 648-2484
Manuscripts, Crafts, Cookery, Gardening, Americana

FLEMING, JOHN F., INC.
322 East 57th Street, New York, N.Y. 10022   (212) 755-3242
Rare Books, Manuscripts, 10th to 20th century

FONDA BOOKS
P.O. Box 1800, Nantucket, Mass. 02554   (617) 228-1821
Manuscripts Relating to Whaling & its Maritime Associations, Nautical Explorations, and Nantuckeriana

FORDHAM BOOK COMPANY
Box 6, New Rochelle, N.Y. 10801   (914) 632-7771
Philosophy, General History, Literature

FRASER, JAMES L.
309 S. Willard Street, Burlington, Vt. 05401   (802) 658-0322
Americana (Business), Business History, Economics, Stock Market, Wall Street

FRENCH, PALMER D., ANTIQUARIAN BOOKSELLER
P.O. Box 2704, Oakland, Calif. 94602   (415) 530-1648 By mail and appointment
General Out of Print & Antiquarian Books, Emphasis on Exploration, History, Americana

FRISCH, HOWARD
Old Post Road, Livingston, N.Y. 12541   (518) 851-7493
(also) P.O. Box 128, Village Station, New York, N.Y. 10014
Illustrated Books, American Fiction, pre-1940

FROHNSDORFF, DORIS
P.O. Box 2306, Gaithersburg, Md. 20760   (301) 869-1256
Rare & Early Children's Books, Illustrated Books, Miniature Books

FRONT, THEODORE
    131 N. Robertson Boulevard, Beverly Hills, Calif. 90211
    (213) 652-9757
    Books on Music, Rare, Old & New, Scores, Sheet Music

GACH, JOHN, BOOKSHOP, INC.
    3322 Greemount Avenue, Baltimore, Md. 21218   (301) 467-6024
    or 467-4344
    Maryland, Menckeniana, Humanities & Sciences, Black Studies

GAISSER, KENDALL G.
    1242 Broadway, Toledo, Ohio 43609   (419) 243-7631
    Art, History, Literature, Military, Rare Books

GATES, W. C., BOOKS
    1279 Bardstown Road, Louisville, Ky. 40204   (502) 451-3295
    Americana (Kentucky, South), Fiction, American Before 1900

GENNS, W. T.—BOOKS
    Studio 1, 116 E. De La Guerra Street, P.O. Box 1328, Santa
    Barbara, Calif. 93102   (805) 965-5817
    Americana, General, Press Books

GILMAN, STANLEY
    237 East 9th Street, P.O. Box 131, Cooper Station, New York, N.Y.
    10003
    American History, Literature, Newspaper History, Out of Print

GINSBERG, MICHAEL, INC.
    P.O. Box 402, Sharon, Mass. 02067   (617) 784-8181

GLENN BOOKS, INC.
    1227 Baltimore, Kansas City, Mo. 64105   (816) 842-9777
    *Western Americana, Aeronautica, Typography, Books about Books,
    Bindings, Press Books, Rare Books*

GLOBE AND ANCHOR BOOKS CO.
    P.O. Box 1173, St. Augustine, Fla. 32084   (904) 834-4717

GOLDSCHMIDT, LUCIEN, INC.
    1117 Madison Avenue, New York, N.Y. 10028   (212) 879-0070
    *Bindings, Illustrated Books, French Literature, Architecture, Prints
    & Drawings*

GOODSPEEDS BOOK SHOP, INC.
    18 Beacon Street, Boston, Mass. 02108, also 2 Milk Street, Boston,
    Mass. 02108   (617) 523-5970
    Autographs, Americana, Genealogies, First Editions, Prints

GORE, MARIAN L.
   Box 433, San Gabriel, Calif. 91775   (213) 287-2946
   Cookery, Wine, Beverages, Gardening, Herbs

GOTHAM BOOK MART & GALLERY, INC.
   41 West 47th Street, New York, N.Y. 10036   (212) 757-0367
   20th-century Literary Manuscripts & Letters, 20th-century Rare Books, Theatre Arts, Film, Poetry & Prose

HAROLD E. GRAVES
   500 Kappock Avenue, Bronx, N.Y. 10463
   Appraisals

GREGORY, K.
   222 East 71st Street, New York, N.Y. 10021   (212) 288-2119
   Illustrated Books, Decorative Old Prints, Horticulture, Valentines & Greeting Cards before 1875, Playing Cards

HALL, NORMAN ALEXANDER
   Mormandie Road, Dover, Mass. 02030   (617) 785-1744
   Appraisals

HAMILL & BARKER
   230 North Michigan Avenue, Chicago, Ill. 60601   (312) 236-9782
   First Editions, Literary Autographs, Early Illustrated Books, Incunabula

HAMMER, MILTON, BOOKS
   819 Anacapa Street, Santa Barbara, Calif. 93101   (805) 966-4666
   Literature, Americana, Art Books, Maps

HAMPTON BOOKS
   Rt. 1, Box 76, Newberry, S.C. 29108   (803) 276-6870
   Cinema-TV in all Languages, South Carolina, Aerospace in all Languages

HANRAHAN, J. & J.
   67 Bow Street, Portsmouth, N.H. 03801   (603) 436-6234
   Rare Books, English & American Literature, New Hampshire, Mosher Press, Modern First Editions

HARDY, GRAHAME—BOOKS
   P.O. Box 449, Virginia City, Nev. 89440
   Railroadiana, Automobiliana, Trade Catalogs, Western Americana, Nevadiana

HARPER, LATHROP C., INC.
   22 East 40th Street, New York, N.Y. 10016   (212) 532-5115

Incunabula, Illuminated Manuscripts, Illustrated Books, History of Science & Medicine, Early Americana, Voyages, Natural History

HARRIS, DORIS—AUTOGRAPHS
5410 Wilshire Boulevard, Los Angeles, Calif. 90036
(213) 939-4500
Autograph Letters & Manuscripts

HAYMAN, ROBERT G., ANTIQUARIAN BOOKS
R.F.D. 1, Carey, Ohio 43316   (419) 396-8104
Americana, Ohio Valley & Midwestern States, Great Lakes, Ohio & Mississippi Rivers, Western Americana

HEINMAN, W. S., IMPORTED BOOKS
1966 Broadway, New York, N.Y. 10023   (212) 787-3154
Africana, Dictionaries, Reference, Technical

HEINOLDT BOOKS
Central & Buffalo Avenues, S. Egg Harbor, N.J. 08215
(609) 965-2284
Western Americana, American Revolution, American Colonial Period, American Indian, American Early Travels & Explorations

HELLER, F. THOMAS
308 East 79th Street, New York, N.Y. 10021   (212) 737-4484
Early Science, Early Medicine, Early Natural History, Psychiatry, Psychoanalysis

HENNESSEYS, THE
4th & Woodlawn, Saratoga, N.Y. 12866   (518) 584-4921

HERITAGE BOOK SHOP, INC.
847 North La Cienega Boulevard, Los Angeles, Calif. 90069
(213) 659-3674
First Editions of 19th and 20th centuries, Fine Printing, Rare Books, Bibliography

HERTZ, ALEXANDER, & CO., INC.
88-28 - 43rd Avenue, Elmhurst, N.Y. 11373   (212) 898-6917
Russia & Eastern Europe, General Slavica, Baltic & Balkan Countries

HICKOK, ERNEST S.
382 Springfield Avenue, Summit, N.J. 07901   (201) 277-1427
American Paintings, Prints, Books (Color Plate), Sporting Etchings

HILLTOP HOUSE
1 The Loch, Roslyn, Long Island, N.Y. 11576   (516) 621-0674
Botany, Horticulture, Orchids

HOFMANN & FREEMAN, ANTIQUARIAN BOOKSELLERS
P.O. Box 207, Cambridge, Mass. 02138
English Books before 1700, 18th- & 19th-century English Litera-ture, Literary Manuscripts & Autographs, Early Historical Manu-scripts, Early Continental Books

HOLMAN'S PRINT SHOP, INC.
28 Court Square, Boston, Mass. 02108   (617) 523-8187
Historical Prints, Fine Prints, Marine Prints & Drawings, Engraved Portraits, Old Maps

HOLMES BOOK CO.
274 Fourteenth Street, Oakland, Calif. 94612   (415) 893-6860, also 22 Third Street, San Francisco, Calif. 94103   (415) 362-3283
California Western Americana, General Literature, First Editions

HOUSATONUC BOOKSHOP
Salisbury, Conn. 06068   (203) 435-2100
General Literature, First & Rare Editions, Scholarly (New & Old)

HOUSE OF BOOKS, LTD.
667 Madison Avenue, New York, N.Y. 10021   (212) 755-5998
Twentieth-century First Editions, Autograph Material

HOUSE OF EL DIEFF, INC.
139 E. 63rd Street, New York, N.Y. 10021   (212) 838-4160
Rare Books & Manuscripts

HOWARD, VERNON—BOOKS
P.O. Box 693, Millbrae, Calif. 94030, also Gamut Book Shop, 723 California Drive, Burlingame, Calif. 94010   (415) 343-7428
Mountaineering, Literature, Western Americana, Scholarly

HOWELL, JOHN—BOOKS
434 Post Street, San Francisco, Calif. 94102   (415) 781-7795
Fine and Rare Books, Paintings, Prints, in all Fields

HOWEY, RALPH T.
Hampton House, 7G, 1600 Hagys Ford, Narberth, Pa. 19072
(215) 664-3886 By appointment

HUNLEY, MAXWELL
9533 Santa Monica Boulevard, Beverly Hills, Calif. 90210
(213) 275-7466

Western Americana, American & English First Editions, Early Juveniles, Fine Press Books, Early American Plays & Poetry

HURLEY BOOKS
Rt. 12, Westmoreland, N.H. 03467   (603) 399-4342
Railroads, New England History, Theology, American Literature & Early Farming

INMAN'S BOOK SHOP
50 East 50th Street, New York, N.Y. 10022   (212) 755-2867
First Editions, Fine Bindings, Standard Sets

INTERNATIONAL BOOK FINDERS, INC.
Box 1, Pacific Palisades, Calif. 90272
Search Service, Western Americana, Horse Books, Literature, Rare Books

INTERNATIONAL UNIVERSITY BOOKSELLERS, INC.
101 Fifth Avenue, New York, N.Y. 10003   (212) 691-5252
Backfiles of Scientific & Scholarly Periodicals (All languages)

JACOBS, DOUGLAS M.
P.O. Box 363, Bethel, Conn. 06801   (203) 748-6222
General Literature, First & Limited Editions, Manuscript & Autograph Material

JELTRUPS' BOOKS
51 ABC Company Street, Christiansted, St. Croix, U.S. Virgin Islands 00820   (809) 733-1018
Caribbean & West Indian Books

JENKINS COMPANY
Box 2085, Austin, Texas, 78767   (512) 444-6616
Texas, Western Americana, Literary First Editions, Bibliography, Autographs

JOHNSON, JOHN
R.F.D. 2, North Bennington, Vt. 05257   (802) 442-6738
Natural History, Botany, Birds, Fish, Reptiles, Zoology, Invertebrates

JOHNSON, WALTER J., INC.
355 Chestnut Street, Norwood, N.J. 07648   N.Y. (212) 947-4560
N.J. (201) 767-1303
Periodicals & Books, Scientific, Medical, Liberal Arts, All Languages
Branch Office: Walter J. Johnson, Inc. Feschaftsstelle in Deutschland, Goldergweg 4, 6 Frankfurt Am Main, West Germany

JOSEPH THE PROVIDER BOOKS
903 State Street, Santa Barbara, Calif. 93101
*Modern Literature, First Editions, Manuscripts, Signed Books &
Autographs*

JOYCE BOOKSHOPS
2187 Salvio Street, Concord, Calif. 94566, also 1116 Franklin
Street, Oakland, Calif. 94612, also 538 – 15th Street, Oakland,
Calif. 94612 (415) 689-7412; (415) 452-2571; (415) 834-8108
*Out of Print, Rare, Periodicals, Antiquarian, Wholesale (Used
Only)*

KANE, NORMAN, THE AMERICANIST
1525 Shenkel Road, Pottstown, Pa. 19464 (215) 323-5289
*American Fiction, Americana, American Poetry, American Drama,
Pennsylvania Books, Pamphlets & Broadsides*

KAPLAN, CAROLYN
P.O. Box 201, Laguna Beach, Calif. 92652 (714) 497-1098
Plays, Drama

KEATS, IRVING
280 Del Mesa Carmel, Carmel, Calif. 93921
*First Editions, Literature, Fine Bindings, Press Books, Color Plate
Books, Literary & Musical Autographs*

KEBABIAN, JOHN S.
2 Winding Lane, Scarsdale, N.Y. 10583 (914) 472-4897
General

KENNEDY'S BOOK SHOP
1911 Central Street, Evanston, Ill. 60201 (312) 864-4449
Out of Print, Scholarly Books, General

KLEMM, GAIL—BOOKS
P.O. Box 1327, Richardson, Tex. 75080 (214) 239-0010
*Early and Contemporary Children's Books, Western Americana,
California, Printing, Papermaking & Typography*

KRAUS, H. P.
16 East 46th Street, New York, N.Y. 10017 (212) 687-4808
*Medieval Manuscripts, Incunabula, Americana, Cartography, History
of Science*

KRAUS-THOMSON ORGANIZATION, LTD.
Route 100, Millwood, N.Y. 10546 (914) 762-2200

Scholarly Periodicals and Books in all Fields & Languages, Bibliographies, Reference & Standard Works in all Disciplines

KREBS, EDGAR
    5849 N. Talman Avenue, Chicago, Ill. 60659   (312) 275-4611
    Americana, History, Literature, Fiction, Out of Print

KRONOVET, DR. MILTON
    881-C Balmoral Court, Lakewood, N.J. 08701   (201) 477-7771
    Autograph Letters, Manuscripts; Historical, Presidential, Literary, Theatrical

LA CHANCE, DONALD
    5105 Bridge Street, P.O. Box L, Cambria, Calif. 93428   (805) 927-4145
    American & English First Editions, Limited Editions, Book Search Service

LEEKLEY BOOK SEARCH
    711 Sheridan Road, P.O. Box 337, Winthrop Harbor, Ill. 60096
    (312) 872-2311
    History & Culture, Sciences & Arts of the Peoples of North America, England & Ireland

LENNIE'S BOOK NOOK
    81–24 Melrose Avenue, Los Angeles, Calif. 90046
    (213) 651-5584
    Literature, Biography, Cinema, Theater, Americana, Fine Editions

LEVINSON, HARRY A.
    Box 534, Beverly Hills, Calif. 90213   (213) 276-9311
    16th- to 19th-century English & Continental Books, Early Travel & Geography, Early Science & Medicine, Incunabula, Bibliography

LEWIS, R. E., INC.
    P.O. Box 72, Nicasio, Calif. 94946   (415) 456-6393
    Old Masters & Modern Engravings & Etchings, Japanese Prints, Illustrated Books and Sets, Indian & Persian Miniature Paintings

LIEBMANN, WILLIAM B.
    2 Blue Ribbon Drive, Westport, Conn. 06880   (203) 227-2240
    Rare Books, Manuscripts, Appraisals

LOWE, JAMES, AUTOGRAPHS
    2 Pennsylvania Plaza, Suite 2870, New York, N.Y. 10001
    (212) 889-8204

Autographs, Manuscripts, Documents in all Fields, Limited Signed Editions, Americana

LUBRECHT, HARRY D.
  4672 Broadway, New York, N.Y. 10040   (212) 942-3086
  General

M & S RARE BOOKS, INC.
  Box 311, 45 Colpitts Road, Weston, Mass. 02193   (617) 891-5650
  19th-century American Thought & Literature, Americana, Science & Medicine

McGILVERY, LAURENCE
  P.O. Box 852, La Jolla, Calif. 92037   (714) 454-4443
  Fine Arts

MacEWEN, AIMEE B.—BOOKSELLER
  Victorian House, Stockton Springs, Maine 04981   (207) 567-3351
  Americana, Maine, Detective Fiction, General

MACKENZIE, ISOBEL
  4162 St. Catherine St. West, Montreal 6, P.Q., Canada
  (514) 933-5575
  Americana (Canadian), Juveniles, Hunting & Fishing, Fine Bindings, Maps & Prints

MacMANUS, GEORGE S. Co.
  1317 Irving Street, Philadelphia, Pa. 19107   (215) 735-4456
  Americana, Literature, First Editions, Autographs, Manuscripts

MAGEE, DAVID, BOOK SHOP
  3108 B Fillmore Street, San Francisco, Calif. 94123
  (415) 567-1888
  Early Printing, Fine Press Books, Western Americana, First Editions

MAGIC, INC.
  5082 North Lincoln Avenue, Chicago, Ill. 60625   (312) 334-2855
  Conjuring, Playing Cards, Punch & Judy, Street Entertainers, Marionettes

MARSHALL FIELD & CO.
  111 North State Street, Chicago, Ill. 60602   (312) 781-1000
  Fine Bindings, First Editions of English & American Literature, Illustrated Books, Antiquarian

MAXWELL SCIENTIFIC INTERNATIONAL, INC.
  Fairview Park, Elmsford, N.Y. 10523

Periodicals—Pure & Applied Sciences, Medicine, Social Sciences, Humanities, Encyclopedias

MENDOZA, ISAAC, BOOK CO.
15 Ann Street, New York, N.Y. 10038   (212) 227-8777
Modern First Editions, Detective Stories, Science Fiction

MINKOFF, GEORGE ROBERT, INC.
Rowe Road, R.F.D. #3, Box 147, Great Barrington, Mass. 01230
(413) 528-4575
Modern First Editions, Private Press Books, American & English Literature, Americana, Manuscripts

MINTERS, ARTHUR H.
84 University Place, New York, N.Y. 10003   (212) 989-0593
Catalogues, Periodicals & Books on the Fine Arts & Affiliated Fields, Architecture, Original Works of Art

MORRILL, EDWARD & SON, INC.
25 Kingston Street, Boston, Mass. 02111   (617) 482-3090
Books pertaining to the American Scene

E. E. MOORE
P.O. Box 243, Wynnewood, Pa. 19096
Autographs, Manuscripts, Americana

MORRISON, W. M.
P.O. Box 3277, Waco, Tex. 76707
Texas, West, Southwest, Civil War (Southern)

MOTT, HOWARD S., INC.
South Main Street, Sheffield, Mass. 01257   (413) 229-2019
Rare Books, First Editions, Autographs, Americana, all 16th to 20th century

MUNS, J. B., BOOKS
1733 Riverview Street, Eugene, Ore. 97403   (503) 345-6357
Fine Arts, Music, Architecture, City Planning

MURRAY, SAMUEL
477 Main Street, Wilbraham, Mass. 01095   (413) 596-3801
Bibliography, Rare Books, Papermaking, Miniature Books, Juvenilia

NEBENZAHL, KENNETH, INC.
333 North Michigan Avenue, Chicago, Ill. 60601
(312) 641-2711
Rare Americana, Voyages & Travels, Atlases, Maps, Prints

NEEDHAM BOOK FINDERS
2317 Westwood Boulevard, Los Angeles, Calif. 90064
(213) 475-9553
General, Search Service, Literature, Sets

NEWMAN, JULIA SWEET
P.O. Box 99, Battle Creek, Mich. 49016   (616) 965-3637
American Historical Materials, Autographs

NORMAN, JEREMY, & CO.
442 Post Street, San Francisco, Calif. 94102   (415) 781-6402
*Medicine, Science, Technology, Natural History, Voyages & Travels,
Fine Arts, Illustrated Books*

NORMILE, JAMES—BOOKS
6888 Alta Loma Terrace, Los Angeles, Calif. 90068
(213) 874-8434
*Arts of Africa, Oceania, Asia, Ancient Americas, Drawings, Prints,
First Editions*

NORTH, PAUL H., JR.
81 Bullitt Park Place, Columbus, Ohio 43209   (614) 252-1826
*American History & Travel, Ohioana, First Editions, Manuscripts,
Paintings*

NORTHWEST BOOKS
3814 Lyon Avenue, Oakland, Calif. 94601   (415) 532-5227
*Western Americana, Fine Arts, Fine Prints, Oriental Art, Color
Plate Books*

O'BRIEN, F. M.
34 High Street, Portland, Maine 04101   (207) 774-0931
Americana, Maine History, Political Economy, Education, Literature

OFFENBACHER, EMIL
84–50 Austin Street, Kew Gardens, N.Y. 11415   (212) 849-5834
*Books of 16th & 17th centuries (General), Early Medicine, Early
Science*

O'HARA, JOSEPH, BOOKSELLER
1311 East 57th Street, Chicago, Ill. 60637   (312) 363-0993
General stock, Used, Out of Print, 100,000 volumes

OLD BOOK HOME
3217 West Cora, Box 7777, Rosewood Station, Spokane, Wash.
99208   (509) 327-2884
Appraisals, Out of Print, Food & Drink, Wine (New & Old)

OLD BOOK SHOP
   3110 Commodore Plaza, Coconut Grove (Miami) Fla. 33133
   General Out of Print, Scholarly, Florida, West Indies

OLD DRAGON'S BOOK DEN
   P.O. Box 186 (352 W. Cuba Road) Barrington, Ill. 60010
   (312) 381-4798
   Dogs: Books, Periodicals, Engravings, Paintings; Hunting & Guns:
   Books

OLD HICKORY BOOKSHOP
   Brinklow, Md. 20727   (301) 924-2225
   Medicine: Old, Rare, Out of Print

OLD MYSTIC BOOKSHOP
   58 Main Street, Old Mystic, Conn. 06372   (203) 536-6932
   Marine, Connecticut, Town & Local Histories, General Americana,
   Crime Fiction

O'NEAL, DAVID L., ANTIQUARIAN BOOKSELLERS
   New Ipswich, N.H. 03071   (603) 878-2232
   Typography, Printing History, Early American Literature, Rare
   Books

OLD OREGON BOOK STORE
   610 South West 12th Avenue, Portland, Ore. 97205
   (503) 227-2742
   Western Americana, Scholarly Books, American & English Litera-
   ture

OLD PRINT SHOP, INC., THE
   150 Lexington Avenue, New York, N.Y. 10016   (212) 683-3950
   Americana in Old Prints, Drawings, Water Colors, Paintings, Maps
   (Old American), Audubon, Dance, Color Plate Books

OLD SETTLER BOOKSHOP
   Walpole, N.H.   (603) 756-3685
   Mountain Climbing, American Literature

O'SHEA, JUNE—BOOKS
   1206½ South Roxbury Drive, Los Angeles, Calif. 90035
   (213) 553-0678
   Psychology, Psychiatry, Criminology

OTTENBERG BOOKS
   724 Pike Street, Seattle, Wash. 98101   (206) 682-5363

Anthropology, Africa below the Sahara, Literary Criticism, Primitive Art

OVERLAND BOOKSHOP
903 E. Hedrick Drive, Tucson, Ariz. 85719 (602) 623-5092
Arizona, West & Southwest, Mexico, Baja California

PACIFIC BOOK HOUSE
2109 D Kuhio Avenue, Honolulu, Hawaii 96815 (808) 923-0547
American & English Literature in First & Limited Editions, Pacific History & Exploration, Hawaiiana History, Exploration, Imprints

PAGEANT BOOK CO.
59 Fourth Avenue, New York, N.Y. 10003 (212) 674-5296
General Literature, Art & Illustrated Books, Old Maps & Prints, Americana, Fiction

PAINE, ALFRED W.
Wolfpits Road, Bethel, Conn. 06801 (203) 748-4125
Americana, Nautical Science, Naval History, Whaling, Voyages

PANGLOSS BOOKSHOP
1284 Massachusetts Avenue, Cambridge, Mass. 02138
(617) 354-4003
Literature, Social Sciences, Fine Arts, History, Philosophy

PARNASSUS BOOK SERVICE
Route 6A, Box 33, Yarmouthport, Mass. 02675 (617) 362-6420
Russia, History, Marine, Latin America, Search Service, Out-of-Print Titles

PARNASSUS BOOK SHOP
Rte. 9, Old State Library, Rhinebeck, N.Y. 12572

PAULSON, ROBERT A.
39 Downing Place, Harrington Park, N.J. 07640 (201) 768-6926
History, Biography, Music, Art, Signed Books

PETELLE'S INTERNATIONAL BOOKSEARCH
56 W. Maple Street, Chicago, Ill. 60610 (312) 787-5533
General, Out of Print, Search Service, Catholica, Miniature Books

PHIEBIG, ALBERT J., INC.
Box 352, White Plains, N.Y. 10602 (914) 948-0138
Foreign Books & Periodicals, Current or Out of Print, Search Service, Building Collections

PINKNEY, WILLIAM & LOIS M.—ANTIQUARIAN BOOKS
241 Mullin Street, Watertown, N.Y. 13601   (315) 788-2125
The West, Americana, American First Editions, New York State

POTTER, NICHOLAS—BOOKSELLER
203 East Palace, Santa Fe, N.M. 87501
Modern First Editions, Southwestern History

RAMER, RICHARD C.
225 East 70th Street, New York, N.Y. 10021   (212) 737-0222, 737-0223 Cable: Livroraro, NY
Luso-Brasiliana, Spain & Latin America, Americana, Nautical Science, Voyages & Travels

RARE BOOK COMPANY
P.O. Box 957, Freehold, N.J. 07728   (201) 780-1393
Christian Science Literature

REED, THEODORE—ANTIQUARIAN BOOKS
3789 Ocean Front Walk, San Diego, Calif. 92109
(714) 488-8001
Art, Californiana, Literature

REGENT HOUSE
108 North Roselake Avenue, Los Angeles, Calif. 90026
(213) 413-5027
Psychology, American Literature & History, Economics

JOANN REISLER
360 Glyndon Street, N.E., Vienna, Virginia 22180
Children's Books

RENDELL, KENNETH W., INC.
154 Wells Avenue, Newton, Mass. 02159   (617) 965-4670
Autograph Letters, Manuscripts, Documents in all Fields, Early American Newspapers, Papyri & Other Forms of Early Writing

WALTER REUBEN & CO.
601 Rio Grande Street, Austin, Texas 78701

REYNOLDS, J. E., BOOKSELLER
16031 Sherman Way, Van Nuys, Calif. 91406   (213) 785-6934
California, Western Americana, General Americana, Literary Criticism

RICHARDS, PAUL C. AUTOGRAPHS
P.O. Box 62, 49 Meadow Lane, Bridgewater, Mass. 02324
(617) 697-8086 or 293-3152

Autographs, Manuscripts, Political Americana, Signed Limited Editions, Inscribed & Associated First Editions

ROBERTS, LESTER—ANTIQUARIAN BOOKS
P.O. Box 6094, Terra Linda, Calif. 94903   (415) 479-0673
California, Americana, First Editions, Rare, Out of Print

ROBINSON, CEDRIC L.
597 Palisado Avenue, Windsor, Conn. 06095   (203) 688-2582
Civil War, Connecticut, Indians, the Sea, Western Americana

ROSENBERG, (MRS.) MARY S. INC.
100 West 72nd Street, New York, N.Y. 10023   (212) 362-4873
German & French; Humanities, Linguistics, Psychoanalysis, Music, Art, Judaica

ROSENTHAL, BERNARD M., INC.
251 Post Street, San Francisco, Calif. 94108   (415) 982-2219
Manuscripts before 1600, Incunabula & Early Printed Books, Bibliography, Paleography, History of Ideas & Scholarship

ROSTENBERG, LEONA—RARE BOOKS
P.O. Box 188, Gracie Station, New York, N.Y. 10028
(212) 831-6628
Renaissance & 17th century: History, Literature, Art, Political Theory, Reformation

ROYER, M. J.
441 North Kings Road, Los Angeles, Calif. 90048   (213) 655-6754
Art Books

SABBOT, RUDOLPH WILLIAM
5239 Tendilla Avenue, Woodland Hills, Calif. 91364
(213) 346-7164
Natural History

SACKHEIM, BEN
5425 East Ft. Lowell Road, Tucson, Ariz. 85712   (602) 327-4285
Modern First Editions, Art Books, Prints

SALLOCH, WILLIAM
Pines Bridge Road, Ossining, N.Y. 10562   (914) 941-8363
Medieval, Renaissance & 17th-century History and Literature: Classics; Rare Books, Manuscripts, Early Music, Emblem Books, Incunabula

SAN FRANCISCIANA SHOP
Cliff House, 1090 Point Lobos Avenue, San Francisco, Calif. 94121
(418) 751-7222, 661-7399
Pictorial San Francisco & California Material, Photos, Posters, Post-
cards, Prints, Maps

SCHAB, WILLIAM H. GALLERY, INC.
37 West 57th Street, New York, N.Y. 10019   (212) 758-0327
Woodcut Books, Science, Americana, Manuscripts, Old & Modern
Master Prints & Drawings

SCHATZKI, WALTER
153 East 57th Street, New York, N.Y. 10022   (212) 688-6116
Illustrated Books, Illuminated Manuscripts, Fine Bindings, Auto-
graphs, Early Juveniles

SCHILLER, JUSTIN G., LTD.
36 East 61st Street, P.O. Box 1667, FDR Sta., New York, N.Y.
10022   (212) 832-8231
Early Children's Books & Related Juvenilia (1640–1910), Bibli-
ography, Literature, American Art-Nouveau and Art-Modern (1885–
1930)

SCHNASE, ANNEMARIE
120 Brown Road, Box 119, Scarsdale, N.Y. 10583
(914) 725-1284
Scientific Periodicals in all Languages, Music

SCHUMAN, HENRY, LTD.
2211 Broadway, New York, N.Y. 10024   (212) 724-2393
History of Science and Medicine

SCHUYLKILL BOOK SERVICE
873 Belmont Avenue, Philadelphia, Pa. 19104   (215) 473-4769
General Prints, Autographs, Manuscripts, Out of Print

SCHWARZ, KURT L., ANTIQUARIAN BOOKSELLER
738 South Bristol Avenue, Los Angeles, Calif. 90049
(213) 828-7927 (By appointment)
Northern Calif. office: 736 Coventry Road, Kensington, Calif.
94707   (415) 524-1274
Social Movements, Art, History, Literature (Europe, Orient), Ori-
entalia

SCIENTIFIC LIBRARY SERVICE
29 East 10th Street, New York, N.Y. 10003   (212) 473-3826

Early Science, Early Music, Music (Books & Scores), Mathematics, History of Science, Early Medicine

SCOPAZZI, JOHN
278 Post Street, Union Sq. Suite 305, San Francisco, Calif. 94108
(415) 362-5708
Fine & Rare Books (General), Art Books, Bindings, Private Presses, Maps

SCOTT, BARRY—BOOKSELLER
15 Gramercy Park South, New York, N.Y. 10003
(212) 677-7842
20th-century First Editions & Manuscripts

SCRIPTORIUM, THE
427 North Canon Drive, Beverly Hills, Calif. 90210, P.O. Box
1290, Beverly Hills, Calif. 90213   (213) 275-6060
Buyers, Sellers, Appraisers of Original Letters, Documents & Manuscripts of Famous People

SEMPERVIRENS BOOKS
Shop address: 207 G St., Eureka, Calif. 95501, Mailing address:
P.O. Box 1083, Crescent City, Calif. 95531   (707) 445-1992 &
(707) 487-2114
*Natural History, Birds, Botany, Zoology, Environmental
Conservation*

SERENDIPITY BOOKS
1790 Shattuck Avenue, 654 Colusa Avenue, Berkeley, Calif. 94707
(415) 841-7455
*Modern First Editions, English & American Literature, Literary
Criticism, Letters & Manuscripts*

SESSLER, CHARLES, INC.
1308 Walnut Street, Philadelphia, Pa. 19107   (215) 735-1086
Rare Books, Prints, Historic & Graphic Arts, Autographs, Paintings

SEVEN GABLES BOOKSHOP, INC.
3 West 46th Street, New York, N.Y. 10036   (212) 575-9257
*American Drama, Fiction & Poetry, English Literature (17th & 18th
centuries) Children's Books, Bibliography*

SHAPIRO, OSCAR
3726 Connecticut Ave., N.W., Washington, D.C. 20008
(202) 244-4446
Music, Autographs, Books, Scores, Violin, Chess Books

Shorey Book Store, The
815 Third Avenue, Seattle, Wash. 98104   (206) 623-0494
Western Americana, Alaska & the Arctic, Indians, Maritime, Shorey Publications Facsimile Reprints

Slater, William
80 East 11th Street, New York, N.Y. 10003   (212) 674-7440
Occult, Yoga

Slifer, Rosejeanne
30 Park Avenue, New York, N.Y. 10016   (212) 685-2040
Autographs, Historical Documents, Manuscripts, Atlases, Old Maps

Smith, Patterson
23 Prospect Terrace, Montclair, N.J. 07042   (201) 744-3291
Crime & Punishment, Gambling, Sociology

Smith, Sydney R.
Canaan, N.Y. 12029   (518) 795-3178
Horses, Foxhunting, Racing, Polo, Dogs, Guns, Fishing, Shooting

Sotheby Parke Bernet, Inc.
980 Madison Avenue, New York, N.Y. 10021   (212) 879-8300
Sotheby Parke Bernet, Los Angeles
7660 Beverly Boulevard, Los Angeles, Calif. 90036
(213) 937-5130
Auctioneers of Art & Literary Property

Specialty Book Concern
3 Dundas St., East, Waterdown, Ont. Canada   (416) 689-1436
Canadiana, Arctica, Yukon

Stanoff, Jerrold G., Booksellers
2717 Lakewood Avenue, Los Angeles, Calif. 90039
(213) 664-0897 (Appointment only)
Buddhism, China, Japan, Missionaries in Asia, Lafcadio Hearn, Asians in America

Starr Book Co., Inc.
37 Kingston Street, Boston, Mass. 02111   (617) 542-2525
Out of Print

Starr Book Shop, Inc.
29 Plympton Street, Cambridge, Mass. 02138   (617) 547-6864
American Literature, Out of Print, Sets, Americana, Press Books

STEELE, GEOFFREY
Lumberville, Pa. 18933   (215) 297-5187
Art, Architecture, Bibliography, Reference & Scholarly Books

STERNE, PAULA—BOOKS
Huckleberry Rd., RFD #2, West Redding, Conn. 06896
(203) 938-2756
Americana, Sporting, Dogs, Guns

STEVENS, HENRY, SON & STILES
Albee Court, Larchmont, N.Y. 10538   (914) 834-7432
Americana, Early Voyages & Travels, Maps & Atlases

STEWART, W. K., CO.
550 South 4th Street, Louisville, Ky. 40202   (502) 584-0147
Kentucky, Americana, Thorobred Horses, Bindings, First Editions, Literature

STIN ON HOUSE BOOKS
Quincy Road, Rumney, N.H. 03226   (603) 786-3211
Americana, New Hampshire, White Mountains

STONEHILL, C.A., INC.
282 York Street, New Haven, Conn. 06511   (203) 865-5141
English Literature (16th–19th centuries), Incunabula, Manuscripts

STRAIGHT, L. S.
P.O. Box 106, Murray Hill Station, New York, N.Y. 10016
(212) 683-1710
Maps (Old)

SUN DANCE BOOKS
1520 North Crescent Heights, Hollywood, Calif. 90046
(213) 654-2383
The American Indian, American Southwest, Mexico, Latin America (any language) Californiana, Southern Pacific Voyages

SWANN GALLERIES, INC.
104 East 25th Street, New York, N.Y. 10010   (212) 254-4710
Cable: Swannsales
Auctioneers: Weekly sales of rare & antiquarian books, autographs, graphics

TALISMAN PRESS
P.O. Box 455, Georgetown, Calif. 95634   (916) 333-4486
California & Nevada History

TAMERLIS, VICTOR
911 Stuart Avenue, Mamaroneck, N.Y. 10543   (914) 698-8950
Bibliography, Early Printing, Scholarly Books, Illustrated Books

TAYLOR W. THOMAS, BOOKSELLER
2200 Guadalupe, No. 224, Austin, Tex. 78705   (512) 472-7739
English & American Literature, Early Printing, Printing Arts

TEMPLE BAR BOOKSHOP
9 Boylston Street, Cambridge, Mass. 02138   (617) 876-6025
Modern First Editions, American & English Literature, Press Books, Photography

TITLES, INC.
P.O. Box 342, Highland Park, Ill. 60035

TOTTERIDGE BOOK SHOP
667 Madison Ave., Suite 305, New York, N.Y. 10021
(212) 421-1040
English and American First Editions, Fine Bindings, Private Press Books, Sporting Books

TRACE, TIMOTHY
Red Mill Road, Peekskill, N.Y. 10566   (914) 528-4074
Architecture, Decorative Arts, Crafts & Trades, Antiques

TUNICK, DAVID, INC.
12 East 80th Street, New York, N.Y. 10021   (212) 861-7710
(By appointment)
Old Master & Modern Engravings, Etchings, Woodcuts & Lithographs, Illustrated Books, Sets of Fine Prints

TUTTLE, CHARLES E. CO., INC.
26–30 South Main Street, Rutland, Vt. 05701   (802) 773-8930
Genealogy, Local History, Heraldry, General Americana, Orientalia, Vermontiana

TWENEY, GEORGE H.—BOOKS
16660 Marine View Drive, S.W., Seattle, Wash. 98166
(206) 243-8243
Western Americana, Alaska & Canada, Voyages & Western Exploration, Maps, Manuscripts, Prints

UNIVERSITY BOOK RESERVE
75 Main Street (also) 815 Nantasket Avenue, Hull, Mass. 02045
(617) 925-0570 & 925-0005
Drama, Social Sciences, Literature, Religion, Philosophy

UNIVERSITY PLACE BOOK SHOP
821 Broadway, New York, N.Y. 10003   (212) 254-5998
Africa, the Negro, West Indies, Early Printed Books, Chess

URBAN BOOKS
295 Grizzly Peak Boulevard, Berkeley, Calif.   94708
(415) 524-3315
Business History, Californiana, Pacific Area, Political Science, Economics, City Planning & Urbanism

URSUS BOOKS, LTD.
667 Madison Avenue, New York, N.Y. 10021   (212) 838-1012
Arts Reference, Bibliography, Historical & Literary Scholarship

VALLEY BOOK SHOP
122 Hamilton Street, Geneva, Ill. 60134   (312) 232-2636
Western Americana, Catholic Americana, Railroadiana, Illinois, & Chicago

VAN NORMAN BOOK COMPANY
422–424 Bank of Galesburg Bldg., Galesburg, Ill. 61401
(309) 343-4516
Americana, American Literature, English Literature, Association Copies, Critical Works

VERBEKE, CHRISTIAN F.
7 Pond Street, Newburyport, Mass. 01950   (617) 462-8740
Bibliography, Literature, 19th-century English Literature, French Literature, Graphic Arts, the Victorian scene and the "Nineties," Appraisals

VICKEY, HENRY J.
9 Brook Street, Stoughton, Mass. 02072   (617) 344-3649
Out-of-Print Books

VICTORIA BOOK SHOP
16 West 36th Street, New York, N.Y. 10018   (212) 947-7127
Children's Books, 16th–20th centuries, Illustrated Books, Drawings & Paintings

VOLKOFF & VON HOHENLOHE RARE BOOKS & MANUSCRIPTS
545 East Mariposa Street, Altadena, Calif. 91001   (213) 797-3342
(By Appointment)
Library Specialists for Rare and Scholarly Books and Periodicals in all Languages and Periods

WAHRENBROCK'S BOOK HOUSE
649 Broadway, San Diego, Calif. 92101   (714) 239-8604
California, Mexico & Baja California, Modern Firsts, Press Books

WALTON, RAYS
P.O. Box 4398, Austin, Tex. 78745   (512) 478-0945
Western Americana, Texas, Press Books, 19th & 20th-century Literature, Manuscripts

WEISER, SAMUEL, INC.
734 Broadway, New York, N.Y. 10003   (212) 477-8453
Occult, Orientalia, Philosophy, Psychology

WEISS, BERNICE—BOOKS
36 Tuckahoe Avenue, Eastchester, N.Y. 10707   (914) 793-6200
First Editions, American & English Literature, Poetry, Private Press, Association & Inscribed Books

WESTERN HEMISPHERE, INC.
1613 Central Street, Stoughton, Mass. 02072   (617) 344-8200
Western Americana, Canadiana, Voyages & Travels, American History, Economics & related areas

WEYHE, E., INC.
794 Lexington Avenue, New York, N.Y. 10021   (212) 838-5466
Art, Architecture

WHITE, FRED, JR.—BOOKSELLER
P.O. Box 3698, Bryan, Tex. 77801   (713) 846-4462
Texas, Range Cattle Industry, Western Fine Presses, Northern Mexico

WHITLOCK FARM—BOOKS
Sperry Road, Bethany, Conn. 06525   (203) 393-1240
Americana, Children's Books, Prints, Maps, Ancient Curiosities, Early Printing & Rare Books

WILSON BOOKSHOP
3005 Fairmount Street, Dallas, Tex. 75201   (214) 747-5804
Americana; Southwest, Texas, Confederacy, Fine Bindings, Sets

WITHERSPOON ART & BOOK STORE
12 Nassau Street, Princeton, N.J. 08540   (609) 924-3582
Rare, Out of Print, Fine Sets & Reference Works

WITTEN, LAURENCE
North St., RFD 2, Monroe, Conn. 06468   (203) 261-2711

Medieval & Renaissance Manuscripts, Incunabula, History of Printing, Fine Books & Bindings

WOFSY, ALAN—FINE ARTS
150 Green Street, San Francisco, Calif. 94111   (415) 986-3030
Old Master & Modern Prints, Illustrated Books with Original Graphics

WOLFE, WILLIAM P.
22 rue de l'Hopital, Montreal, Canada H2Y IVS   (514) 288-5732
Canadiana: Books, Manuscripts, Maps, Topographical & Historical Views, Paintings, Broadsides, Early Imprints

WOOD, CHARLES B., III, INC.
The Green, South Woodstock, Conn. 06267   (203) 928-4041
Architecture: English & American, Early American Science & Technology, History of American Art, Early Photography

WOODBURN, ELISABETH
Booknoll Farm, Hopewell, N.J. 08525   (609) 466-0522
Gardening Landscape, Herbs, Wine & Other Beverages

WOOLMER, J. HOWARD
Gladstone Hollow, Andes, N.Y. 13731   (914) 676-3218
20th-century Literature, Poetry, Autograph Letters & Manuscripts in this field

WORMSER, RICHARD S.
Wolfpits Road, Bethel, Conn. 06801   (203) 748-4125
Early Science, Non-European Incunabula, Type Specimen Books, Horology, Americana

WREDEN, WILLIAM P.
200 Hamilton Avenue, P.O. Box 56, Palo Alto, Calif. 94302
(415) 325-6851
Western Americana, Literature, Bibliography, Manuscripts, General

XIMENES: RARE BOOKS, INC.
120 East 85th Street, New York, N.Y. 10028   (212) 744-0226
English & American Literature, English Books Printed Before 1700, Americana, Voyages & Travel

YOUNG, WILLIAM & Co.
P.O. Box 282, Wellesley Hills, Mass. 02181
Modern First Editions

ZAMBELLI, ALFRED F.
156 Fifth Avenue, New York, N.Y. 10010   (212) 734-2141

Bibliography, History (Medieval, Renaissance, Reformation), Philosophy, Rare Books

ZEITLIN & VER BRUGGE
815 North La Cienega Boulevard, Los Angeles, Calif. 90069
(213) 655-7581
Early Science, Natural History, Fine Arts, History of Medicine, Fine Press Books

ZEITLIN PERIODICALS COMPANY, INC.
817 South La Brea Avenue, Los Angeles, Calif. 90036
(213) 933-7175
Back Issue Periodicals & Learned Society Publications, Reprints, Microforms Prints, Appraisals

ZUCKER, IRVING—ART BOOKS
256 Fifth Avenue, New York, N.Y. 10001   (212) 679-6332
Books on the Fine & Applied Arts, Color Plate Books, French Modern Illustrated Books

Index